Understanding the War Between the States

 W9-DAG-976

A Supplemental Booklet by 16 Writers that Enables
A More Complete and Truthful Study of American History
(Middle School, High School, College and Beyond)

Written in 2015 by Sixteen Members of The Society of Independent Southern Historians as a gift to America:

Editors: Society co-founders Clyde N. Wilson, Ph.D. of SC and Howard Ray White of NC.

Writers: Wilson, White, Joyce Bennett of MD, Vance Caswell of NC, William Cawthon of AL, Paul C. Graham of SC, Earl L. Ijames of NC, Gail Jarvis of GA, Patrick J. Kealey of CA, Steve Litteral of IL, Barbara G. Marthal of TN, Karen Stokes of SC, Joseph Stromberg of GA, Egon R. Tausch of TX, Lesley R. Tucker of OK, and H. V. Traywick of VA.

Understanding the War Between the States, commonly called the Civil War, the War of Rebellion, etc., requires a broad view going back to settling the British colonies of North America, beginning at Jamestown, Virginia Colony, in 1607. Readers need to go back 254 years (8 to 10 generations) and move forward to the year 1861 to properly experience the cultural and political divisions that led to Political Sectionalism, State Secession, War, and Political Reconstruction. So, our authors take you back to the beginning and rapidly move forward. Stated another way, this gift to America will enhance understanding of the Revolution and westward expansion; the 1850's political sectionalism in the Northern States that created its Republican Party and resulted in State Secession; a Federal Invasion and 4-years of horrific war; plus the aftermath: Political Reconstruction, which replaced State Rights with an all-powerful Federal Government.

The Society has written this booklet for diligent and inquisitive youth of Middle School and High School age who have inquiring minds and are engaged in formal study of history in public school, charter school, private school and home school. It is also helpful to young men and women in college studies, as well as parents, and even inquisitive older adults.

This booklet does not replace the student's assigned textbook. But the expense of engaging the student also with this booklet is minimal because it is provided at cost in print form and free of charge in computer download and e-book form. No authors have earned any money from their contributions; they have volunteered their time in hopes of benefiting you, the inquiring student or adult.

Who are we? The Society of Independent Southern Historians is a non-profit, web-site-based, educational association registered in North Carolina. Although membership is concentrated in the Southern States, it encompasses all of the American States. The copyright for this work is held by the Society, which only requires that no one alter this booklet or copy and/or reprint it for resale.

Approximately 600,000 Africans were imported into North America, primarily in ships operated out of Great Britain and New England. By the time of the War Between the States (1860 census), the population of African immigrants and their descendants had expanded by approximately 700 percent: to 3,950,528 who were bonded to owners (slaves) and 476,748 who were independent (free), a little over half of the latter living in the Southern States. These men and women can take pride in the role they played in raising families and building America. We also present their history and how their lives were impacted by the war and the Political Reconstruction that followed. We also tell how Native Americans suffered.

This booklet imparts a clear and truthful understanding of the most horrific war ever suffered in North America. Sadly, that is bloody business. If the bodies of the 400,000 Federal dead were stretched from Washington, DC southward, with arms stretched upward holding a bouquet of flowers, laid down, toe to flower, the line of bodies would reach to Charleston, South Carolina. That defines a Horrific War! What political disintegration caused it? You are about to find out.

In print form, this booklet is made up of 40 chapters presented on 44 sheets of 8-1/2x11-inch paper, printed front and back. The chapters are organized into seven Sections, the first titled, "How to Make this Booklet Your Personal Adventure," where, in stand-alone Chapter 1, Mr. White and wife Judith tell war-time stories within their families and give guidance for personalizing your journey through this booklet. Section Two presents "The Evolution of Two Cultures – North and South – from 1607 to 1846." Here, Dr. Wilson, Mr. White and Vance Caswell present relevant history in 7 chapters. Section Three, "African Americans in the Southern Culture," contains 3 chapters written by Caswell, Barbara Marthal and Les Tucker. Section Four, "The Rise of Political Sectionalism in the Northern States – Inciting Secession," contains 5 chapters by Egon Tausch, Wilson and White, all essential to the student's understanding. Section Five, "The War Between the States . . ." contains 12 chapters by Dr. Wilson, White, Caswell, Steve Litteral, Karen Stokes, Patrick Kealey and Earl Ijames, which present all necessary facets of the history, leaving none untouched. Section Six, "After the Conquest – Consequences of Political Sectionalism and Horrific War," contains 7 chapters by Litteral, Tausch, William Cawthon, Joe Stromberg, Joyce Bennett and Gail Jarvis, and none doubt the importance of their writing. Section Seven, "Discussion Subjects and Concluding Information," contains 5 chapters by White, Marthal, Paul Graham and H. V. Traywick, wrapping up the history and encouraging thought and discussion. Each chapter ends with suggestions for class discussion and a few recommended reading resources, for reflection and discussion are keys to good understanding.

The primary way historians mislead students is not by telling untruths, but by omitting history critical to truthful learning, what the Society calls "the sin of omission." We correct that deception. Here you learn the truth, **the whole truth** and nothing but the truth. If not already of age, you will soon be voting. Please apply the wisdom gained here, for you are America's future. We, the authors, hope parents, teachers, students and those "beyond" accept the approach we have taken to enhance everyone's understanding in all 50 states.

Understanding the War Between the States (WBTS) – The Table of Contents

The 7 sections and 40 chapters in *Understanding the War Between the States* (noted as WBTS) are as follows, most chapters limited to two pages, a few to one page, a few more. In these chapters we authors are not presenting a comprehensive history of the eras and regions involved, but only those portions of the histories that are not readily available but keenly relevant and so essential to achieving the thorough understanding we hope you are seeking.

Section One: How to Make this Booklet Your Personal Adventure

Chapter 1 – Your Starting Line and a Personal Navigation Strategy.

By Howard Ray and Judith Willis White, S. I. S. H.

Introduction

When beginning a new adventure, always push off at your Starting Line. We will help you find it and do that. But first, we offer these personal stories about our family ancestors.

The Bloodstains, Howard Ray White's Story

My grandfather lived on a farm in Middle Tennessee near Murfreesboro where the terrible Battle of Murfreesboro (Stones River) was fought on this and surrounding farms as 1862 concluded and 1863 began. Using our farmhouse as a field hospital, Federal surgeons had sawed off irreparable arms and legs, tossed them out the window, drawn the skin tight against the stump and stitched them closed. The battle had been terribly brutal; about 3,000 men had been killed, and a much higher number had been wounded.

My family lived on Granddad's farm in 1948. I was ten years old. My brother and I slept in the upstairs bedroom amid the bloodstains. Our school bus traveled beside the Federal graveyard as rows and rows of gravestones filed past the window. I mourned all those dead men – over 6,000 Federal soldiers – as my childhood mind sought the answer to what I considered then a simple question: "*Why?*" Why did men from the northern States come to Tennessee bent on conquest? Had not their grandparents fought beside my Tennessee, Carolina and Virginia ancestors to make everyone's state independent?

Living in that old battlefield farmhouse, amid the bloodstains, changed my country's war history into a very personal story of terrible times 85 years back into the past. But I tucked those pictures safely in the back of my mind as I resolved to one day undertake a *determined study* of the political history of that era, to understand "why?". Eventually, my time for serious study arrived. Perhaps you too will develop such a passion to understand truthful history, to understanding "why?". You desperately need to understand "why?" because "War is Hell."

Ancestors Who Suffered So Much, Judith Willis White's Family Story about the War Between the States (WBTS)

My Bowen ancestors on my maternal grandfather's side were Carolinians of Welsh ancestry. Lt. Reese Bowen was killed leading a charge in the Revolutionary War battle at Kings Mountain, near Charlotte, NC, the first major Patriot victory that eventually led to British surrender at Yorktown, Virginia. And six other Bowen relatives fought alongside Reese. Later my Bowen ancestor, John Bowen and wife Elvira Hunt Bowen, of Pickens County, SC, saw five of six sons off to war in defense of the Confederacy: Colonel Robert, William, Captain John, Samuel and Sergeant Thomas. Captain John Bowen was with Hampton's Legion and survived one year in a Federal POW prison. Sergeant Thomas Bowen was twice seriously wounded, each time recovering to rejoin the fight, surviving to the end. The Bowen parents were unusually fortunate to see all five sons return home. Lieutenant William Uriah Hunt was another Confederate officer on my maternal grandfather's side. Also of Pickens County, SC, he was captured at Missionary Ridge above Chattanooga, TN and sent to the Federal POW prison at Johnson's Island on Lake Erie where he almost froze to death, almost starved to death, but survive by determination and eating rats. Also of Pickens County, my maternal great grandfather David Ervin Hendricks was called into service late in the war, and after one battle, contracted measles and was sent home where he recovered. But two brothers had already been killed at Chancellorsville, VA: John Baylus Hendricks and William Fields Hendricks.

On my father's side of the family, Daniel and Elizabeth Willis saw five sons off to war, to fight in the WBTS, one being my great grandfather James. John was killed in the Wilderness Battles in VA in May 1864. Marcus was killed near Petersburg, VA in September 1864. Erastus was killed in the Battle of Bentonville, NC in March 1865. Perry and James survived. I exist because James Willis, an artilleryman near Charleston, SC survived the war.

A Personal Approach to Engaging this Booklet.

The title on the cover says, "Understanding the War Between the States." So, if a student, how do you fit in? Are you diligent about your studies and by nature inquisitive – inquisitive about your state, its people today and those that came before? How old are you: 13, 15, 17, 20 or beyond? Do you thirst for Understanding? If 13 or 15, you may not yet be ready to tackle this booklet's more difficult pages. Guidance below will help. But, before completing your education and becoming a responsible voter, you should earnestly engage all of the pages, all of the chapters and soak up the valuable wisdom to be gained – wisdom essential for good citizenship.

Perhaps you are beyond school age but have never gained the understanding within this booklet. Perhaps you are a teacher or a parent or grandparent of a teenager, or maybe a college professor or college student? Or maybe you are unlike those mentioned above, but are by nature diligent, inquisitive and hungry to finally understand how America's politics degraded into State Secession (then thought legal), horrible War between the States (then thought illegal) and Political Reconstruction (which escalated into an all-powerful Federal Government). You could be anyone pondering the reading of *Understanding the War Between the States.* So our first job is to, together, think about how to make this booklet your personal adventure.

Your Personal Adventure

The stories on the front and back cover are great starting points; read them twice. If you are young and think the total 40-chapter set is too much, go for 20, marked with "*", as follows: Chapter 3* (Revolution); Chapter 5* (1801-1824); Chapters 7* and 8* (Expansion); Chapter 9* (Slavery World View); Chapters 13*, 14*, 15* and 16* (Northern States Political Sectionalism); Chapter 18* (Secession); Chapter 19* (Lincoln Incites War); Chapters 20*, 21* and 22* (War History); Chapters 25* and 28* (Total War), and Chapters 29*, 30*, 33* and 36* (Political Reconstruction). This reading plan involves 20 of the 40 chapters. To this plan add chapters 2, 4, 17 and 23 about limits to government power; 6 and 12 for the rest of westward expansion; 10, 11, 26, 27, 34 and 37 for African American history, and 24, 31, 32, 38, 39 and 40 for the rest of the story. Yet, many people will choose to just start with chapter 2 and read sequentially to the end. You decide.

Chapter 2 – Origins of the Northern and Southern Cultures, 1600s and 1700s

By Clyde N. Wilson of S. C., Ph.D., S. I. S. H.

Introduction

Most historians today, whether they realize it or not, write about the War Between the States (WBTS) from the Northern viewpoint. They assume that their task is to explain why the South was so misguided, warped, or evil that it fought to break up "the greatest nation on earth." But proper historians should not be judges assuming guilt before the facts are heard. They should be like members of a jury examining all the evidence before deciding. Confederate President Jefferson Davis said of Southern secession that it "illustrates the American idea that governments rest upon the consent of the governed." His father had been a soldier in the Revolutionary War. The Confederacy's greatest general, Robert E. Lee, not only had a father fighting in the Revolutionary War, two of his uncles signed the Declaration of Independence and his wife was the granddaughter of Martha Washington. Clearly Davis and Lee did not regard the Confederacy as un-American.

Relevant History

To really understand how the WBTS happened, we have to go back to the earliest days of the founding of the thirteen English colonies in North America that became the United States. Between the first permanent English colony at Jamestown, Virginia, in 1607 and the beginning of the Revolution in 1775 is 168 years. In this long period each of the colonies developed its own representative legislature, militia, economy, and religious institutions. Everyone at the time of the Revolution recognized these differences and understood that the major difference was between the North and the South. John Adams spoke of Massachusetts as "my country," and General Washington had uncomplimentary things to say about the New England and Pennsylvania (PA) soldiers in his army. The differences between North and South were very much on people's minds before, during, and after the Revolution. Most of the considerable opposition to ratification of the U.S. Constitution involved the potential sectional costs and benefits.

A relatively small number of English settlers founded Maryland (MD), Virginia (VA), North Carolina (NC), South Carolina (SC), and Georgia (GA). Population increased greatly, mainly because the settlers had big families and many children. (George Washington would be the fourth generation of his family in Virginia.) Also present were a significant number of Huguenots (French Protestants) in SC. In the early 1700s the population was increased by a great in-migration of Scots-Irish, along with some Germans. At first there were tensions between the English settlers of the coastal South and the new settlers of the Upcountry. By the early 1800s they had merged comfortably into one Southern identity. Some writers have portrayed Southern pioneers as almost entirely Scots-Irish. These people were important, but other Southern groups settled the frontier as well.

At the time of the Revolution the South was the most dynamic and fastest growing part of the 13 colonies and the region most actively expanding westward. Before there was a U.S., North Carolinians and Virginians were planting settlements across the Appalachian Mountains in what was to become Kentucky (KY) and Tennessee (TN) and Charleston traders were sending mule trains to the Gulf Coast and the Mississippi River.

During the 1700s Southern tobacco was by far the most important export of North America, supplemented by other Southern crops such as rice, indigo, cotton, and lumber and tar – "naval stores" for the wooden sailing ships of the time. There were bonded Africans in all 13 colonies (as well as all the other European colonies in the Caribbean and Central and South America). African-American people were most common in the South, more than half the population in SC and about a third in the other Southern colonies. The South has always been a biracial society, whereas the North had few black people before the 20th century (although we should not forget that slaves made up 10% of the population of New York Colony (NY), Connecticut (CT), and Rhode Island (RI) when the Constitution went into effect).

The Middle Colonies (New York, New Jersey, Pennsylvania and Delaware) were diverse in population, religion, and economy. There were English from the Midlands, Welsh, and many Germans in PA and Dutch in NY. There were so many different religious denominations – Anglican, Quaker, Baptist, various German churches – that they had to tolerate each other. The economy was diverse with shipping, fur trade, wheat, and an early start on iron manufacturing. The North was by no means culturally united until a few decades before the WBTS. Remember how, in Washington Irving's most famous story about a "Headless Horseman," the Hudson Valley Dutch people disliked and ran out the obnoxious Ichabod Crane, who had come over into NY from CT. Another great early American writer, James Fenimore Cooper, satirized the "Yankees" who invaded his NY lands. In the beginning the landowners of NY and the pioneer farmers of PA had more in common with the South than with New England, which was reflected in their political support of Southern men and policies. As time went on, the Middle States, and later the Midwest, became more "Northern," as we will describe in Chapter 6.

New England (NH, MA, CT, RI) definitely was regarded and regarded itself as distinct, much more so than the South. The core population, who settled Massachusetts Bay in the 1630s, were Puritans from eastern England, the heartland of Puritanism, while the first Virginia settlers were from southern and western England. (Later on New Englanders became Congregationalists and then Unitarians, without changing their basic attitudes.) They were strong on religious conformity, the clergy were political leaders, and civic life was tightly organized and supervised. When Southerners moved west, an extended family and their neighbours went out to make new farms in the wilderness. New Englanders tended to move as whole congregations, taking their institutions with them. Economically, New England could produce and export little that Europe could not produce for itself. It turned to shipping – carrying goods between the many English and other colonies. One very lucrative aspect of this was the slave trade, which made many fortunes. New England ships continued to carry African slaves to Cuba and Brazil right up to the WBTS although it was illegal for Americans from 1808.

Virginia and Massachusetts colonies were the seeds from which separate and conflicting Southern and Northern cultures grew. The expanding Southern colonies were dominated by landowning agriculturalists. They were settled by people hoping to improve their lives. In the South they found a land with a milder climate than Northern Europe. In England all the land was taken and only the eldest son could inherit. Cutting down trees and hunting on the lord's land were serious criminal offenses. In Virginia land was abundant and easily obtained and lumber inexhaustible. In England food was scarce – in Virginia even the bonded people had meat every day and more vegetables than they could eat. An English poet wrote that Virginia was "the earthly paradise." The Church of England was officially established in the Southern colonies, but Baptists, Presbyterians, Lutherans and Methodists flourished and enjoyed practical freedom of religion.

The inspiration and motivation of the settlers of Massachusetts were very different from those of people in the South. They had already been fairly prosperous townspeople in England. They considered themselves to be on "an errand into the wilderness" to establish their religion where it was not interfered with by government or other churches. Their leader John Winthrop, as the first settlers landed, preached a lay sermon in which he said that New England was to be "a city on a hill," a shining beacon of righteousness to illuminate the world. Puritans had a firm sense of their righteousness and of their moral and intellectual superiority to the rest of the world. Later they strayed from orthodox Christianity, but they kept their sense of righteousness and superiority. We can see this clearly later when they were to assert that other Americans were obligated to go along with the tariff that made them rich. And bow to in the abolition movement and the activities of generals like Sherman, which condemned their fellow American citizens in the South as evil people to be chastised by their betters.

A vivid illustration of the difference in ways of life and attitudes between Massachusetts and Virginia is given by two diaries from the late 1600s and early 1700s. Cotton Mather was a leading clergyman, scholar, and influential man in MA. William Byrd II was a large landowner and prominent man in VA. Both were born in America of English parents and both kept diaries of their life. Mather's diary is about how God is either constantly favouring him or thwarting him, but at any rate minutely concerned with him, about the lack of appreciation for his books and sermons, about the evil doings of other people. It is a depressing read – the record of a self-righteous man with no affection for or real interest in other people. Byrd's diary records his prayers and studies, but it also presents a lively social life, a strong interest in other folks and in nature, a sense of humour about himself and the world, and even admissions of his own sins and shortcomings. It is a delightful read.

The plantation became a prominent feature of Southern life. It has been extensively written about by those who find it attractive (think of the worldwide popularity of *Gone with the Wind)* and by those who think of the plantation as the most horrible thing in American history. What is a "plantation"? Originally it meant a new settlement – the English spoke of "plantations" in Ireland and RI was chartered as "Rhode Island and Providence Plantations." In time the word came to describe a particular kind of agricultural establishment -a large one where bonded labour lived and worked to produce "staple" crops. Meaning crops that were not for local consumption or sale but for export in large quantities to the world market. In the 18th century Southern tobacco and in the 19th century Southern cotton were the most important "staple crops." Indeed, they provided the overwhelming part of American exports and the economic development of the United States would have been much retarded without them. Plantations also flourished on the Caribbean islands and in South America in the various European colonies, producing sugar, coffee, and other valuable products that Europe could not easily produce for itself.

The plantation was a significant feature of Southern life, an independent community in itself. But we should never lose sight of the facts that most plantations were small: a dozen or fewer bond people rather than several hundreds, and that most white Southerners were farmers of modest but independent means and without slaves.

Summary

When the U.S. Constitution was adopted Americans had long been divided into two lasting different cultures of the North and the South. They had much fellow feeling as Americans but they also realized that they differed considerably in ways of life, means of making a living, values, and attitudes. Perhaps most importantly they differed in expectation of how the power of the new Federal Government would be used. These differences had nothing to do with African-American slavery, which only became a contentious issue decades later. We can understand much of the history that leads to the WBTS (and later American history as well) when we remember that people came to Virginia to find a good life and to Massachusetts with a mission to build "a city on a hill" that was superior to all other existing societies.

Suggestions for Class Discussion

Are the Northern and Southern cultures still significant today? In what way?

Does the idea of America as "a city upon a hill" with a special mission in the world still carry weight?

Recommended Readings

- *Albion's Seed: Four British Folkways in America*, by David Hackett Fischer, pub. 1989.

- *The Scarlet Letter* and more. Sometimes creative writers can give us a more realistic and vivid idea of historic events, places, and people than dry historians. Nathaniel Hawthorne's famous novel, *The Scarlet Letter,* shows what life was life in colonial Puritan New England. The novels of Inglis Fletcher set in colonial North Carolina do the same for the South.

Chapter 3* – The First American War for Independence

By Vance Caswell of N. C., S.I.S.H.

Introduction

The Great Seal of the Confederate States of America carries the image of George Washington. The Americans who fought in 1861-1865 against Northern Republican conquest very much felt themselves to be following the example of the earlier War of Independence against British conquest. The American Revolution had been only two generations past. It was to them not a matter of theoretical speculation about what it meant but a living heritage clearly understood.

It will be helpful to clarify briefly the often discussed history of the path that led from 1763 to the 13 colonies' fight for independence. Many colonial families had been in America for several generations. Most Americans did not regard themselves as clients or servants of the British government. They had come on their own initiative and at risk of life, limb, and capital to conquer a wilderness. They were willing to allow the British to make rules for external matters but very much insisted on the right of Englishmen to govern themselves by elected representatives and to be free of arbitrary power. Every colony had an elected assembly. These bodies were sometimes in conflict with the governors sent from Britain, especially over matters of taxes, land, and Indian relations. It was a burden to wait months for the laws they passed to be approved in London. The colonies were full of very able, successful, well-educated men. They resented that third-rate politicians were sent from Britain to fill offices that Americans could fill more ably.

A New British Agenda

At the victorious conclusion of a world war with France in 1763, Britain was deeply in debt while shouldering far-flung imperial responsibilities. It was also suffering from an unusual period of low-quality statesmanship. Unwisely, the government attempted to clamp down on the North American colonies, insisting on more taxes and more obedience, setting off a chain reaction that led to revolt and war.

The factors driving Americans toward independence were many. All had a strong sense of their hereditary right as Englishmen to be ruled by consent. For Northern colonies, where shipping was the primary industry, there were economic grievances – they resented restrictions on who they could trade with and what commodities they could ship. They wanted more access to European and American colonial markets. New Englanders feared that the Church of England might send bishops that would interfere with their Puritan churches.

Southerners had no economic loss in being part of the British Empire. For the right of self-government they sacrificed economic benefits. For example, the indigo industry was deprived of British subsidy and never recovered. By contrast, New England temporarily lost government subsidy of its fishing industry. It demanded in the very first U.S. Congress that the federal government continue the British subsidies, which was granted.

Besides the right of self-government the matter of access to new land was large in the thinking of Southerners. Virginia, North Carolina, and Georgia, from their colonial charters, held vast unsettled lands, all the way west to the Mississippi river and north to the Great Lakes. Here was clearly the future strength, prosperity, and freedom for their burgeoning population. But, in 1763 the British government issued a Proclamation forbidding settlement on all land west of the Appalachian mountain watershed divide – an unacceptable restriction to free and adventurous Southerners.

Armed opposition confronted British military force in 1775. The revolting Northern States badly needed the support of the Southern States. The Continental Congress chose George Washington of Virginia to lead its army. In a brief modest speech Washington accepted this daunting mission, for which he refused any pay. The war at times seemed hopeless, but Washington was able to keep an army in the field despite defeats and hardships and finally achieved victory. He certainly deserved the tribute that was made by Robert E. Lee's father: "First in war, first in peace, and first in the hearts of his countrymen."

Incidentally, Southern volunteers fought in all the Northern campaigns of the war, but no units from north of Delaware fought for the Patriot cause in the South. Later historians have tended to minimize the extent to which the States financed and fought the war with little help from the Continental Congress.

Why Independence?

Many Americans were reluctant to break ties with the beloved Mother Country. But, support for self-government solidified when, in the words of the Declaration of Independence, British troops were sent "having in direct object the establishment of an absolute Tyranny over these States." In a very similar way, in 1861, those Southerners initially reluctant to secede would become solid in their resistance when Lincoln made clear he would send armies to enforce obedience to his rule.

We suggest that students of American history undertake to actually read the Declaration of Independence from start to finish, without any preconceptions of what it says. Not long after the American Revolution, the French Revolution, a very different affair, broke out. French Revolutionaries sought to overthrow society and remake it through a government with total power. The people who achieved American independence were not at all like that. But many later commentators, dwelling on "All men are Created Equal" have asserted that the Declaration initiated a world revolution for "equality." Abraham Lincoln suggested such in the Gettysburg Address, but he misstated history and put an interpretation on the Declaration not at all intended by those who signed it. The Declaration is about government by "consent of the governed."

American Independence is Won in the South

New York and Philadelphia were occupied during most of the war, but the situation in the North was stalemated. The British could not control the countryside or eliminate Washington's army. The Southern colonies had been relatively free of British rule for the first four years. South Carolinians by their own efforts had driven off a major British attack on Charleston in May, 1776, and NC Patriots had defeated a Tory uprising by recent Scots immigrants at Moore's Creek Bridge. The Southern colonies of Virginia, North Carolina, South Carolina, and Georgia were crucial in the third and final phase of the conflict.

The third phase began at the dawn of 1779 when 3,500 British troops under Archibald Campbell landed at Tybee Island and advanced to successfully conquer Savannah. Georgia had never before been threatened. On September 2 a French fleet under Comte d'Estaing joined with Continentals under Benjamin Lincoln in an attempt to liberate Savannah. But the effort failed. The French lost 637 men, the Continentals lost 264, the well-protected British lost only 54.

Four months later, 7,600 British troops under Henry Clinton, having departed from their New York base, succeeded in forcing the surrender of Charles Town, South Carolina in January 1780. From these two seaport bases, British set out to conquer Georgia and the Carolinas with the help of Loyalists and the Cherokee. The British effort to defeat the Revolution by conquering the South was fearsome, but holding two seaports and establishing a string of inland forts did not ensure the conquest of that vast region and its rugged inland settlers, already experienced in battle with Native Americans.

Yet, British advances were impressive, even after Clinton left and British commander Charles Cornwallis took over. British troops were brutal to Patriot civilians, especially cavalry commander Banastre Tarleton. When 270 of Tarleton's men swooped down upon 400 Virginia militia under Abraham Buford at Waxhaw, near Charlotte, NC, the Virginians, caught by surprise, attempted to surrender. Not allowed. All 400 were slaughtered. One of Tarleton's men would later write of "a scene of indiscriminate carnage never surpassed by the ruthless atrocities of the most barbarous savages. The demand for quarters, seldom refused to a vanquished foe, was at once found to be in vain. Not a man was spared." There would be one more British triumph. On August 15, at Camden, SC, 2,000 British troops under Cornwallis engaged 3,050 Continentals under Horatio Gates. Tarleton's cavalry was key to the British victory, killing 1,000 and capturing 1,000 Continentals. Then Tarleton's cavalry located Thomas Sumter's 800-man partisan force and scattered it, killing 150 and capturing 200. News of the American defeats at Camden and Waxhaw shook Patriot resolve in many sections. Not so among partisans under Francis Marion, Thomas Sumter and other heroic leaders. Not so among settlers beyond the mountains on the Watauga region of what is now East Tennessee. The toughest had just begun to fight and British forces had just enjoyed their last victory.

Cornwallis advanced into North Carolina with 1,000 troops, arriving at Charlotte on September 26 and finding the town resembled "a hornet's nest." Not surprising, since five years earlier, on May 20, 1775, Mecklenburg County had declared its independence from British rule, an action not challenged until Cornwallis' arrival and one still celebrated as "Meck Dec Day." Meanwhile, a thousand man force of Loyalists under Patrick Ferguson crossed into NC and found itself being pursued by the "Over the Mountain Men," a volunteer army made up of rugged settlers west of the King's Proclamation Line, men with long rifles and keen marksmanship. Ferguson's army climbed King's Mountain and prepared to defend itself on the high ground. It was October 6, 1780. No match for the "Over the Mountain Men," the Loyalists were soundly defeated, 225 killed and 879 taken prisoner. Ferguson

was killed. "This battle dispirited Loyalists and almost demolished their hopes." A month later, on November 9, Tarleton lost a fourth of his cavalry at Blackstock's Farm. By this time George Washington had sent his best general, Nathanael Greene, to take over from the disgraced Horatio Gates, setting up his headquarters in Charlotte. Now the Continentals in NC had an excellent leader. On January 17, 1781 Continentals under Daniel Morgan dealt a severe blow to the British cause at Hannah's Cowpens, near Spartanburg, SC, killing 110 and capturing 800. Meanwhile, Maryland, satisfied that Virginia would give to the general government its claim to its vast land north of the Ohio River, signed the Articles of Confederation – by Maryland's pen those United States of America were born. Cornwallis consolidated his troops into one force and set out after Nathanael Greene's forces. On March 15 a terrific fight involving 4,500 patriots took place at Guilford Court House, NC. Weakened, Cornwallis decided to retreat toward the coast and further consolidate his forces.

By summer Cornwallis had 7,000 men at Yorktown to build a British military base on the Chesapeake Bay. On August 14 George Washington learned that a large French fleet of 29 ships, under de Grasse, had left the Caribbean for the Chesapeake – capable of blocking a British retreat or re-enforcement by sea. So, the armies of Washington and French Commander Rochambeau began a rapid march south to join up with French forces under Lafayette and Southern continentals. Consolidating a 16,000 man army at Williamsburg, Washington lay siege to Yorktown while the French navy blocked entrance into the Chesapeake. The British surrendered on October 19. Marie-Joseph Marquis de Lafayette turned to a friend and remarked, "The play, sir, is over."

Summary

Although the British had a 30,000-man force in America, Parliament decided to abandon its recolonization effort. On September 3, 1783, the Treaty of Paris granted independence to each of the 13 former British colonies, each clearly recognized as an independent, sovereign state. From this point forward you learn how these independent states united under a Federal Government with clearly limited powers and how settlement of land west of the Appalachians accelerated. Kentucky would be a state in 9 years, Tennessee in 13.

Suggestions for Class Discussion

Compare the importance of two passions motivating Patriots to fight and die for Independence: 1) for American control of land out to the Mississippi River, versus 2) for American control over international commerce (escaping British mercantilism).

Recommended Reading

- *The Life of Francis Marion*, by William Gilmore Simms, pub. 1844.
- *Redcoats and Rebels, the American Revolution through British Eyes*, by Christopher Hibbert, pub. 1990.
- Eight Revolutionary "Romances" by William Gilmore Simms: *Joscelyn, The Partisan, Mellichampe, Katherine Walton, The Scout, The Forayers, Eutaw, and Woodcraft.* Probably nobody has ever known more about the Revolution in the South than the great Southern writer Simms (1806 – 1870). His great collection of irreplaceable original documents was destroyed during Sherman's invasion.

Chapter 4 – Thirteen Free and Independent States Join in a Constitution; George Washington Presides Over the New Common Government; Alexander Hamilton Has an Agenda and Thomas Jefferson Disagrees, 1783 – 1800

By Clyde N. Wilson of S. C., Ph.D., S.I.S.H.

The Constitution

In 1783 Great Britain gave up its war to retain control of the 13 States and granted a treaty that recognized the former colonies as "free, sovereign, and independent States." Britain also acknowledged the States' rights to the land that they claimed, up to the Mississippi river border of the Spanish Empire. This latter benefit to Americans came largely because VA had sent George Rogers Clark out to defeat British occupation of the territory above the Ohio River and Southerners had already planted settlements in Kentucky (KY) and Tennessee (TN).

During the Revolution the colonies joined in a constitution called the Articles of Confederation, under which a Continental Congress was empowered to handle certain common matters. In this Congress, as in the Constitutional Convention later, each State had one vote, whatever number of delegates it chose to send. (Bet you didn't know that.) Ordinary actions required a majority of the States voting affirmative. Important matters required unanimity.

The Continental Congress formed a Continental Army under Washington that provided a core of military power, though it must be remembered that a great deal of war was carried on by State forces. It started a small navy and sent its ablest men as representatives to European governments. Britain's hereditary enemy France came in on the side of the Americans.

The Congress had no source of revenue except what it asked the States to contribute. It had trouble paying the soldiers and suppliers of its army and its paper promises had little market value. At the end of the war there was a large outstanding debt, no standard money for business, potentially hostile European empires on every side, and some quarreling among the States about boundaries, currency, and trade. Historians who dub this "the Critical Period" and say that everything was falling apart are guilty of exaggeration. However, many people felt the need for "a more perfect Union," that could act effectively in the common interest. The Congress asked the States to send delegates to a convention, meeting in Philadelphia in1787, to draft amendments to the Articles.

This was by no means a universally popular move. Rhode Island (RI) did not send delegates and several prominent men like Patrick Henry mistrusted what was going on and refused to go. When the delegates met, advocates of a strong central government took the initiative and proposed a whole new instrument rather than amendments to the Articles. The centralizers' specific plans met major opposition and less extreme proposals were considered. A major compromise was reached when it was agreed to have a two-house legislature. In the Senate the States would be equal. In the House of Representatives they would be weighted according to population. There were brilliant discussions on many matters of government, although these were not known to the public until forty years later when the proceedings of the Philadelphia Convention and of the State ratifying conventions were published. This has allowed politicians, judges, and historians to claim that the Constitution is a more centralist document than it was intended to be.

One compromise caused considerable North/South friction later on. In determining representation in the House, it was agreed to use three-fifths of the bonded African-American population. This did not mean, as was later claimed, that a black man was considered 3/5ths of a man. There were still slaves in the North. Women, children, men without property, and many others were counted for representation but could not vote anywhere or exercise full citizenship rights. Property qualifications for voting disfranchised half the white men in some States. The 3/5ths rule was also to be used for taxes and could be considered a Southern concession.

Many later people, including one silly Chief Justice of the U.S. Supreme Court, like to pretend that the Philadelphia Constitution was a "miracle" delivered by saintly Founding Fathers – that it created liberty for Americans and promulgated freedom for all mankind. Nonsense! Americans were already free with their freedoms protected by State constitutions. The men who wrote the Constitution were not saints, they were learned but also experienced and practical men, who disagreed on numerous points. When issued from the Convention, the Constitution was nothing more than a piece of paper. It had no validity until it was ratified by the sovereign peoples of each State. It could go into effect when nine States had ratified – *among those nine States.* The ratifying States were thus potentially seceding from the Articles and from the States that did not ratify.

There was a great deal of learned discussion for and against the Constitution that is worthy of study by every American. Ratification was far from universally popular. Smaller States concerned about defense ratified quickly. Coastal business areas were for the Constitution. Suspicion and opposition occurred in independent-minded back country regions. Some New Englanders feared that a central government might interfere with their unique religion and way of life. Many thoughtful people everywhere said that they had just fought to be free of remote rulers and did not want to set up another bunch. Many Southerners felt that Northern business would use a central government for its own profit rather than mutual benefit. North Carolina (NC) rejected the Constitution the first time and there was a very close vote in several States. The change of a few votes in three States would have defeated the Constitution.

Finally, all the States agreed to join together and give the new Constitution a try. They did not regard the government established as eternal and unlimited, but as an experiment. Alexander Hamilton, the strongest proponent of a powerful central government, stated clearly that, of course, the new Federal Government would never be able to coerce a State against its will.

In ratifying, a number of States demanded amendments. These were proposed in the first Congress and quickly approved by the States. These first ten amendments are known as the Bill of Rights. Read these Constitutional provisions: as is clear from its language, the Bill of Rights was intended to restrain the Federal Government, which was viewed as the chief danger to the freedom and rights of American citizens. Since the War Between the States (WBTS), the Bill of Rights has been interpreted as empowering the Feds to overrule State laws. Strange!

Hamilton and Jefferson

The 12 years from ratification of the Constitution to Jefferson's election as President in 1800 contain much of interest. Population, economic productivity, Western settlement, and culture flourished without any significant immigrant input (see chapter's 6, 7 and 8). Space allows us only to consider things relative to the WBTS. These things were economic/political and cultural. Southerners entered the new government with open minds and a cooperative spirit. After a while they discovered that there was a highly organized party determined to force through measures profitable to the wealthy of the Northeast. This was essentially the program of Alexander Hamilton – a national debt with interest-collecting bondholders, a "national" bank, various business subsidies, and the Constitution stretched as far as possible to make the Federal Government supreme over the States and the people. Hamilton had been close to Washington during the war, was brilliant, and had married into one of the wealthiest families of New York State. At the Constitutional Convention he had advocated a British-style monarchy and left in disgust when his proposal got no support. As the first Secretary of the Treasury he made use of his post to initiate his agenda and form supporters into what became the Federalist Party.

Gradually an opposition party developed which came to be called Republican. (No relation to the later "Republican Party" of Lincoln, which was its exact opposite.) Thomas Jefferson became the leader of this party, which was based on the agricultural South and the less financialized areas of the North. When Hamilton levied a tax on Western farmers to make them obey the heavy hand of the Federal Government, he caused "the Whisky Rebellion." He led soldiers into western PA and arrested people, but they were all freed by juries.

As Washington left the Presidency in 1797 he urged Americans to observe two rules: avoid dividing into political parties and avoid "entangling alliances" with foreign countries. The first principle was already abandoned when he spoke. And 20th century Americans would discard the second. In the 1790s and the years immediately after, Americans could not ignore involvement in the 20 years of war between the great powers Britain and France that followed the French Revolution and the rise of Napoleon. American trade was with Europe and with many nearby European colonies, and imperial British power in Canada seemed threatening. This situation was to lead the U.S. into the War of 1812.

The forces released by the French Revolution created conflicting and heated opinions among Americans which added to the fire already started by Hamilton's agenda. While Jefferson lived at ease among his 300 bonded African Americans, the Federalist John Adams fortified his house and armed his servants in fear that an American mob might imitate their French counterparts and attack the privileged. Federalists wanted Federal officials to be regarded with awe, the upper classes be kowtowed to, and majority rule held within tight limits by the executive and courts. As President, Adams rode about in a coach with white horses and insisted on being addressed as "Your Excellency." When Jefferson became President in 1801 he got rid of all that and lived casually like any Virginia gentleman. He exemplified "republican simplicity" to later generations.

The Federalist Congress in order to quash opposition passed "Alien and Sedition Acts." The "Sedition Act" punished people for criticizing President Adams. A number of newspaper editors were imprisoned or fined. This was clearly in violation of the recently passed First Amendment. How was it justified? The Federalists claimed, falsely, that English Common Law was part of the Constitution and therefore they could punish "sedition." They had already been filling the Federal bench with judges devoted to centralization and to assertion of unelected judicial power. These, with lifetime tenure, were to continue to promote Hamiltonian philosophy long after it had been repudiated at the polls.

The Alien and Sedition Acts were too much. Jefferson and Madison began to respond to demands to form political opposition. On a "botanical research" trip to Pennsylvania and New York they happened to meet with people who were organizing against Federalist rule. Politics became hot. Jeffersonians accused Federalists of working to establish a monarchy, and Federalists likened Jefferson to the Jacobins who were merrily cutting off heads in France.

In 1798 the Kentucky legislature passed resolutions written by Jefferson that stated unequivocally that the Federal Government was not supreme but the agent of the States with powers specifically delegated in the Constitution and no others. When federal officials exceeded their powers, as in the Sedition Act, the sovereign State could "interpose" between their people and federal usurpation. Madison wrote similar resolutions passed by Virginia the next year. These statements formed the background to Jefferson's election in 1800. For long after "the Principles of '98" were watchwords of Jefferson's party and the succeeding Democrats.

The controversies of the 1790s were quite fierce but they differed considerably from the sectional conflict engendered later by the Republican Party. The Federalists were patriots who had a genuine vision of how America could become strong and prosperous. Their vision of a strong government and economy has mostly come to pass today. They did not engage in disguising their agenda with demagogic diversions like the later Whig and Republican parties that pursued the same policies (see Chapter 15). Unlike the Republican Party they sought support throughout the Union and did not condemn the Southern Culture as something to be annihilated.

Cultural Conflict

Many Americans hoped to develop an art and literature that was "American," not imitative of Europe. This took various forms. Unfortunately, one form was a product of New England's Puritan arrogance of superior virtue and wisdom, although the theology was now post-Puritan. (The Adamses and many other New Englanders became Unitarians.) New Englanders viciously opposed the Louisiana Purchase and other territorial growth and threatened secession. During the War of 1812 they came close to treason. They were losing power, relatively, as the West, largely Southern, grew. The Connecticut poet William Cullen Bryant condemned the Louisiana territory as a swamp only useful for Jefferson's strange scientific pastimes. Daniel Webster of Massachusetts, later touted to be a great spokesman for "Union," said: "What do we want with this vast and worthless area, of this region of savages and wild beasts, of deserts, of shifting sands and whirlwinds, of dust, of cactus and prairie dogs; to what use could we ever hope to put these great deserts, or those endless mountain ranges?"

Conscious of their loss of status, New Englanders began a campaign to take over American culture. In 1789 Jedidiah Morse from Connecticut published the first American geography book. He portrayed New Englanders as educated, pious, and industrious people, and the rest of Americans mainly as lazy, backward, and immoral. When Noah Webster, also from Connecticut, published his first "American" dictionary he took the same tack: New Englanders spoke and wrote the best and purest English of any people in the world. Historians joined in to portray the War of Independence as a New England achievement with the contributions of other regions denigrated. The message in all this was that New Englanders were the true and real "Americans" and everybody else was marginal. Two years before he was elected President, Jefferson wrote a friend about the economic and cultural imperialism coming from the North: "It is true we are completely under the saddle of Massachusetts and Connecticut, and that they ride us very hard, cruelly insulting our feelings, as well as exhausting our strength and substance." At first many Northerners disdained this Yankee ethnocentrism as much as did Southerners. But in time it succeeded, spreading across New York State, Pennsylvaina and the upper Midwest. At first, New Englanders had no anti-slavery feelings. One of the leading lights of their early literature, Timothy Dwight, wrote a long poem about how well-treated African American bonded people were in New England compared to other States.

The drive for cultural dominance would be joined in the North in the 1830s by abolitionism. Then in the 1850s, the growth of industry and finance across the North would create a new and powerful Hamiltonian fervour for government promotion of private profits. Together, these elements created a new and revolutionary sectional party – the Republicans.

Conclusion

When he became President in 1801, Jefferson encouraged a damping down of political antagonism. It was not immediately successful, but as the "Virginia Dynasty" of Jefferson, Madison, and Monroe matured, politics eventually became less fiery. The time of Monroe (1819-1825) was often referred to as "The Era of Good Feelings." Ambitious politicians, however, made certain good feelings would not last. When the War Between the States came, many people on both sides saw in the conflict of Hamilton and Jefferson an early hint of the great crisis.

Suggestion for Class Discussion

Contrast the above description of American history in the period of 1783—1801 with the way it is presented in most textbooks.

Recommended Reading

- *A Better Guide than Reason*, (pub. 1977); *Original Intentions*, (pub. 1993); and *Founding Fathers*, (pub. 1994), all by M. E. Bradford.

- *The Life and Selected Writings of Thomas Jefferson*, by Adrienne Koch and William Peden, eds., pub. 1944.

- *From Union to Empire*, (pub. 2003), and *Defending Dixie*, (pub. 2006), both by Clyde N. Wilson.

- *Nullification: A Constitutional History*, *1776—1833*, by W. Kirk Wood, pub. 2008.

Chapter 5* – The Virginia Dynasty: Spectacular Growth of the Union of the States, 1801 – 1824

By Clyde N. Wilson of S. C., Ph.D., S.I.S.H.

Introduction

During the administrations of three great Virginia statesmen and friends, Thomas Jefferson, James Madison, and James Monroe, Americans created new States across almost half a continent and acquired vast new territory for future States. The population tripled without much immigration, and the Jeffersonian party and most Americans favoured and lived happily with a limited central government that in peacetime interfered very little with the States and the citizens.

Growth of the Union

Even before Jefferson took office in 1801, Kentucky (from land ceded by VA) and Tennessee (from land ceded by NC) had become States and were already exercising influence in Union affairs. There was a post-Revolutionary flood of settlers across the Appalachians. Between 1790 and 1820 the population of KY increased from 73,677 to 581,434 and that of TN from 35,691 to 422,823. In 1811 a Kentuckian, Henry Clay, was elected Speaker of the House. In 1824 two of four presidential candidates were from the new States: Clay from KY and Andrew Jackson from TN. Before Monroe left office five new States had been admitted to the Union from western territories of the 13 States. Three of these OH, IN, and IL – were from the Northwest Territory ceded by VA for the use of all Americans. (By 1820, OH had 581,434 people.) Two new States, AL and MS, came from Georgia's western lands. And two more new States, LA and MO, came from the Louisiana Purchase.

The Louisiana Purchase

The Union in 1800 was surrounded on the south and west by sparsely populated territories of the once great but now weak Spanish empire. Dynamic Americans could not help but look longingly at the unused land and resources beyond the Mississippi River. Even more importantly, free use of the river and its great port at New Orleans were essential to the prosperity of the Americans west of the Appalachians. In 1803, by a secret treaty, Spain transferred the vast territory north and west of New Orleans to Napoleonic France. Jefferson heard of this and sent Monroe to Paris to see what could be done in the interest of the western States. As it turned out, Napoleon decided not to try to launch a new empire in America but instead sold what became known to Americans as the Louisiana Purchase for money to support his European campaigns. This added to the Union a vast territory from the Mississippi to the Rocky Mountains. The borders were somewhat vague – by some interpretations Texas was included. In 1810, American settlers in what was known as West Florida declared independence from Spain. This added the Gulf Coast and the port of Mobile to what would become the States of Alabama and Mississippi.

Jefferson sent two young Virginia friends, William Clark and Meriwether Lewis to explore the new territory, then largely unknown to civilization. They ascended the Missouri River, crossed the Rocky Mountains, and reached the Pacific at the mouth of the Columbia River. They brought back a vast amount of information about geography, weather, flora, fauna, Indian tribes, and potential resources. A similar expedition in a more southern region under Zebulon Pike got only as far as "Pike's Peak" (in present Colorado). It brought back the news that sparse rainfall would make the region problematic for agriculture.

The War of 1812

Britain and France were engaged in a world war for 20 years before and during the administrations of the Virginia Dynasty. Both powers declared blockades that attempted to prevent neutral shipping from trading with their enemy. Much of the U.S. Northern economy was based on shipping and suffered from impositions by both powers in trade with Europe and European colonies in the New World. British offenses were more numerous because Britain ruled the seas. American merchant ships were seized. British warships stopped American vessels on the high seas and took away into harsh service seamen they considered to be British. In 1807, off Hampton Roads, a British warship *Leopard* fired on and boarded the U.S. Navy vessel *Chesapeake,* killing several sailors and carrying off others. This created fiery grassroots indignation among American patriots.

The Jeffersonians tried a series of boycott policies to force the great powers to respect American neutral rights on the seas. These were not successful and were harmful to New England, which protested vigourously and evaded the laws. In fact, New Englanders resented Jeffersonian attempts to secure American rights peacefully far more than they did British impositions. Even if they got only every other ship through they were still making huge profits off trade with wartime Europe. New England leaders cared little if some of their sailors were impressed. These were lower class people whose lives were likened by John Adams to those of Southern slaves. Southerners and Westerners, who had no ships, resented British atrocities more than did the merchants. There was a rising sentiment outside the commercial areas, eloquently expressed by young John C. Calhoun of SC, that the Union could not allow itself to be treated so dishonourably and must make a less cowardly response.

Another consideration contributed to the declaration of war by the U.S. against Britain in 1812. The British had not completely withdrawn from the Northwest Territory as they had promised. There they incited some of the Indians to war against Americans. In 1811 General William Henry Harrison from VA defeated the largest uprising, led by Tecumseh, at Tippecanoe in what became Indiana. Some Americans even envisioned "liberating" and annexing Canada, although this proved to be a pipe dream. Canadians, both British and French, did not want to be "liberated."

The war that followed was not a success, although the infant American navy had some heroic exploits to record. In the northeast, an American invasion of Canada was defeated and repulsed. A British fleet sailed into Chesapeake Bay, bombarded Baltimore, and sent soldiers to burn Washington, forcing President Madison and the government to flee. In the Northwest things began badly when General William Hull, from CT, surrendered Detroit to the British without firing a shot. By hard fighting with mostly Southern volunteers, the Virginian General Harrison was able to recover the Northwest Territory.

In the South, things went better. Andrew Jackson of TN had already established himself as a successful commander. In 1810 he had defeated a major Indian uprising at Horseshoe Bend in what became Alabama. (Davy Crockett and Sam Houston were among Jackson's soldiers in that battle.) In 1814 a large British fleet sailed to New Orleans. On board was a complete set of officials for a British government for the Louisiana Territory and veteran soldiers who boasted that they would soon be in possession of "booty and beauty." Jackson's TN and KY volunteers, behind cotton bale defenses, decimated the attacking British invaders. Finally Americans could take some pride in the war which had changed nothing. They even celebrated it as "the second War of Independence" because they had asserted themselves against British power. Harrison and Jackson became presidential contenders.

A further consequence of the war was the discrediting of New England and the decline of the Federalist Party. New Englanders with a few exceptions rabidly opposed and undermined the war effort. They traded with the enemy. Massachusetts refused to allow its militia to leave the state in answer to a constitutional Federal call for help in defending the northern border, although for years afterward it demanded that the Federal Government pay its militia expenses. In 1814, the MA, CT, and RI legislatures sent delegates to meet at the "Hartford Convention" to consider secession. Secession was not recommended, but demands were made for five amendments to the U.S. Constitution to reduce the weight of the South in Congress.

A footnote to the war in the Southwest is the acquisition of East Florida (now the State of Florida). East Florida was a Spanish territory without any effective government. The territory was a continuing threat to GA – bands of marauding Indians and criminals crossed the border, kidnapped, murdered, looted, and disappeared back into East Florida. In 1818 Andrew Jackson, as army commander in the South, pursued hostiles into East Florida, seized two Spanish forts, executed two British subjects accused of encouraging the raids, and remained in control. Although Jackson had undoubtedly exceeded his orders and threatened to involve the U.S. in war with European powers, President Monroe was able to secure the purchase of East Florida from Spain. Along with the earlier acquisition of West Florida, this meant that the U.S. ever after would unavoidably be involved in the Caribbean.

The Missouri Controversy: A Fire Bell in the Night

The treaty acquiring the Louisiana Purchase required that the French residents retain citizenship and property rights, including slaves. In 1812 the southern portion of the territory was admitted to the Union as the State of Louisiana. New England Anglo-Saxon Protestants raged unsuccessfully against a new State with French-speaking and Catholic people but they fit easily into the Southern Culture. The next new State from the Louisiana Purchase was Missouri, quickly populated by people from the South. The people adopted a constitution based on that of KY and applied for admission to the Union. A Northern majority in the House of Representatives voted that slavery be eliminated in MO as a condition of admission. The Senate refused to go along and Congress and the country were thrown into turmoil that lasted two years.

Everyone understood that this move had nothing to do with sympathy for bonded African Americans. It was an attempt to create a division that would bring about a new Northern political party to replace the Federalists. The elder statesmen Jefferson and Madison understood this. Jefferson lamented that the Northern move had come on the country like "a fire bell in the night" and was likely to ruin the work of the Founding Fathers. The attempt to dictate a constitution and society to a State which the people had founded was unprecedented and violated the true nature of the Union of sovereign States. As always, Jefferson wished the country could be rid of slavery, but "we have a wolf by the ears," which could not safely be let go. The best policy for the welfare of the African American bonded people and for American society was allowing them to spread out rather than bottling them up.

Eventually, politicians engineered a "compromise." MO was admitted to the Union without the restriction and ME, which until then had been a part of MA, became a separate State. It was provided that within the Louisiana Purchase no bonded African Americans could be held in territory above an east/west line drawn from the southern border of MO, leaving only the Arkansas territory to the South. Legally, the compromise did not apply to FL or to any territory beyond the Purchase that the U.S. might later acquire. It was not much of a true "compromise" because different majorities voted separately for each part. Northerners largely voted against it and in 1846 would try to prevent the territorial division principle from being applied again to territory gained by the Mexican War. Still later, when the Kansas/Nebraska acts were passed, the same people who had opposed the compromise raged that a sacred pact had been violated. A considerable number of Southern leaders opposed the settlement also, asserting that the South had made a fatal mistake by allowing the Northern majority to make conditions for future sovereign States. Most Americans, probably, hoped that a troublesome issue had been settled for good. But the Union would never be the same again. The IL legislature in the 1820s seriously considered legalizing slavery, but Midwesterners were mostly determined to keep black people, free or slave, elsewhere.

Suggestions for Class Discussion

What characteristics of the Southern Culture produced statesman like Thomas Jefferson and leaders like Andrew Jackson?

Recommended Readings

- *The Missouri Controversy, 1819-1821*, by Glover Moore, pub. 1953.

- *The Old Northwest, A Chronicle of the Ohio Valley and Beyond*, by Frederick L. Ogg, (#19 in *The Chronicles of America* series), pub. 1919.

- *The Rise of the New West, 1819-1824*, by Frederick Jackson Turner, (vol. 14 of *The American Nation: A History* series), pub. 1906.

Chapter 6 – Expansion and Conflict of the Northern and Southern Cultures to 1860

By Clyde N. Wilson of S. C., Ph.D., S. I. S. H.

Introduction

As stated in Chapter 2, understanding the War Between the States is sharpened by knowledge of the characteristics of the two American cultures present before, during, and after that horrific conflict. From the founding of the U.S. under the Constitution to the election of Abraham Lincoln as President by the Northern Culture in 1860, the basic underlying theme of American history was expansion. The population increased from 4 million to 31.5 million, the States increased from 13 to 33, and the territory increased from 865,000 square miles to almost 3 million. The Northern Culture and the Southern Culture played different roles in this great growth and experienced it in different ways. This we will need to understand as we pursue the events leading to the WBTS.

Relevant History

When the American Revolution broke out in Boston in 1775, it took a month for the news to reach Andrew Jackson, a lad in upcountry South Carolina. When Jackson passed away in TN in 1845 the news was telegraphed and was reported in a few hours in the larger cities by the new daily newspapers peddled on the streets. Life was vastly different in some ways than it had been in the 13 colonies, although in fundamental ways the core Northern and Southern cultures remained. By 1860 fleets of steamboats plied the Mississippi, Ohio, and Missouri rivers and traveled many miles inland from port cities. Railroads spread over much of the country. Banks, factories, churches, schools and colleges were numerous and Wall Street was in full flower. There were two new American States on the Pacific coast, California and Oregon.

Many Americans had become accustomed to moving west. New Southern States admitted to the Union: 1790s, KY and TN; 1810s, LA, MS, and AL; 1820s, MO; 1830s, AR; 1840s, FL and TX. New Northern States: 1790s, VT; 1803, OH; 1810s, IN and IL; 1820s, ME; 1830s, MI; 1840s, IA and WI; 1850s, MN; and KS with Northern control in 1861.

The Southern culture moved west and reproduced itself in a vast territory. In 1860, half the people born in the Carolinas, both black and white, were living somewhere further west. This was natural. Families were large and did not want to break up their property among many sons; new lands were more fertile; there was a vast and ever increasing world demand for cotton; and Southern Americans were spirited and adventurous.

Southerners were always in the lead in acquiring new territory. Virginia by its own efforts had conquered the Northwest Territory (Midwest) and generously gave the land to the Union to be enjoyed by all Americans. Southerners were responsible for the Louisiana Purchase, the acquisition of Florida, and the American settlement of Texas, all of which were vigorously opposed by dominant Northern leaders. Northerners did not need new land; they wanted the Federal Government to support their industry and commerce.

During most of this period, up to the 1850s, Southerners dominated national politics. Eight of the first 12 Presidents were Southern plantation owners and another, Harrison, though elected from the Midwest, was born on a VA plantation. However, population increases tended to make for more control of the House of Representatives by the Northern culture.

During this period also, Southern crops made up the vast majority of American exports. The foreign commerce of the U.S. was Southern based, although New York City enjoyed much of the shipping, financing, and insuring, and had good relations with the South. The South had relatively little industry. This was not because Southerners were ignorant and lazy, as New Englanders loudly proclaimed, but because they could enjoy more prosperity and a more comfortable way of life without it. Thomas Jefferson had warned that farmers were the mainstays of freedom and that urban workers were not desirable. When the Confederacy was threatened by invasion Southerners showed great skill in inventions, engineering, and industrial production.

The North retained its Puritan roots but changed dramatically in its economy and population during the period before the war. Chapter 4 explains how economic conflict dominated the politics of the Union in this period because the Northern and Southern cultures had different ways of making a living and different ideas of how the power of the Federal Government should be exercised.

The Northern economy had at first been mercantile – shipping and trading. During the War of 1812 shipping had been curtailed and New England capital had been turned to textile factories and production of war materiel. They had water power, surplus labour, raw material from the South, and money to invest (much of it accumulated earlier in the slave trade). PA developed iron industry. From 1816 onward Northern industrialists demanded a "protective tariff" on imports, constantly increased, in order to "protect" their industries by pricing foreign goods out of the market and forcing all Americans to buy their products. It is worth noting that one of the leading Radical Republicans, Thaddeus Stevens, owned iron furnaces. The tariff on British imports was very profitable to him although it added $6,000 to the cost of every mile of railroad built in the U.S.

During the 1850s industry spread to the Midwest. Chicago and Detroit, which not long before had been insignificant villages, grew into teeming industrial cities and Chicago was a great railroad center. The Federalist and Whig parties both advocated a tariff, a national bank, and "internal improvements" at Federal expense. All these measures took wealth from the South and transferred it to capitalists in the North. As industry, banking, and stock trading became more and more important in the North, the demand for such measures grew stronger. The Republican Party got much of its strength from Northern resentment at Democratic vetoes of Federal subsidies they considered to be beneficial to them.

The economic conflict between North and South that is discussed in Chapter 4 was important and was present from the beginning. It was the root of the disagreement between Alexander Hamilton and Thomas Jefferson that was the first serious political conflict of the Union. But the undoubted importance of economics was no more central to conflict than the persisting and evolving differences in values and ways of life. Southerners had first developed the Midwest by settling the southern parts of OH, IN, and IL. As time went on, this region changed character as industry and great cities developed and as New Englanders and European immigrants swarmed in. From the 1840s large numbers of impoverished Irish came to the U.S. and settled everywhere, especially in the cities. After the failed revolutions of 1848 many Germans and other central Europeans came, and settled largely in the Midwest. They had strongly centralist, progressive, and authoritarian attitudes and knew nothing of the South or American Constitutional traditions. They would be zealous supporters of the Republican Party and the Federal Army. Abraham Lincoln secretly bought a German language newspaper to support his presidential candidacy. By the 1850s a majority in the Midwestern States no longer identified with and voted with the South as they had traditionally. The Northern people were one-fourth foreign-born.

Hard as it is for people today to understand, the pre-war South was far more tolerant of ethnic and religious "diversity" than the North. Immigrants to the South came as individuals and were quickly assimilated and became loyal Southerners. During the years before the war the anti-immigrant "Know-Nothing" party rose in the North. Catholic convents were attacked and burned down by mobs in Philadelphia and Boston (with the collusion of local officials). Nothing like that happened in the South. The Catholic bishop of SC was an honoured and well-liked citizen of Charleston. The South elected many Catholics to public office. In 1860 two Senators from the South were Jewish, unheard of in the North.

It must be understood that Northern abolitionists had little sympathy for black people – they considered them an obstacle to what they wanted as American "progress." Most Northern states denied rights to the few black people who lived there. In Lincoln's IL, before and during the WBTS, free black people *were not even allowed to move into the State.* If slaves were freed in the South, as abolitionists demanded, they were still not allowed to move North. The majority of free black people of the U.S. were in the South and demonstrably better off than those in the North. For a long time New Englanders made the "racist" boast that they were "pure Anglo-Saxons" and thus superior to other Americans. It is simply wrong to think that antislavery was for racial equality. It was against black people and even more against those who held them as bonded labour. To assume otherwise is to make the mistake of reading the later 1900s back into that time. Abolition had little to do with the actual life lived by people, white or black, in the South. No abolitionist every made any constructive suggestion.

Religion was an important difference. The South grew more and more orthodox and devout in this period, although tolerant among the different denominations. The North went in the opposite direction, developing dubiously Christian sects. Harvard, founded by Puritans, became Unitarian. Many new churches, like Mormons and 7th Day Adventists, appeared in the North. (General Lee prayed frequently during the war; there is no indication that General Grant ever did.)

The North developed a class of "intellectuals," people who were rich enough that they did not have to work but could spend their time hectoring others. The perfect example is Ralph Waldo Emerson. He started as a Congregational minister but decided that the ministry was invalid and went to Germany to study advanced philosophy. When he returned he married the daughter of a rich banker and became a guru. He taught that "the American" was a "New Man" who could lead the world to perfection if the barbaric South could be got rid of. He announced that the inhabitants of the MA penitentiary were superior to Southern leaders. Another of the type was Henry David Thoreau, whose father owned a factory, and who likened the psychopath John Brown to Christ. The "Secret Six," who financed John Brown's murderous escapades, were independently wealthy men, mostly from inheritance. It seems that MA was still the righteous and superior "city on a hill" although Christianity was no longer part of the vision.

The differences between the Northern and Southern cultures grew greater and more obvious as the antebellum period went on. The Baptist, Methodist, and Presbyterian churches split into Northern and Southern groups. For 30 years prior to secession many influential Northerners constantly denounced their Southern fellow citizens as evil barbarians who were inferior in intellect and morals. We cannot over-estimate the extent to which this hostile atmosphere contributed to secession. Southerners knew their fathers had joined the Union for mutual benefit of all the States. They grew weary of a Union in which they were relentlessly exploited and slandered by the other parties.

Republicans claimed that the South was dominated by a few rich planters they called "the Slave Power." This was not true. Most Southerners were proud and independent in spirit and property. They could vote, make up their own minds, and choose their own leaders. Planters had much less influence in the South than bankers and industrialists in the North. The difference was that the bankers and industrialists controlled the politicians but stayed in the background.

Standard Republican propaganda said that the backward, lazy, ignorant, and uncivilized South was an intolerable drag on the welfare of the North. But in 1860 in NYC there were women and children working 16-hour days for starvation wages, 150,000 unemployed, 40,000 homeless, 600 brothels with girls as young as 12, and 9,000 saloons where the poor could drown their sorrows. Half the children died before the age of 5 while black children proliferated in the South. By this time many Southerners had been to NYC, some to London. When they got home and looked around, they saw no reason to listen to abolitionists who wanted to destroy Southern life at no cost to themselves.

Conclusion

The South did not need the North and had no desire to interfere in its life, but the North found the South indispensable as a source of profits and a political and moral whipping boy. This is the background for the Republican Party's rise.

Suggestions for Class Discussion

Why would respectable Northern clergymen liken John Brown to Christ?

When campaigning for the Republican Presidential nomination, Lincoln made a famous "House Divided Speech" in which he said that the U.S. had to become "all slave or all free." Discuss.

Recommended Readings

- *The Coming of the Civil War*, by Avery O. Craven, pub. 1942.

Chapter 7* – Westward Expansion to the Pacific and Efforts by Two Cultures to Control Political Power.

By Howard Ray White of N. C., S.I.S.H.

History Relevant to Understanding the WBTS

You read in Chapter 4 how westward expansion added 5 states during the James Monroe Administrations (MS, IL, AL and MO, plus ME, which was carved out of MA) This chapter continues that history, covering the days of Presidents John Q. Adams, of MA; Andrew Jackson, of TN; Martin Van Buren, of NY; John Tyler, of VA, and James K. Polk, also of TN. This era spanned 24 years – from 1825 to 1849. During this time western expansion continued out to AR, FL, WI, IA and vast Texas. Pioneers of the Southern culture were at the forefront in most of the region being settled, but not along the Great Lakes and upper Mississippi Valley.

During this one-generation span of 24 years, as before in America, pioneers continued pressing westward, most to acquire land of their own upon which to raise large, well-fed families, an opportunity denied relatives and ancestors in densely populated Europe. Today, few schools have students who are being raised on family farms. If you be one, you can appreciate a passionate love of the land that motivated the pioneering spirit. If not of a farm family, just dream back to 1825 and visualize the pioneer family's love of the land.

President John Quincy Adams, Independent of Massachusetts, 4 Years, 1825-1829 (States Admitted: None).

Setting aside constitutional prohibitions, Adams advocated far more Federal spending on roads and canals to facilitate westward expansion, but only managed to win approval of the Cumberland Road into Ohio and the Chesapeake and Ohio Canal. But these two would greatly aid westward expansion from the north. He also advocated a huge hike in taxes on imports, far higher rates than constitutionally acceptable, to raise prices on manufactured goods. Opponents called this the "Tariff of Abominations." Vice President John Calhoun of South Carolina condemned it as "unconstitutional, oppressive, and unjust." Rates were soon cut back. But this fight between the northern and southern cultures over import tax rates would continue and become a cause of the WBTS.

President Andrew Jackson, Democrat of Tennessee, 8 Years, 1829-1837 (States Admitted: Arkansas and Michigan).

The newly-founded Democratic Party took control in 1829, with solid majorities in the House and Senate and with President Jackson and Vice President John C. Calhoun in the Executive. Westward expansion continued. Jackson supported extension of the National Road westward, but railroads would become the answer. During Jackson's era, the Cherokee and the four other "Civilized Tribes" would be directed to migrate to a new homeland in what would become Oklahoma. These able Native American's would migrate, many forcibly, to a new homeland where they were promised sovereignty, a promise broken after the WBTS.

President Martin Van Buren, Democrat of New York, 4 Years, 1837-1841 (States Admitted: None).

Jackson's Democratic Party elevated Vice President Van Buren to President. Just two months after Van Buren took office, the financial panic of 1837 sent America's economy into a tailspin. This serious economic depression would last six years, until 1843. Even though America's financial center was in the northeast, urban and manufacturing regions suffered the most. Farm families and pioneering families were more resourceful, more able to put food on the table, but still fearful of losing their farms for inability to pay mortgages. Meanwhile, the relocation of southeastern Native Americans to what would become Oklahoma continued.

President John Tyler, Embattled Whig of Virginia, 3 Years 11 Months, 1841-1845 (States Admitted: Florida).

The financial panic elevated the Whig Party to power in the House and Senate and put in office President William Henry Harrison of Indiana and Vice President John Tyler of Virginia. But President Harrison died a month after taking office and Tyler completed the term. It was not a happy time. In control of Congress and eager for greater Federal enhancement to banking, Whigs twice submitted bills to establish a National Bank. Sharing Andrew Jackson's concerns about empowering centralized banking, Tyler twice vetoed these National Bank bills. In protest, all but one of his Cabinet resigned. Tyler was a man without a party. But pioneers seeking land could cheer: Tyler signed a bill making it easier for settlers to purchase 160 acre tracts of public land for $1.25 per acre.

President James K. Polk, Democrat of Tennessee, 4 Years, 1845-1849 (States Admitted: Texas, Iowa and Wisconsin).

We now arrive at the last time the Southern Culture exerted power over the Federal Government, the four-year term of President James K. Polk of Tennessee. The big story concerns the Republic of Texas, a vast land indeed. In hindsight, Texans giving up their Republic for statehood might be judged unwise. But they did. President Tyler had championed the merger. Northeastern politicians had opposed, fearing further loss of power. But "Statehood for Texas" had elected Tennessee Democrat James K. Polk. On February 16, 1846 at Austin, Texans lowered their Republic flag, the Lone Star, and raised their new state flag. Addressing the crowd, Republic of Texas President Anson Jones said in part: "The Lone Star of Texas. . . has passed on and become fixed forever in that glorious constellation, which all freemen and lovers of freedom in the world must reverence and adore, the United States of America. Blending its rays with its sister states, long may it continue to shine and may generous Heaven smile upon this consummation of the wishes of the two Republics, now joined in one." But Texans would not see the anticipated "smile" from a "generous Heaven." Fearing loss of its sparsely settled northern lands, Mexico challenged American expansion and the Mexican War was fought. Fifteen years later Texans would suffer the WBTS.

But President Polk proved that diplomacy could trump war in America's effort to expand to the Pacific Northwest. Great Britain and the United States had been sharing control over the region that would become British Columbia, Washington State and Oregon. Some had advocated war to secure much of the land above the Columbia River. But John Calhoun, John Tyler's Secretary of State, had negotiated a compromise boundary. Polk agreed and the boundary was set at the 49th parallel. Peaceful relations with Canada would endure.

Suggestions for Class Discussion

The American population doubled to over 22 million during this 24-year era and available land expanded to the Pacific. Should we praise the Southern Culture for this achievement?

Chapter 8* – Southerners Found the Republic of Texas

By Howard Ray White of N. C., S.I.S.H.

What an exciting story this is! What heroes Texans have in Stephen Austin and Sam Houston! Our story begins in Mexico City. But wait. Are you asking, "How can the history of the Republic of Texas, a foreign nation, pertain to understanding the War Between the States?" Good question. Answer. You are learning about the persistent political and economic conflict in the US between the Southern and Northern cultures. Well, in the Republic of Texas you experience the climax of the great westward expansion of the Southern Culture, the conclusion of a very important story, now presented here.

Mexicans declared independence from Spain and successfully defended it in 1821, bringing Augustin de Iturbide to power as Emperor of Mexico. Soon afterward Moses Austin, an American, received permission to bring immigrants from the United States into Mexican Tejas (Texas), the northern part of what was soon to become the vast, sparsely settled Mexican state of Coahuila y Tejas. Under the guidance of Moses's son Stephen, pioneers, mostly from the Southern states, left America to settle Mexican Tejas and become Mexican citizens. Why? – Because Mexico needed hardy settlers to come to vast Tejas and defend Mexicans against Apache and Comanche raids and Mexican land against future U.S. westward expansion. Emperor Iturbide was deposed in 1823 and a republican government was established under the new Constitution of 1824, which established states with elected governors and legislatures. Guadalupe Victoria was elected President. But soon, frequent political upheavals in Mexico City threatened to return Mexico to an all-powerful central government. After several *coup d'etat* overthrows, in May 1833, Antonio López de Santa Anna gained power and began killing the Constitution of 1824. He imprisoned Stephen Austin who was in Mexico City seeking improved relations for Tejans. In May 1835 Santa Anna brutally crushed a revolt in the state of Zacatecas, slaughtering 2,000 non-combatants. Opposed to centralization, Agustin Viesca, the governor of Coahuila y Tejas, disbanded the state legislature on May 21 and retreated northward with his government. But he was arrested in October at Béxar (San Antonio), Tejas. In late October Santa Anna completed the demolition of federalism, abolishing all state governments and reorganizing the nation as departments administered from Mexico City. Finally released from jail, Austin was back in Tejas on September 1, advising, "War is our only hope." The War for Texas Independence was just beginning.

Trouble was brewing by November 3, 1835 when Texas leaders convened a "Consultation" in San Felipe and a 1,400-man Mexican army under Martin Cos was occupying Béxar (San Antonio). Meanwhile, the "Consultation," approved one last attempt to establish a Mexican state of Tejas with assured State Rights. Sam Houston was named the state's commander of military forces. But the Mexican State Movement was soon abandoned. Meanwhile, in early December at Béxar, Tejans forced Cos' to surrender his army and depart Tejas. A spirit of independence and confidence was growing.

On March 1, 1836, the Texas Independence Convention opened at Washington-on-the-Brazos, Tejas. Working rapidly, delegates drew up a Republic of Texas Constitution (6

Southern States, VA, NC, TN, KY, SC and GA, provided nearly three-fourths of the signers). Dead was the idea of a Mexican State of Tejas. Elected Commander-in-Chief of Texas Armies, Sam Houston departed on March 6 to gather his forces. The Convention had just learned of the massacre at the Alamo in Béxar. Only a Texian for three years, Houston, a former Tennessee governor, had left his Cherokee wife Tiana for Tejas in December 1832. Volunteers were arriving with arms from LA, GA, MS, TN, KY and other American states.

Santa Anna had been personally leading 1,500 soldiers to Béxar, first arriving on February 23. Considered the government center of Tejas, the town's major feature was the Alamo, a rugged and old Spanish Mission structure. Considering the Alamo a death trap, Sam Houston had sent James Bowie to Béxar with orders to salvage the cannon and destroy the building while time permitted. Instead, Bowie and William Travis had rallied the Texians within to stay and reinforce the building. A final message from Travis announced that Santa Anna "has demanded surrender at discretion, otherwise the garrison are to be put to the sword. . . . But I shall never surrender or retreat. I am determined to sustain myself as long as possible. . . . Victory or Death!" The army overran the Alamo on March 6. No defenders were allowed to surrender. When the walls were breached, about 80 Texians fled, but were killed by Mexican cavalry. Almost everyone was slain; the number killed estimated at 182 to 257 men. Among the dead defenders were leaders William Travis of AL, James Bowie of LA, and David Crockett of TN. Yet the heroism of those brave men accomplished much: Santa Anna was delayed at Béxar for two weeks, giving the Convention time to declare independence and form a government for the Republic of Texas. And they inspired Texans to fight harder to defeat Mexican forces. All would "Remember the Alamo" and derive enhanced justification for their rebellion against tyranny. All of them were heroes.

Santa Anna had three Mexican armies in Texas, viciously destroying the independence movement, not allowing surrender, not taking prisoners. The army under Antonio Gaona was moving northeast from Béxar. Santa Anna was leading an army eastward from Béxar and, since January, Jose Urrea had been leading an army, nearly 1,000 strong, along the Gulf Coast, which had already inflicted heavy damage by the time Houston had been named Commander-in-Chief of Texas Armies. Urrea's main opposition were the much smaller Texian forces under James Fannin and others, which had taken control of the town of Goliad in October and its Spanish fort, Presidio La Bahia. Believing the Republic needed to consolidate its troops and avoid capture, Houston ordered Fannin to destroy the Goliad fort and march eastward toward Victoria. Receiving the order on March 11, Fannin declined, unwilling to leave any men behind. Unfortunately, his men suffered the Goliad Massacre two weeks later. Like at the Alamo, the Mexican command refused to take prisoners. Those who surrendered were killed. On Palm Sunday, March 27, Fannin of GA, William Ward of GA, Ira Westover of MA and their men were marched out of the Presidio and shot. Almost 350 Texians died. The Texas Independence Movement gained another war cry, "Remember Goliad."

Houston planned to avoid the West and Gulf armies and find a way to defeat the middle army, which was under Santa Anna himself. Retreating with purpose, Houston was patient and intent on preserving his army. He finally found his chance at the San Jacinto River. His men surprised Santa Anna's army at 4:30 pm on April 21, overran their camp and captured Santa Anna. In remembrance of the Alamo and Goliad, about 650 Mexican soldiers were killed. Texans only lost 6 killed and 24 wounded, one being Houston, whose right leg was "shattered above the ankle."

Santa Anna accepted surrender and ordered the other two Mexican armies to leave Texas. On May 21, 1836 he signed a document at Velasco, Texas recognizing the Republic of Texas and establishing the boundary at the Rio Grande River. Santa Anna would be forced to travel overland and by steamboat to Washington, DC to meet with President Andrew Jackson and discuss Mexican recognition of the Republic of Texas. They would meet in January 1837 and Jackson would formally recognize the Republic of Texas on March 3. Santa Anna would be free to return to Mexico City and resume his political career. France would recognize Texas in late 1839.

On September 5, 1836, Texans approved the Constitution and elected Sam Houston as President. Not allowed re-election, Houston's vice-President Mirabeau Lamar served as President from December 1838 to December 1841. Houston returned as President, serving to December 1844. Anson Jones was President until February 1846.

The Republic of Texas was a vast expanse of land, much larger than the present State of Texas. The Republic claimed rights to the present state, plus westward to the Rio Grande River (now over half of the state of New Mexico, including Santa Fe), plus northward to the Arkansas River (now southern and western Colorado, including Grand Junction), plus a small slice of south-central Wyoming. To view a map, Google: "Map of Texas and Countries Adjacent, 1844, U. S. War Department." Although huge in land, Texas was small in population and growing by only 7,000 per year. In 1836, the central, settled region of Texas contained 30,000 people of US background, mostly Southerners, 5,000 slaves of African descent, 3,478 people of Mexican ancestry and 14,000 Native Americans. So, Texas had insufficient population to rule over the upper Rio Grande Valley and Santa Fe, already 225 years old. Pueblos and Mexicans there saw no Texas authority.

But the Republic was a success even through debt was troublesome. By December 1843, President Houston took pride in progress: Mexico was not threatening, agriculture was growing, trade was expanded, the Texas dollar was strong, and diplomatic relations with Great Britain and France had been secured. But Santa Anna returned to power in Mexico City for a time in 1844, threating again to conquer Texas. Although Texas was a viable Nation, soon to be 10-years old, this combination of troublesome debt and invasion threat caused President Houston and then President Anson Jones to explore transitioning to statehood.

President John Tyler of Virginia thrice submitted merger treaties to the U.S. Senate; but northern Senators rejected it every time, the last in early June, 1844. But Tyler's term in office was coming to a close. Democrats nominated James K. Polk of Tennessee and Whigs nominated Henry Clay of Kentucky. The contest for President was heated and pivoted around the issue of "to admit" or "not to admit" Texas. The Whig Party opposed admitting Texas. The Democrat Party favored it. Democrat Polk was elected. Tyler viewed Polk's

election as a mandate for immediate admission. In his annual message on December 2, he urged Congress to approve admission by a joint resolution (this was different from a treaty). The bill passed the House. The Senate concurred. Tyler signed the Texas Merger Bill on March 1, 1845.

Andrew Jackson Donelson, a nephew of Andrew Jackson, was dispatched to Texas with instructions to present the Texas Merger Bill to President Anson Jones. The terms were generous. Texas would be admitted as a slave state rather than as a territory (only land north of the Missouri Compromise latitude must exclude slavery). She would keep her public lands and pay her own public debts. She could divide herself into as many as four additional states with population growth.

Upon getting news of the Merger Bill ("Annexation"), British and French diplomats rushed to President Jones encouraging that Texas remain a Republic with guarantees of military support from their two nations. Also, fearing the Americans more than the French and British, Mexican President Santa Anna indicated he would make peace with Texans if they remained a Republic. Jones was impressed. So U.S. diplomat Andrew Donelson had to campaign for merger votes. Progress was evident by May: Houston was supportive and President Jones relented, calling the Texas Congress into session.

A Texas Constitutional Convention, made up of delegates elected by Texas voters, gathered in July and framed a State Constitution for the State of Texas. The result was submitted to voters. On October 13, 1845 Texas voters approved the merger by 94% and the State Constitution by 93%. Apparently Texans felt secure under the Democratic administration of James K. Polk of Tennessee. It seemed like a good deal. They were promised that the boundaries of the State of Texas would match the boundaries it claimed for its former Republic. At this point the population was barely sufficient for one state; the 1847 census would count 102,961 whites and Mexicans and 38,753 slaves.

The First Texas State Legislature convened in Austin on February 19, 1846. In a ceremony in front of the Capitol, President Jones gave a valedictory address, the flag of the republic was lowered, and the flag of the United States was raised above it. The ceremonies concluded with the inaugural address of the newly elected governor, J. Pinckney Henderson. Texas would send two men to the US Senate: Sam Houston, formerly of Virginia and Tennessee, and Thomas Jefferson Rusk, formerly of South Carolina and Georgia.

Summary

Texas is a story of the Southern culture and hardy Southern pioneers. It is a fast-moving story that stirs the emotions – 1821, first settlement – 1835, independence and war – 1836, Republic of Texas – 1846, State of Texas.

Suggestions for Class Discussion

Did Texans understand the grave danger in giving up their rights under a Republic in exchange for U.S. statehood?

Recommended Readings:

- *Dream of Empire: A Human History of the Republic of Texas, 1836-1846*, by John Edward Weems, pub. 1971.

- *The Raven, A Biography of Sam Houston*, by Marquis James, pub. 1929.

Section Three: African Americans in the Southern Culture

Chapter 9* – African-American Bondage in World Perspective

By Vance Caswell of N. C., S.I.S.H.

Introduction

Before the invention and widespread use of machinery in the 1800s, servitude was commonplace in civilized societies everywhere. It was one of the chief means of controlling labour to get the world's work done. In the ancient Greek cities, credited with the invention of democracy, slaves were abundant. Citizenship was hereditary and freed slaves and immigrants did not take part in public life. In medieval Europe many people were serfs, hereditarily tied to a particular piece of land and to service to its lord. For several centuries Islamic pirates from North Africa raided the European shores of the Mediterranean and carried off thousands of people to slavery. Serfdom in Europe and the enslavement of white people in the Islamic world did not end until well into the 1800s. Slavery was also commonplace in Africa. According to United Nations reports it can still be found today in parts of Africa. Some form of dependency on and obedience to a master was the lot of much of humanity for most of history.

New World African Slavery

In the 1500s and 1600s, in one of the most important and remarkable events in history, intelligent and hardy Europeans explored the globe, discovering new lands and peoples. The most important discovery was of the New World – North and South America and the Caribbean Islands. This vast territory was sparsely inhabited by mostly nomadic Indians who spoke a multitude of different languages and were constantly at war with each other. The New World held vast resources. What it needed was labour to exploit those resources. In the course of their explorations, the coasts of Africa had become familiar to Europeans. For three and a half centuries (1500s to 1800s) several million Africans were brought to the various European colonies in the New World to work. Every European country that had ships engaged in this activity, including the English colonists of New England. Enslavement of native Indians had not worked. The great Spanish bishop of South America, Las Casas, known as a protector of the Indians, said that slavery was inappropriate for the Indians but was a benefit to "pagans" from Africa. European colonists drove themselves hard, and others even harder.

Both the east and west coasts of Africa supplied slaves. Black slaves went not only to the New World but throughout the vast Islamic world and even to China. This trade could not have been carried on without African chiefs who traded with coastal stations and supplied captive enemies and sometimes their own people for export. Such was the need of America for labour that the slave trade was extremely profitable to seamen, although also extremely dangerous, since the west coast of Africa was full of devastating diseases and was known as "the white man's graveyard." Interestingly, the black leader of the slave revolt portrayed in the film *Amistad* returned to Africa and became a slave trader himself.

North America was a less important destination in the international slave trade than such places as Brazil (Portuguese), Cuba (Spanish), Jamaica (British), and Haiti (French). Only about 5% of the imports came to North America. Even so, African slaves were legally held in all of the 13 colonies at the time of their independence and plantation slaves were numerous in the Southern colonies. Few people had any strong feelings against this, including respectable Northerners who owned many house servants and farm workers. The first official record of slavery in what became the United States is from the court records of Northampton County, Virginia Colony, in 1653. A free African-American named Anthony Johnson was given permanent right to the labor of African-American John Casor. From a fairly early period it was well established in the English colonies that white servants were apprenticed for a fixed period of years and blacks were to be bonded for life. That the Africans were of a different race and culture was an important social fact. At law a master did not own the bonded person, but had a permanent right to his labour and an obligation for his care.

People these days who discuss American slavery fail to note an important point. The history of slavery in North America differs in significant ways from the remainder of the New World. From very early on most Americans sought to end further importation of slaves. They petitioned the British government to end the trade but were refused. This was one of the American grievances cited in the Declaration of Independence. The reason for this American position is clear – the black population was proliferating. Like the white population in the colonies, the black population was more than reproducing itself (an indication of relatively good treatment). Opposition to the foreign slave trade did not mean criticism of slavery. It meant: "We already have a large enough black population." The Constitution gave Congress the right to end slave importations after twenty years – keeping it temporarily open at the request of a combination of SC and GA with New England shipping interests. In 1808 importations were ended by federal law, and Americans were forbidden to engage in this trade. Southerners supported this ban on the international slave trade. Some slaves came into U.S. jurisdiction with the Louisiana Purchase and the admission of Texas as a State, and some were smuggled in. But by 1860 most African American bonded people were native born to America and had known no other life.

Republican propagandists and historians have harped on the charge that the Confederacy was inspired by Southern determination to reopen the foreign slave trade. There were indeed some political radicals who talked this up, but they were put down by overwhelmingly contrary Southern opinion. These same historians don't get around to mentioning that the Constitution of the Confederate States of America plainly forbids importation of African slaves.

Slave importations to Spanish and Portuguese possessions in the New World continued long after the American ban. Although it was illegal for Americans, New Englanders were greatly involved in carrying Africans to Brazil and Cuba, where slavery did not end until the 1880s. The last ship captain hanged for this crime was from Maine, just before the WBTS. Southerners honourably accepted and worked to enforce the suppression of the international slave trade. Henry A. Wise, later to be Governor of Virginia and a Confederate general, was active in this while he was U.S. Minister in Brazil. Here is an interesting story that never gets into your textbooks but illustrates the complex nature of the slavery question. In 1860 a U.S. coast guard vessel near the Cuban coast intercepted the ship *Echo* from Providence, RI. There were 400 Africans on board, many of them in miserable condition, the mortality rate on the voyage having been 30%. The coast guard vessel was commanded by John N. Maffitt, who a few years later would be commanding the Confederate Navy raider *Florida*. The skipper of the *Echo* was a well-educated and affluent man named Edward Townsend, from a "respectable" RI family. He alleged that he had saved the Africans from death in their homeland, and let slip that he expected to clear $130,000 from his voyage, a staggering sum in those days. Maffitt took the Rhode Islander to the U.S. Judge in Key West to be prosecuted. The Northern-born Federal judge there (later a Unionist) refused to take jurisdiction and sent Townsend to Boston, the supposed point of origin of his voyage. The judge in Boston let Townsend, who had influential friends, walk free of a crime equivalent to piracy in American and international law. Meanwhile, the *Echo* and its captives were taken to Charleston, SC, where they were received sympathetically and provided with food and clothing. The U.S. District Attorney in Charleston was James Conner. Unable to get hold of Townsend, he vigorously prosecuted the *Echo* crew. A few years later Conner was a general in the Confederate army and lost a leg in battle defending the South. One writer claims falsely that the *Echo* Africans were enslaved in SC, indicating that hatred of Southerners outweighs the truth for him (and many others). In fact, the captives were sent back to their homeland, although many did not want to go.

Perspective

In what is now the United States, African American bondage existed for about two and a half centuries, perhaps ten generations or so. It involved millions of people spread over a vast territory. In this history one can find an incident to prove anything one wishes to prove, but historians should look at the general picture. It would be a mistake to think that slavery remained static and that easy generalizations can be applied. Like all human institutions, African American slavery evolved over time and was not the same in 1860 as in 1660.

Some historians have asserted that slavery was milder in South America than in the U.S. because the Catholic culture encouraged emancipation and racial distinctions were not so tightly drawn. But this is belied by the figures. In Latin America a constant new importation of slaves was needed to make up for high mortality. The slave population there was largely male, while in the Southern U.S. the balance of numbers between the sexes was normal. White Southerners were overwhelmingly serious Christians. The black population by 1860 was Christian while Christianity was almost unknown in Africa. Southerners by and large encouraged monogamous family relationships, unknown in African cultures. Most Southern clergy insisted on this and had made great if not complete progress toward the goal.

It has been often pointed out that slavery ended everywhere in the New World without bloodshed except for Haiti and the United States. Southerners were well aware of what had happened in Haiti. The ideology of the French Revolution in the 1790s brought on a slave revolt which led to the torture and extermination of the white population, including women and children, and to war between the people of mixed race and the pure Africans. What was once the most valuable island in the New World for its sugar production descended into poverty and disorder that remains till this day. Prewar Southerners were also aware of Britain's emancipation policy in its New World colonies. There emancipation was compensated. Slave owners collected their money and returned to England. Once rich colonies like Jamaica underwent rapid economic decline. The great British thinker Thomas Carlyle excoriated British leaders who showed great compassion for slaves who lived easy lives in a warm climate and were indifferent to the immense sufferings of their own people in the mines and factories of the time.

Much evidence shows that by 1860 African American bondage was moving toward a peaceful end in the Southern culture. Many African Americans were skilled craftsmen – masons, carpenters, sailors, overseers, chefs, butlers, seamstresses. More than among the freed people in the North then (and very possibly today). Quite a few were allowed to hire themselves out and enjoyed considerable freedom. On the plantations sturdy if modest dwellings were common and most workers were allowed personal gardens from which they made money. Invading Northern soldiers were astonished to find that African Americans had watches and fine clothes. They did not hesitate to loot the slaves along with the whites.

Some people today have likened prewar bondage in the Southern Culture to the concentration camps of totalitarian governments in the 20th century. This is a malicious and willfully false contention. The prisoners in 20th century camps were snatched from normal lives and imprisoned by governments with negative interest in their welfare. The Old South had domestic servitude, an institution as old as the Bible. The bonded people were not the property of governments, they belonged to families who cared for their well-being, with whom they attended the same churches and were treated by the same doctors. There was no barbed wire around the plantations, no guard towers, no armed guards. In the early 20th century many people, black and white, looked back on the plantations before the WBTS as happy places. Plantations were farms, where people lived and worked together to grow crops to feed themselves and perhaps make a little profit.

Perhaps most people today think of African American bondage in comparison to the safe and prosperous life of Americans in the late 1900s and early 2000s. But the Old South ought to be viewed in its own times. Life expectancies for every one were lower than today. Many families saw half their children perish before adulthood. Women frequently died in childbirth from infections today easily treatable. Devastating epidemics struck the cities every few years. There was no welfare, no unemployment pay, no antibiotics, good anesthetics, or microsurgery. People grew their own food with hard labour and raised and killed their own livestock. The American frontier was not settled without a lot of tough people and tough behavior. Corporal punishment existed on plantations. It also existed in families, factories, the army, the navy, schools, and in local criminal punishment.

The Southern Culture was far from perfect and its people were aware that much of the civilized world had changed its attitudes and by the mid-1800s regarded them as backward. Outside critics were harsh in denunciation but conspicuously lacking in constructive suggestions. The Northerners who condemned slavery were also adamant that they did not want black people living among them. Southerners were doing the best they could and were creating as humane a way of life as they could. The great Massachusetts statesman Daniel Webster said that the abolitionists were to blame for diverting the South from early movement toward emancipation. What better evidence of the nature of the Old South than the absence of any slave revolt during the war when most white men were away from home. Thousands of black men accompanied and helped sustain the Confederate armies and often took their wounded and dead masters home. Conservative clergymen, North and South, knew that Scripture did not condemn servitude – it urged masters to be good masters and servants to be faithful servants. The Episcopal Bishop of Vermont, John Henry Hopkins, wrote a book on slavery just before the war by which he hoped to dampen down the fire directed at the South among his fellow Northerners. Abolitionists, he said, had never done anything really helpful to African Americans, while white Southerners had done more to advance them than any people in history.

Suggestion for Class Discussion (Let students decide.)

Recommended Readings

- *Roll, Jordan Roll: The World the Slaves Made,* by Eugene Genovese, pub. 1976.
- *Our Fathers' Fields: A Southern Story*, by James E. Kibler, pub. 1998.
- *Life and Labor in the Old South* by Ulrich B. Philips, pub. 1929.

Chapter 10 – More on Americans of African Descent.

By Barbara Marthal of Tennessee, M. Ed., S. I. S. H.

Editor's Introduction

In 1619 a ship arrived in Jamestown, Virginia Colony with 20 indentured servants of African ancestry. Purchased by tobacco farmers, thus began the history of people of African ancestry living in what would become the United States of America. But before long African laborers were purchased as bonded persons, slaves for life, and laws soon permitted owners to also own the children of their female slaves. Puritan Separatists began the northeastern colonies at Plymouth in 1620 and soon afterward joined British and others in the trans-Atlantic slave trade business. They sailed to African seaports, purchased Africans captured by rival tribes, brought them back across the Atlantic and sold them at New World seaports, including the 13 British colonies. People in all the 13 colonies were buyers, but most were purchased in the southern colonies. Descendants of African ancestry living today in the US are here, not Africa, because of this slave trade. They would not have been able to come otherwise. We estimate that 25,000,000 were captured by fellow Africans and enslaved; 12,000,000 were sold for the trans-Atlantic crossing; 10,000,000 arrived in the New World, and only 575,000 (the lucky ones) were legally imported into what became the United States (beyond 1807, about 25,000 were smuggled in). The 1810 census reported 1,304,151 people of noticeable African ancestry. Not all were slaves, for 97,284 were living in the Southern states as independent persons and 76,086 were living independently in the Northern states. Considering that life was hard back then for most people, this population growth is evidence that Africans were far more resistant to disease than were Native Americans and, by and large, were receiving sufficient care to live then-normal life spans and raise children. Over the next 200 years, to 2010, the African American population grew 6,173 percent to 37,035,333. With few exceptions, these people are descended from the original 600,000. But historian Barbara Marthal tells that the history of people of African ancestry in America is not that simple.

The Broader History, by Barbara Marthal

Current biology and scholarship proves there is a larger story – thanks to the science of DNA and too-often ignored historical documents, literature and art, we find that the history of people of African descent is broad and fascinating. You see, DNA follows the wanderer no matter where he or she goes. We can analyze tissue samples from today's African Americans and easily identify their African-specific DNA traits.

The Moorish Empire, centered in North Africa, was present in Spain from 713 to 1492, a span of 781 years. Those Africans living in Spain and Portugal during the Moorish Empire contributed much to the scholarship, science and geography of the New World. Even after Queen Isabella demanded the removal of African Muslims and Jews from Spain, they continued to man the ships of Her Majesty as crew, pilots and captains, and some as slaves. Trading contacts between the Iberian Peninsula and Africa remained. Some in Africa had wealth and gold to finance explorations. In this way, people of African descent helped discover the New World. Not all were slaves. Many sought to rebuild their lost wealth in the New World, then return to Morocco, Algeria, Libya, Egypt, Mauritania, Mali, Niger and other North Africa and West Africa countries. Through such existing contacts with Africa, Portuguese and Spanish rulers and adventurers undertook profitable slave trading, which became the engine that drove the development of the New World. You see, people of African descent did not simply come as slaves. They played an important part in the discovery and building of the New World and of what would become the United States.

In the southern colonies that had early ties to Spain, Portugal and France, indentured Africans were freed after working off their indentures. Because of such early cross-cultural interactions, the South became a much more tolerant society than the one begun by Puritan Separatists in the Northeast. Southerners opened their doors to slaves, indentured, freemen, Jews, Protestants, Catholics, a significant population of African Muslims, and people of mixed ancestry with the promise of success to those who were willing to work. People with African DNA pioneered and provided a vast amount of agricultural knowledge and physical labor in the building of America – providing the skills and work which built the foundational wealth of our country and made available the resources required for sufficient health care and community support to live then-normal life spans and raise children.

When the call for arms was made to defend the southland, people of African descent, for the most part, responded throughout the south in support of their state. They served as support troops and unofficially as soldiers. Many, like the author's third great grandfather, remained on the plantation and did his best to protect everyone living there, both his family and the master's family. Another of the author's family relations accompanied his young master to the war, served the entire length of the war and received a Confederate pension.

Can you better understand why the vast majority of southern black people, both slave and free, considered the South as their home and opposed the agenda of the American Colonization Society, which, in reality sought to deport them? – why they considered America "my home where my ancestors have bled and died long before many others arrived on these shores?" and – why many who had served the Union as civilians and as troops returned to the South to reclaim their southern roots?

Over one million white Americans are unaware that they are of partial African descent. I tell people, if you can't handle surprises, do not get a DNA analysis. People of African ancestry should be proud of these ancestors who played a major role in discovering the New World and in building the United States – continuing to add to that great legacy today.

Summary

One needs to look back over 1,000 years to understand how people of African descent helped discover the New World and build what is considered today "the greatest country on earth."

Suggestions for Class Discussion

Does thinking deeply about America's racial background help in understanding who built America and how they did it?

Recommended Readings

- *The Making of New World Slavery: From the Baroque to the Modern, 1492-1888*, Robin Blackburn, pub. 1997.
- *Slave Ships and Slaving*, George Francis Dow, pub. 1968.

Chapter 11 – Characteristics of the African American People During the 1850's

By Leslie R. Tucker, Ph.D. of Oklahoma, S. I. S. H.

Introduction

The 1860 census of American population shows 3,950,528 bonded persons of African ancestry and 476,748 people of African ancestry who were independent, meaning not slaves. Slightly more than half of the free black people were in the South, having been emancipated by their own efforts or by masters for personal or conscience considerations. A considerable number of African Americans, North and South, had some European or Native American ancestry. Northern states had eliminated slavery by gradual processes which generally allowed time for owners to move their bonded people to the South if they wished, or to free those born in bondage when they came of age. (There was a sizable group of CT slaveholders who migrated to sugar plantations in LA.) Unlike the situation in the slave States, few thriving communities of free black people developed after emancipation in the North. African Americans in the North generally lived in impoverished, segregated communities, and the newer Northern States did not even allow black people as residents. Every good student of history needs to mentally transport himself or herself back into the times under study to properly understand those times, when people did not live or think as we do today.

Overview

There are three important points to keep in mind in the study of the African-American population of the 1850's. First, we should avoid presentism. Attitudes toward working people of all races were different at that time than those we find acceptable today. The Dutch did keelhauling of sailors as late as 1853 and the British did not ban the flogging of soldiers until 1860. The working classes in industrialized areas such as Manchester, England, worked under conditions that left many crippled and maimed from injuries or breathing dust from textile mills and mines. This left most unfit for work at 40 years of age, and almost none at 50. Children as young as 7 or 8 worked up to 12 hours, some "seized naked in bed by the overlookers, and driven with blows and kicks to the factory."

Second, regardless of good treatment, being a slave has many costs which few of us would be willing to pay. Third, trying to have a realistic understanding of slavery is not an apology. It is a mistake to oversimplify slavery to chains, whips, and division of families; it is likewise a mistake to say that they were better off as slaves. The objective should be to understand as best we can. A difficulty is finding objective records at a time when Northern writers emphasized the horrors of slavery in a continuing regional attack, Southern writers emphasized slavery's benefit to the African, and the bonded people themselves left few written records. The slave narratives collected by the Federal Writers' Project in the 1930s offer the best testimony we have by slaves themselves, although, of course, memories of 70 years ago have problems of certainty.

History Relevant to the WBTS

By 1850 all of the Northern states had abolished slavery, making a sharp difference separating North from South. Agricultural improvements in the older Southern areas and the worldwide demand for cotton had ensured the continued economic vitality of the plantations into the 1850s. Cotton production increased from 750,000 bales in 1830 to 2.8 million in 1850, to 3.2 million in 1860. Like the white population, the slave population moved westward in large numbers. Some accompanied owners on their migrations. Others were sold. New Orleans was the largest slave market in North America.

Slaves lived in such varied situations that it is impossible to describe what it was like for all of them. There were slaves who employed white workers, there were slave doctors who treated white patients, and there were some slaves who rented out their labors. Some were house servants who exercised considerable influence in the running of the household and plantation, and were thought of as members of the family. Many, perhaps a fourth, were skilled craftsmen; however, most worked as plantation field hands.

We sometimes see assertions that only one in ten of prewar white Southerners were slave-owners. This is not strictly correct. If we count by families, approximately one-fourth were slave owners, more in some States and areas and less in others. Half of the slave owners owned fewer than five slaves. Those who owned 20 or more were considered "planters." In 1850, 73 percent of the agricultural slaves were on cotton plantations, 14 percent on tobacco, 6 percent on sugar, 5 percent on rice, and 2 percent on hemp plantations.

Southern writers submitted that the slaves lived more comfortably and happily than workers and urban dwellers who were enduring the industrial revolution in the North and Europe. Economists Robert W. Fogel and Stanley L. Engerman (a Nobel Prize winner) made an intense and controversial economic study of slavery, *Time on the Cross*. They found statistics relating to food, housing, clothing, and medical conditions which support the Southern point of view. The total calories consumed by slaves were slightly higher than the general population in Europe and America, with more potatoes and grains and slightly less meat and milk. They evaluated the housing using plantation records and comments by travelers. They found that the "houses of slaves compared well with the housing of free workers." At that time most Americans lived in log cabins on farms and the workers in the northern cities lived in crowded and filthy tenements, many without even a window. Common sense dictates that the medical care of slaves would be better than that of free workers who, if sick or injured could simply be dismissed to fend for themselves. Plantation medical care, food, and living conditions resulted in an African American survival rate in the American South superior to any other region in the Western Hemisphere. In fact, the rate of natural population growth among the slave population was greater than whites in any nation in Europe, and was nearly twice as much as in England, then the richest and most powerful nation on earth.

Some slave families were forced to separate and many individuals were subjected to cruel punishments. Many slave owners tried to keep families together knowing that it impacted the performance of their workers, and also because they were Christians. There were internal slave markets carried on by slave traders who generally had less concern about preserving families, although some, such as Nathan Bedford Forrest, were known to make considerable efforts to keep them together. Fogel and Engerman reported, "Most slave sales were either of whole families or of individuals who were at an age when it would have been normal for them to have left the family." Most slaves lived in nuclear households, at 64 percent, while 21 percent were single parents and 15 percent non-family. Corporal punishment was practiced among the free population but was becoming less common by the 1850s. Without a doubt it was more common among the slaves.

More than ten percent of the black population in America were free, with slightly more than half of those living in the slave states. Free "Coloreds" living in the U.S. in 1860 came from various backgrounds including mulatto children born to indentured or free women, any born to a free African woman, mixed-race born to Native-Americans, slaves who had been freed by their masters, those who bought their freedom with money they earned working on their own time, and those who had run away and managed to stay away. North or South, free blacks did not have the same full citizenship rights. The Dred Scott Supreme Court Decision of 1857 declared that Africans, free or slave, were not citizens.

Many Americans, including Abolitionists, advocated that Africans be sent to Africa or to some place in the New World where they would be removed from American society. This impractical scheme was sometimes thought of as voluntary emigration by free blacks. Toward this goal, the American Colonization Society, to which many prominent Northern and Southern Americans belonged, established the western African nation of Liberia. The attitude of most Americans of the time was summed up by Abraham Lincoln during the Lincoln-Douglas debates of 1858, "I will say, then, that I am not, nor ever have been, in favor of bringing about in anyway the social and political equality of the white and black races – that I am not, nor ever have been, in favor of making voters or jurors of negroes, nor of qualifying them to hold office, nor to intermarry with white people; and I will say in addition to this that there is a physical difference between the white and black races. . . I, as much as any other man, am in favor of having the superior position assigned to the white race."

It would not be until January of 1863 that the North would allow black men to serve in the Union Army, and then in segregated units at lower pay and with white officers. U.S. "Coloured Troops" were often used as labor or in "forlorn hopes," such as fighting at the Crater and Battery Wagner.

Some free blacks found opportunity in the North, and some of them became active in the Abolition movement, the most famous being Frederick Douglass. President Lincoln long held to the policy of colonization. Concerning that belief, Union General Benjamin Butler reported that President Lincoln said in April 1865 (a few days before his death), "I can hardly believe that the South and North can live in peace, unless we get rid of the Negroes."

Summation

Many writers have strongly objected to the findings of economists Fogel and Engerman on conditions in the Old South, thinking it was defending slavery and offensive to African Americans. Fogel and Engerman, however, felt that their findings showed a positive picture of black people wisely making the best of their situation by contributing greatly to the success of their plantation home. "The typical slave field hand," they wrote, "was not lazy, inept, and unproductive. On average he was harder-working and more efficient than his white counterpart." Slavery is today the most difficult and contentious subject in American history. This is at least in part because of feelings and political agendas that are more a part of our own times than of history. Current literature reflects the position of those who insist that the WBTS was entirely "about" the evil of slavery. A smaller and less fashionable group of writers defend the Confederacy and the honor of the Southern people and point to motives other than antislavery as cause of the great bloodletting. History is about what people thought, did, and said before we were born. It is and always should be open to different perspectives and interpretations.

Suggestions for Class Discussion

What factors make the discussion of American slavery difficult today? After all, it ended a century and a half ago.

Recommended Reading

- *Time on the Cross: The Economics of American Negro Slavery*, by Robert Fogel and Stanley Engerman, pub. 1974.
- *Slavery Remembered: A Record of Twentieth-Century Slave Narratives*, by Paul D. Escott, pub. 1979.
- *"What Shall We Do with the Negro?": Lincoln, White Racism and the American Civil War*, by Paul D. Escott, pub. 2000.

Chapter 12 – The Mexican War, Expansion to California, and the "Compromises of 1850"

By Egon Richard Tausch of Texas, S. I. S. H.

Introduction

Texas became a State of the U.S. on 16 Feb 1846, leaving the Polk administration with a major problem – Mexico refused to recognize its previous grant of Texas independence. Further, Polk and many other Americans looked longingly at the Mexican territories north and west of Texas and west of the Louisiana Purchase, all the way to the Pacific coast. These territories were sparsely settled and remote from Mexico City. There was much talk in the air about the need of the U.S. to control all of North America. There soon came a war with Mexico and the acquisition of vast new territories, the future of which ignited a conflict between the Northern and Southern Cultures.

Perspective

When Texas joined the Union, Americans were divided in their feelings about it. Southerners were happy to have new land to grow with and increased power in Washington by two U.S. Senators and who knew how many more U.S. Representatives in the future? After all, most settlers in Texas had come from the South. But many influential people in the northeastern United States were unhappy about Texas. More power for the South meant less power for *them*, and sectional differences and hostilities had been growing. Northerners and Southerners were becoming more aware that they were different peoples. The South was agricultural, socially traditional, favored free enterprise, and was fiercely independent-minded – personally, locally, and as States. The North was becoming more and more commercial and industrial. It wanted power for the central government at Washington and the "internal improvements" (infrastructure) and corporate subsidies that flowed from that government. The North also wanted unconstitutionally high tariffs to protect its industries from foreign competition, at the expense of domestic consumers (especially Southern farmers).

When the original thirteen States banded together to create the U.S. Constitution, the Federal (or Central, or General) Government was given certain delegated powers, and the States retained all powers not delegated to the Federal Government. But central governments always tend to try to increase their power, as the framers of the Constitution well knew and thought they had guarded against. While the people of the Northern States encouraged this trend to expand Federal power, Southerners began to look to the defense of freedom and independence through the rights and powers of their States, preferably within the Union. Southern States adhered to their sovereignty, as declared by James Madison and Thomas Jefferson in their "Kentucky and Virginia Resolutions," including the right to separate from the Union if necessary. This independent position went double for the Southerners in Texas. The people there had fought and won a war for their rights under the Mexican Constitution of 1824 and had been forced to secede from Mexico. They joined the U.S. only with the understanding of Union protection of their State's Rights. Texas was the only independent country ever to join the U.S. as a State. Unlike other States, Texas entered the Union without granting *any* of the land within its "final" borders to the United States.

War with Mexico

Meanwhile, in Mexico, General Santa Anna, who liked to think of himself as the Napoleon of the Americas, was again seizing power (he was to do so four times in his 20-year career of coups and dictatorships). In his previous rule he had overthrown the Mexican Constitution of 1824 and caused a general uprising throughout Mexico, which he suppressed by bloody massacres, only to force Texas into secession and independence. This time, he denied the peace-treaty with Texas he had signed a decade earlier and sent small military units across the Rio Grande to appear to maintain Mexico's claim to all of Texas. President Polk sent emissaries to negotiate with the Mexican Government, offering to settle disputes and to buy land useless to Mexico. The government refused even to meet with Polk's negotiators.

Mexican army units attacked a small U.S. force north of the Rio Grande that was part of Zachary Taylor's small army. President Polk declared that a state of war existed, and Congress, with some reluctance on the part of Whigs, declared war against Mexico on 13 May 1846. Gen. Taylor asked for reinforcements and marched southward. He captured Monterrey in northern Mexico and then defeated Santa Anna soundly at the Battle of Buena Vista. That victory owed much to the fast thinking and courage of Taylor's son-in-law, Col. Jefferson Davis of the 1st Mississippi Volunteers. The Mexican Army at that time was no pushover. It had been in combat almost constantly crushing revolutions and was well trained and supplied, especially in artillery and engineers. The American regular army was small and had not seen major combat since the War of 1812. The U.S. fought the war with volunteer regiments, predominantly from the Southern States.

President Polk decided to send Gen. Winfield Scott south with a force much larger than Taylor's. Scott captured the heavily-fortified port of Vera Cruz and fought his way overland to Mexico City. Though far outnumbered, the Americans succeeded in conquering Mexico City after the fall of Chapultepec – a victory which owed much to a dangerous one-man reconnaissance by Capt. Robert E. Lee. Meanwhile, a U.S. force, consisting mainly of Missouri volunteers, captured Santa Fe. In California the Mexican people had long been estranged from and had resisted Mexico City. With the resident Americans they declared independence and were soon joined by U.S. army and navy forces. By 1848 the U.S. was in possession of most of the territory that had been wished for.

The Wilmot Proviso

In the beginning some Americans of the Whig Party had opposed the war, falsely claiming that it was a plot by the South to extend slavery, but most Americans felt pride when the Far West was won. By the treaty of Guadalupe-Hidalgo, Mexico's vast northwestern lands were sold to the U.S. for $15,000,000 and U.S. payment of the extensive Mexican debts owed to American citizens for earlier seizures of their property.

But the war had barely gotten underway when Congress was turned into warring Northern and Southern camps. On 8

August 1846, Representative David Wilmot of PA introduced an amendment to a pending war appropriations bill. Wilmot's amendment would ban slavery in any and all territory that might be acquired as a result of the war. (Wilmot was a Democrat in trouble with his constituents for not promoting their demand for a higher tariff.) The "Wilmot Proviso" passed the House and was defeated in the Senate. It was later introduced two more times with the same result. Some peaceable Northern representatives tried to overcome the antagonism by proposing that the old Missouri Compromise line be used to divide the territory acquired from Mexico between the North and South. Southerners declared they would accept this, but advocates of the Wilmot Proviso rejected it.

A new and fervently evangelical abolitionist movement had appeared in the North in the 1830s. It was growing but still small and held in contempt by most Northerners. The movement to ban slavery from the territories profited from growing abolitionism but it had nothing to do with the welfare of African Americans in bondage. "Free-soilers" wanted the land for "free white men." They wanted no black people, free or slave. It might be argued that the Proviso controversy began the chain of events that made the WBTS likely if not inevitable. Northern business interests were made happy and more aggressive by a sense that they now held power over the South and the future of the Union. Southerners knew that the semi-arid lands of the Mexican Cession would not be conducive to plantation agriculture, but they resented being deprived of their equal status in the Union and understood that they were becoming a minority dominated by an alien and hostile power.

Formerly Mexican lands – present-day Arizona, Nevada, Utah, Wyoming, and parts of Colorado and New Mexico – were virtually unpopulated except by fierce, nomadic Indian tribes. Texas settlement had not expanded past its eastern third. (After the WBTS it became cattle country, with the herds of wild longhorns rounded up and driven to market in the North. The population did not spread widely until the oil-boom of the 1900s.) Northerners were uninterested in moving west except where profits were to be made. California itself was already populated, and the Gold-rush there brought more Americans, a majority from the North. It did not take long for Northerners to realize that control of the new territories would benefit their interests.

Passions inflamed by the Wilmot Proviso led to the "Compromise of 1850," which was actually a series of separate Acts passed by Congress, each meant to advantage either North or South. The first Act admitted California as a non-slave State. Another Act concerned Texas land west of the *present* State of Texas, which had not been given to the U.S. upon statehood, but kept. This Texas land included half of the modern State of New Mexico. Northern Whigs did not like Texas and were delighted to whittle away at it. Gen. Stephen Kearny was a nationalist from New Jersey, and his Army of the West simply pretended Texas did not exist. His army assembled a few Northerners and Mexican settlers into a convention in Santa Fe, which petitioned Washington to become a separate U.S. territory. When the Texas Legislature sent emissaries, Kearny's army threatened war against Texas unless they left. Pres. Taylor's Whig successor, Millard Fillmore (New York), also threatened force against Texas. Texans who had opposed statehood were proven right, and

even secession from the U.S. was seriously threatened. An interesting thought: What if the War Between the States had begun then, in the Southwest, rather than in the East?

The U.S. had even failed in its major obligation for Texas Statehood: the defense of Texas against hostile Indian tribes. Austin, the capital, was raided by Comanches, and over 200 Texas civilians were kidnapped in 1849 alone. For decades before and after the WBTS, the Texas frontier was a bloody wound which the U.S. government did little to heal. The Texas Rangers would hunt these Indians down after an atrocity and recapture women and children who had been taken away. The U.S. Army would make a show of force, chase them a bit, then build a useless camp. As one of the "compromises" of 1850, Texas gave up her lands beyond the present State boundaries. In exchange the U.S. paid off the $10 million Texas debt, although this was of more benefit to Northern bondholders than to Texas.

Another Act allowed for "popular sovereignty," which permitted each new territory to decide for itself for or against legalizing slavery before becoming a State. Congress thus passed the buck. Southerners had always insisted that only a sovereign State, not a temporary territorial government, could decide on slavery. A final "compromise" meant to mollify the South, strengthened the "Fugitive Slave Act," requiring Northern States to return escaped slaves to their owners. The South was not impressed. Actually, the law already existed, but only a small number of African-Americans were ever involved in the much-exaggerated and glorified "underground railroad." Southerners had been victimized by so many dubious interpretations of the Constitution that they wanted the North to abide by this very clear one. But Northern States passed laws forbidding free *or* escaped African-Americans from remaining in their States, from employment, and from any civil rights.

Summary

People were beginning to realize that the Union was in serious crisis. The Whig elder statesman Henry Clay worked hard for the Compromise, helped by the rising Democratic star Stephen A. Douglas. Daniel Webster aroused bitter hatred in his own Massachusetts by supporting compromise. The third elder statesman of "the Great Triumvirate," John C. Calhoun of South Carolina, who would be dead in a few days, rejected the "compromise." The Union could not survive, he said, unless the North stopped its exploitation of the South. The South was now hemmed in by the West and North. The United States continued as a federation, unseparated, for another decade. The North was discovering its political power, and the Federal Government it favored was growing more powerful.

Suggestions for Class Discussion

What if the War Between The States had begun in the Western Territories?

Recommended Reading

- *Lone Star, A History of Texas and the Texans*, by T. R. Fehrenbach, pub. 1968.
- *The Repressible Conflict: 1830-1861*, by Avery Craven, pub. 1939.

Chapter 13* – Understanding the conflict between the North and South over the Role of the Federal Government in the Economy.

By Clyde N. Wilson of S. C., Ph.D., S.I.S.H.

Introduction

The economic issues that created conflicting sectional interests and helped bring on the WBTS are often not very well understood, even by those who write about them. There are many roadblocks to understanding the complexities of economic history. Certain economic policies lead to some people making money. These people, and the politicians who speak for them, are eager to obscure the truth and make it appear that such policies are good for everybody. I might argue that President A created good economic times (B) that followed his administration. But just because B follows A does not prove that A is the cause of B. In the vast conditions and actions of a large national economy, what caused B may be something unrelated to the actions of President A. Politicians and special interests neither know nor care about the truth, they are seeking advantage. And much history is written as if politicians' arguments tell us the truth about economics.

Relevant History

We have it on very high authority that the love of money is the root of evil. Yet almost all of us would like to have a comfortable amount of it. The saying is perhaps aimed at those who always want more and more. Money can be inherited. It can be earned by hard work, brains, and good luck. But another way to get money is from the government. The government holds the sword and the purse. It can collect from the people all the money it wants and give it away to whoever it wants. Throughout history, in every form of government, there have been those who rely on influence and cleverness to get rich out of government. America is largely a story of the success of free enterprise, of hardworking and smart people who have spread prosperity and improved life for all of us. But there also runs through American history a strong element of the other kind of enterprise – getting money from government.

At the ratification of the U.S. Constitution, everyone knew that the Northern and Southern States had different and sometimes conflicting economic interests, arising from their different ways of making a living. In the first days of the government Alexander Hamilton proposed a regime of public debt, national bank, tariff, and business subsidies. Thomas Jefferson saw this program as a scheme for certain people, Northern capitalists, to make money out of the taxpayers, to create an elite class of special beneficiaries of the government. The contested philosophies of Hamilton and Jefferson dominated national politics from their time until the WBTS. Each side had victories and defeats until the Republican Party took power in 1861, and, with the South not voting in Congress, implemented Hamilton's ideas with a vengeance. They said their policies were benevolent, good for everybody, and necessary for progress. The South thought they were being exploited to make certain loud and influential Northerners rich.

The most important matter in our discussion is the tariff. A tariff is a tax on goods imported from another country. It is collected at an official port by customs officials when the products are unloaded. To land cargo without paying this tax is illegal smuggling. The drafters of the Constitution agreed that the proposed new Federal Government needed a source of money to pay for its necessary officials and delegated powers. The Constitution provided that to raise this money Congress might legislate and collect a tariff on imported goods. It was a customary kind of tax and one that generally affected only people affluent enough to import luxuries. It required no levies on the States or direct taxation of citizens. In regard to taxes, it is important to note that the Constitution provided: 1) that there be no trade barriers between states; 2) that products *exported* by any State could never be taxed; and 3) all taxation was to be equal among the States.

Some Southern statesmen saw a problem with this. George Mason, who had been an important player in drafting the Constitution, refused to sign or support it for this reason. He pointed out that it would be used by the wily businessmen of the Northern States to place unfair taxation on Southerners. Mason demanded but failed to get a provision that tariff laws should require a 2/3rds rather than a majority vote to pass. The first tariffs were 5-10 per cent. But from 1816 on we find constant clamor that the rate be raised. Textile, iron and other manufacturers demanded a "protective tariff." What is a protective tariff? It is raising the tax so high that nobody can afford to buy imported goods. People will have to buy manufactured goods from Northern factory owners. The truly "Abominable tariff" of 1828 raised it to 50% on many products. South Carolina referred to Jefferson's Kentucky Resolutions and nullified the law as unconstitutional. The tariff came down for awhile but there was constant pressure to raise it. "Protection" was a major plank of the Whig Party and then of the Republicans. Democratic President Polk managed in 1846 to get the tax down to a "revenue" rather than a "protective" level. This caused angry discontent among many if not all Northerners and added greatly to the growth of the Republican Party. Especially since Polk also ended the national bank and vetoed a huge "internal improvements" boondoggle for the Great Lakes area.

What did the South have to say about the protective tariff? First, the South supplied the overwhelming part of U.S. exports. Its economy rested on supplying cotton, rice, sugar, and tobacco to the outside world. There would hardly have been any foreign trade otherwise. Always the great bulk of federal revenue, at times up to 5/6ths, was collected by the tariff at the Southern ports. Northerners paid little in taxes, although the tariff did raise the price of goods for Northern consumers while it profited factory owners. What is going on here? Let us suppose a Southern farmer wants to buy a bolt of cloth for clothes for his bonded people. He can buy this for $10 from British imports even after a 5% tariff. The merchant who ships his cotton can also bring in the cloth in exchange so that he does not have to pay any cash money, which he has little of anyway. Britain led the world in manufacturing and sea transport. A similar bolt, purchased from MA, cost $11. But when you put a 50% tariff on imports the British cloth now costs $15. The MA factory owner is no longer going to charge $11 for his product when his competitor is out of the market. He is going to charge $14.95. The Southern statesman John Randolph and others asked why factory owners, among all the other occupations in the country, required the special "protection" of the government. The Union was intended to be beneficial to all the States, but instead was being used to extract prosperity from the South for the benefit of wealthy Northerners. Worse, New Englanders snarled that Southerners had declining prosperity because they were lazy and extravagant, not wise and industrious like Yankees. Senator Calhoun replied that the South sold its products for what it could get in the open world market while New England had government guaranteed profits. Senator Benton said that that the South used to be known for good living and hospitality. Thanks to the tariff all that was left was the hospitality.

Note that the demand for tariff had nothing to do with the bonded people in the South except that it potentially detracted from their standard of living by making their masters poorer. This was a battle between an industrial region and an agricultural region that could have happened if there had not been a single African-American bonded servant. Note also that the wisest observers of the time and later said that the South was exactly correct about the results of the tariff, that it did not create prosperity but transferred wealth from one group to another, that free trade among countries was best for all.

"Internal improvements" meant building roads, railroads, canals, harbours, river improvements at Federal expense. This provided large subsidies for private corporations, some of which did not fulfill their promises. Almost all the money was spent in the North. Southerners from Jefferson on said they could not find anything in the Constitution that gave Congress such power and that State and private enterprise could meet any real needs. "Internal improvements" were popular. In his earlier career Lincoln pushed through the IL legislature a canal building program which was never finished and threw the State into bankruptcy.

Few people understand that bankers and other wealthy people like government debt. The government has a large income and should not normally need to borrow money. But the rich like for the government to sell them bonds from which they get risk free and tax free interest. Hamilton said that public debt is a public blessing because it meant that the rich and powerful would support the government. Southerners noted that they paid most of the taxes that conferred this benefit on wealthy Northerners. Throughout the antebellum period Democrats tried to pay off the Federal debt and almost succeeded. Wall Street bankers and brokers enthusiastically supported Lincoln's war and congratulated each because they knew a large debt would be created. While young boys and old men in the South fought to defend their homes, the financiers enjoyed their yachts, fast horses and women, and lit their cigars with $50 bills while dining on thick steaks at Delmonico's.

The question of banks and money is the most poorly understood economic controversy of all. First off we must understand that the "national bank" was not a government bank, although the government appointed its head and put up 1/5 of its stock. It was a private bank that had the privilege of handling the government's money and of issuing paper money (banknotes) that, with assumed government backing, could circulate as currency. Critics asked why Congress should give away its power and responsibility to provide a sound currency? Most people then and later did not understand the invention of "fractional-reserve" banking. They assumed that people deposited real money in banks for interest and banks loaned out the money. But bankers discovered that at any one time all depositors would not ask for their deposits in real money (gold and silver). They could loan out 20 times more money than they had on deposit simply by printing out paper banknotes that supposedly represented real money. This gave the bankers effective and extremely profitable and irresponsible control over the country's credit and currency. The fluctuating value of unbacked bank money was responsible for the inflation and deflation that caused depressions, known in those days as "panics." The Republicans in 1861 spread around the loot by creating a chain of "national" banks rather than one, but the principle was the same.

Nothing in the Republican platform, which was implemented in full during the WBTS, had anything to do with Northern interest in the welfare of Southern black people, which casts an interesting light on many historians' insistence that the war was all about "slavery." Lincoln said that he was opposed to slavery in the abstract but that he did not have any power to do anything about it and wouldn't know what to do if he did. All that he and the party insisted on was that there would be no "expansion of slavery," i.e., that there would not be any new States that would be settled by Southerners who would vote against the North's economic interests. Jefferson had pointed out that the spreading out of the slaves over more territory was a good thing for them because it improved their lot and chances for freedom.

Summary

Anyone who leaves out the significance of what happened in early 1861, between Lincoln's election and Fort Sumter, and insists it was all about "slavery" will never know the truth about the WBTS. Congress passed the Republican tariff of 50 to 60% on most imports. The new Confederate government voted a tariff of 5% and announced that Northerners could have free navigation of the Mississippi river and use of the port of New Orleans. Influential Northerners realized what this would mean (because tariffs were then only being collected at seaports). They would lose their captive source of revenue and market in the South. Their profits would nose-dive. They might even have to pay taxes themselves. Not only would they lose the South, but it was obvious that the whole Mississippi Valley would prefer to trade through the low tariff Confederacy rather than the United States. In public speeches and private letters, in newspaper editorials and petitions to Congressmen, and in every other way, influential Northerners let it be known that war was preferable to allowing the South to escape. One could fill several books with such statements. When asked why the South could not be allowed to peaceably secede, Lincoln invariably referred to the loss of revenue – not "slavery."

Suggestions for Class Discussion

What are the arguments in support of high tariffs in contrast to the arguments in support of low tariffs or free trade?

Recommended Readings

- *When in the Course of Human Events: Arguing the Case for Southern Secession*, by Charles Adams, pub. 2000.
- *Hamilton's Curse: How Jefferson's Arch Enemy Betrayed the American Revolution – and What It Means for Americans Today*, by Thomas J. DiLorenzo, pub. 2008.

Chapter 14* – *Uncle Tom's Cabin*, the Anti-Slavery Movement in the Northern States and the Necessity of Understanding the Divergent Passions for Exclusionism, Deportationism and Abolitionism.

By Howard Ray White of N. C., S.I.S.H.

Introduction

In this and the next two chapters you will witness passionate sectional political agitation aimed at defeating the dominant Democratic Party in the Northern states. And you will learn that agitation of that sort won elections and forced Democrats in the Northern states to abandon old ties to brethren in the Southern states, as they struggled to combat the political pressures within their localities and their states. The passions and prejudices political organizers were exploiting and the propaganda they were dispensing was varied in nature, but historians today rather lump their message under a single banner, called "Anti-Slavery." That over-simplification is a disservice to we who wish to learn, for in the study of political movements it is of primary importance that we ascertain what a movement was "for," not what it said it was "against." We need to find out what those Anti-Slavery agitators were "for?" Not only do we need to know what they said they were "for," more importantly, we must be able to conclude, by their actions and by evidence, what, in truth, they were "for." Toward that understanding, we will determine who among the Anti-Slavery agitators were "for" keeping African Americans out of the Northern states and the National Territories, and those will be called, for our purposes, "Exclusionists." Secondly, we will determine who among those agitators were "for" sending African Americans to South America, Africa or somewhere far away, and those we will call "Deportationists." Thirdly, we will determine who among them were "for" forcing owners to emancipate their slaves, allowing them to live in any state they chose, perhaps even offering help with the relocation. Those we will call "Abolitionists." We will look for benevolent "true" Abolitionists in the Northern states with money and means and not find a significant number. That is the sad story coming out of the Anti-Slavery Movement. It was "holier-than-thou," readily denouncing slavery, but doing nothing to help the people of African ancestry they pretended to care about.

History Relevant To Understanding the WBTS

One's understanding of American political history is incomplete until he or she has factually studied the fictional novel that unquestionably exerted the greatest literary influence on the emotional political controversy that eventually erupted into the horrific War Between the States. I am speaking of the 1852 novel, *Uncle Tom's Cabin; or Life among the Lowly*, by Harriet Beecher Stowe, of Connecticut and Ohio, daughter of the famous Congregational minister, Lyman Beecher, and sister to an equally famous preacher, Henry Ward Beecher. I am speaking of a novel that embraces all three passions: Exclusionism and Deportationism, these two shrouded in a religion-inspired Abolitionism. Of the thousands of books and magazine articles, and of the tens of thousands of newspaper stories, that accused the people of the Southern culture of inhumane treatment of bonded African Americans (slaves), Stowe's *Uncle Tom's Cabin* was by far the most influential. Although pure fiction, it was a propaganda masterpiece that became bigger than life and painted for many northern States people their mistaken perception of the people of the southern States. After serial publication in *The National Era* during 1851, the novel was published in 1852 as a book. By the end of the excitement, 3,000,000 to 4,000,000 copies would be sold in America, over 1,500,000 in Great Britain, and, after translation into 40 languages, 4,000,000 more worldwide. Within months playwrights created copyright-free dramatic plays, which were popular. This fictional novel was by far the most influential Exclusionist-Abolitionist-Deportationist propaganda publication to ever influence the American mind. At the time of publication, Abraham Lincoln was just another lawyer in Springfield, Illinois. But ten years later he was President and Commander in Chief of the Federal Military. It was then that Lincoln and Stowe first met, the President greeting the novelist with these telling words: "So this is the little lady who made this big war?"

So what was the story in this fictional novel that so excited the mind of so many people of the Northern culture – that caused President Lincoln to view her as "the little lady who made this big war?" Well, strange as it may seem, since Harriet had not traveled to a significant extent in the Southern states, her understanding of relationships between slave families and master families was only framed by second-hand stories heard from others and her own imagination. That observation underscores how tragic was the fictional novel's impact.

There is insufficient space in this chapter of two pages to discuss the characters and relate the story in the novel, but we must view Stowe's closing, where she asks: "Do you say: 'we don't want them here; let them go to Africa?'" Her answer speaks volumes: "Let the Church of the [northern States] receive these poor sufferers in the spirit of Christ; receive them to the educating advantages of Christian republican society and schools, until they have attained to somewhat of a moral and intellectual maturity, and then assist them in their passage to those shores, where they may put in practice the lessons they have learned in America." So we realize that Stowe is not an Abolitionist, not even an Exclusionist – she is just a Deportationist, conjuring impossibility!

Then, as if forecasting a future War between the States, Stowe warns that the people of the United States cannot be saved from disaster "by combining together, to protect injustice and cruelty, and making a common capital of sin," but only "by repentance, justice and mercy; for, not surer is the eternal law by which the millstone sinks in the ocean, than that stronger law by which injustice and cruelty shall bring on nations the wrath of Almighty God!" But, we need to ask ourselves this: "Since laws governing slavery were State laws, not Federal laws, how can Stowe worry that the Wrath of God would be hurled down upon, say, the people of Massachusetts for the sinful behavior of, say, the people of South Carolina?

We now examine the passion for Exclusionism in greater detail. It is sufficient to go back to May 13, 1846, the day that Congress and President James K. Polk of Tennessee declared war against Mexico. The invasion of Mexican land began quickly afterward, especially just south of Texas and westward out to Mexican California. Everyone realized that, with men of both the Southern and Northern cultures joining together in this military invasion, resistance would be impossible, and the United States would quickly take vast Mexican lands out to the

Pacific Ocean. Question: would the invaders of the Southern culture share in settling the vast lands acquired? Politicians of the Northern culture answered: not with African American slaves! The North wanted the South at its side fighting for the land, but wanted all of the land for itself. This became apparent when Democrat Representative David Wilmot of Pennsylvania presented an amendment to a war appropriations bill stipulating that all African American slaves were to be excluded from living in any land taken from Mexico. This would become known as the "Wilmot Proviso." In the Treaty of Guadalupe Hidalgo, approved on March 10, 1848, the Mexican Government relinquished all of its land west of Texas in exchange for peace and $15,000,000. With this vast land in American legal possession, the fight began to restrict settlement to the Northern culture, characterized by the exclusion from this vast land of all African American slaves. In its campaign the North was successful and Exclusionism ruled American politics. But Exclusionism was not confined to land taken from Mexico. In the same year of 1848, in Illinois, the land of Lincoln, the newly revised State Constitution, in Article 14, directed the General Assembly to pass a law prohibiting "free persons of color from immigrating to and settling this state and to effectively prevent owners of slaves from bringing them into Illinois for the purpose of setting them free." In the next chapter, you will learn about terrorist attacks by Exclusionists in Kansas Territory from 1854 to 1860. So, while recalling that importation of African slaves had been outlawed since 1810, ask yourself the question: "Did the Northern insistence on Exclusionism benefit the African American slave?" Keep that question in mind during class discussion.

Having examined Exclusionism, we look at Abolitionism. We must assume that a true Northern Abolitionist, worthy of the name, was passionate about helping African American slaves become free and become successful at independent living in a Northern state. A "true" Abolitionist, if wealthy, would simply purchase a slave family and help them become resituated. Sadly, the Northern culture did not produce any like that. A "true" Abolitionist, if devout, would help a slave, often a runaway, adapt to independent living and shelter him from authorities, not hasten him north to Canada. A significant number of Quakers were of this stripe. But, overall, "true" Abolitionists, by the definition provided in this chapter, were a rarity in the Northern culture. But for now, we move forward to an examination of Deportationism.

When historians report on American Deportationism, they first mention "The Society for the Colonization of Free People of Color of America," called the "American Colonization Society" for short. Begun in New Jersey in 1816 and supported by both slave owners of the Southern culture, including Henry Clay of Kentucky and John Randolph of Virginia, and Quakers and Evangelicals of the Northern culture, the Society facilitated the deportation or transfer of African Americans to lands elsewhere, mainly to the colony it helped organize on the West African coast they named "Liberia." In some cases the Society purchased slaves, made them independent and put them on ships bound for Africa. But more often they were already free or freed by their owner for the purpose of deportation. The first arrived at Liberia in 1820. By 1830, 2,600 had been transferred to the colony. By 1867, two years after the conquest of the Confederacy, the number transferred had exceeded 13,000, representing one sent to Liberia to every 400 remaining in the States. In subsequent years very, very few African Americans even gave serious thought to leaving for Africa. Deportation was considered by many to be the ultimate solution to the "Negro problem" in America, but it took a lot of wishful dreaming to explain how and why millions would volunteer to relocate to an Africa they had never known, full of perils to be sure. Only forced deportation seemed a possibility.

Let's examine the "Underground Railroad." Which "ism" best classifies it? The name helps us figure that out. A railroad runs from "A to B," right? Well, "A" was somewhere near the boundary separating the "free" and "slave" states. "B" was in Canada. Because Exclusionism was the primary passion in the Northern culture, secret conveyance northward of run-away slaves was supported by the Northern culture, as long as the "passengers" on that train kept moving north to Canada. Perhaps as many as 30,000 made the journey, there left to fend for themselves. The Fugitive Slave Law empowered persistent political agitation helpful to Republicans seeking to exploit incidents to demonize Southerners and Democrats.

Actually, President Lincoln, fundamentally a Deportationist, promoted deportation in the first two years of his presidency. In December 1861, knowing that the North faced a protracted and brutal war, Lincoln proposed to Congress that his Government sponsor and finance a major African American deportation program. The following year his Administration actively sought resettlement sites in Africa, the Caribbean and Central America, including Chiriqui. Various emancipation schemes in Maryland, Kentucky and Missouri, followed by deportation, were hotly debated in 1862, then allowed to die away. But in April 1863, 430 African American men, women and children from occupied Virginia were deported to Ile A'Vache, Haiti, the beginning of a planned 5,000 deportations. The Haiti project failed (the survivors were eventually rescued). If the Confederates had been overwhelmed by late 1862, history suggests substantial deportation might well have occurred. But, by 1863 the war became so horrific and African American men were consequently viewed as too important to the military as soldiers and to politicians as voters in the future conquered states.

Summation

Anti-Slavery was not simply Abolitionism. It was also Exclusionism and Deportationism. Empowered by political gain-seeking, these three Anti-Slavery passions were diverse and not very caring for the welfare of the African American. An inquiring mind is needed to fully understand it.

Suggestions for Class Discussion

With no government welfare programs, life was hard in the 1850's for people of every race who were in need of help. With that in mind, discuss the good and the bad of Exclusionism, Deportationism and "true" Abolitionism.

Recommended Reading

- *Understanding "Uncle Tom's Cabin" and "The Battle Hymn of the Republic,"* by Howard Ray White, pub. 2003-2014.
- *Lincoln*, a biography by David Herbert Donald, pub. 1995.
- *Legend of the Underground Railroad*, by Larry Gara, pub. 1961.

Chapter 15* – Bleeding Kansas, the Emigrant Aid Societies and John Brown – a Story of 1850's Political Prejudice, Terrorism and Propaganda, pitting the Northern against the Southern Cultures.

By Howard Ray White of N. C., S.I.S.H

Introduction

Understanding the War Between The States requires knowledge of the competition, between the Northern Culture and the Southern Culture, for political control of Kansas Territory, which began in 1854 – the year of the first Republican parties in the Northern states – and lasted into 1861, the year Republicans completed their takeover of the office of Governor in every Northern state, plus the office of President. Here also is the important story of terrorist John Brown. Prior to 9/11, America's greatest experience with terrorism had occurred in Kansas Territory during the 1850s, fueling political sectionalism and propaganda useful to the rapidly expanding Republican Party of the Northern states.

An Honest Sampling of the History Relevant to the WBTS

At first, Kansas Territory was not to be, suggesting that America might have avoided Bleeding Kansas, because in early 1854, Congress was moving toward authorizing a larger territory composed of the combined lands of present-day Nebraska and Kansas. The Missouri Compromise of 1820, which was struck to gain admittance of Missouri as a state, had stipulated that afterward bonded African Americans would not be allow to live in any new states north of the Arkansas-Missouri boundary latitude, and Nebraska and Kansas lay north of that boundary. Had the agreement been broken by admission of California, far south of the boundary? Southerners said "Yes." So, Stephen Douglas, Senator of Illinois and the most powerful Democrat in Congress, drafted a bill dividing this proposed Nebraska into two territories, the northern half to be called Nebraska, the southern half to be called Kansas – vote by settlers would decide yes or no on bonded African Americans. Douglas's main political concern was ensuring that his home town Chicago was the hub of westward railroads, for no Senator focused more on railroad deal-making than the North's most powerful Democrat. Anyway, Douglas figured the Southern culture would settle Kansas while the Northern culture settled the other territory and his railroad schemes would be the better for it. On May 29, 1854, Democrat President Franklin Pierce signed the Kansas-Nebraska Act, making it Federal law. Of his leadership over what would prove to be reckless legislation, Douglas would boast:

> "I passed the Kansas-Nebraska Act myself. I had the authority and power of a dictator throughout the whole controversy in both [the House and the Senate]. The speeches were nothing. It was the marshalling and directing of men . . ."

That summer, settlers of the Southern culture, mostly of adjacent Missouri and generally comfortable with including African Americans, slave or free, had established 3 towns on the west bank of the Missouri River, named Leavenworth, Kickapoo and Atchison. But there was no organized effort to fund and encourage rapid settlement by Southerners.

On the other hand, an organized effort to organize and fund settlement from far-away Massachusetts was launched during that summer of 1854 when Eli Thayer convinced the Massachusetts State Legislature to grant him a Charter to establish the "Massachusetts Emigrant Aid Company," with authority to raise up to $5,000,000 to finance the venture. Thayer reasoned that Kansas settlers from Massachusetts would need organized political, financial and military support to win control of the future Kansas Territory Legislature and thereby empower the Exclusionist cause. He also hoped to make a lot of money on Kansas land sales and other opportunities. The stock prospectus promised to sell off all company assets and pay a dividend to stockholders when Kansas became a state. Christian and Unitarian ministers, the latter a major force in the Massachusetts Abolition Movement, were supportive. In July, 29 men, aiming to be the Company's first group of Kansas settlers, were sent off from Boston with much the same fanfare with which heroes are sent off to war.

By the way, in that same month, Cassius Clay, son of a Kentucky slave-holding family and a well-known Abolitionist, denounced the Kansas-Nebraska Act before a gathering in Springfield, Illinois, while local lawyer Abe Lincoln lounged on the grass, listening to the denunciations and exhortations.

When the group of 29 Massachusetts men arrived at St. Louis, they were directed to a town site about 40 miles up the Kansas River, where Company leader Charles Robinson wanted to build the outfit's first town. Robinson announced the town's name would be "Lawrence" in honor of Amos Lawrence, the treasurer of the Massachusetts Emigrant Aid Company. Robinson was heaping flattery on the wealthy Lawrence in hopes of even greater financial aid.

Appointed by President Franklin Pierce to be Governor of Kansas Territory, Andrew Reeder of Pennsylvania set up office in October 1854 near Fort Leavenworth, which had been built by the U. S. Army in 1827. Of Leavenworth town, the February 1855 issue of the Leavenworth *Herald* said: "Five months ago there was not a building in the place."

There is insufficient space in this chapter to cover events in 1855, when many settlers of the Southern culture arrived, so we skip forward to the crucial year of 1856. By that summer, Republican political leaders and Republican newspapermen were intent on winning fall elections in the Northern states. At stake were Northern state elections not yet in Republican hands (governors, legislators, Congress and President). And political agitation over Bleeding Kansas was near the forefront of Republican propaganda efforts. We will examine three happenings that summer which focused on Bleeding Kansas.

First, we look at Senator Charles Sumner of Massachusetts. During May 19 and 20, 1856, Sumner stood before the Senate delivering a 120-page thoroughly memorized and preprinted, 120-page speech, demonizing the people of the Southern states and their political leaders. The speech, called "The Crime against Kansas," was delivered to a packed Senate crowd and printed in many Republican newspapers in the Northern states and as a pamphlet. In this 120-page memorized speech, Sumner twisted into a "crime" the story of efforts by Southerners to peacefully and lawfully settle in Kansas Territory and to allow African Americans to live there. In my epic history, *Bloodstains*, I wrote, "It is amazing that a mind capable of memorizing 120 pages was incapable of recognizing false propaganda, yet, that is the case with Charles Sumner." By the way, during the two-day speech, Sumner also defamed the name of fellow Senator Andrew Butler, of South Carolina, prompting his nephew, Representative Preston Brooks, also of South Carolina, to beat the defamer with a walking cane, for Sumner would have refused to duel. How did Sumner respond? He pretended to be gravely and permanently injured by the "Southern ruffian," transforming himself into a well-publicized martyr for the Republican Party over the next 4 years. Yes, over a span of 4 years he returned to his Senate seat once, then to vote for a higher tariff. This political episode was called the "Caning of Charles Sumner."

Secondly, we look at a May 21 attempt by Kansas Territory authorities to arrest a group of Exclusionist terrorists who had been previously indicted by a grand jury, but shielded by Exclusionists in Lawrence, headquarters for the Massachusetts Emigrant Aid Company and its propaganda newspapers. Sheriff Jones had attempted to arrest these terrorists in December 1855, but had been shot and wounded by the town's defenders. This time arresting authorities were led by Federal Marshall Israel Donelson and supported by a large, well-armed Territory posse and Sheriff Jones. Unlike the defiant response encountered in December, arresting authorities found that Emigrant Aid Company leader Charles Robinson and most prominent terrorists had fled north to escape arrest. But the posse could not be restrained from doing a bit of damage about town. It burned the fortress-like Free State Hotel, demolished the buildings housing two newspapers, the *Kansas Free State* and the *Herald of Freedom*, threw their type into the river and, for good measure, burned the vacant house belonging to Charles Robinson. No Lawrence resident was hurt. But, Republican newspapers across the Northern states were eager for propaganda that supported allegations that Southern people were violent "ruffians." So, the burning of the four vacated buildings in Lawrence was trumpeted as the "Sack of Lawrence," projecting horrors reminiscent of the "Sack of Rome" by Barbarians over 1,000 years ago.

Thirdly, we examine the May 24 terrorist murders by the Kansas Territory gang led by John Brown of New York and Ohio, and secretly supported by six well-to-do and influential northeastern Republican Exclusionists. At this point, Brown's gang consisted of sons Watson, Oliver and Frederick, his son-in-law Henry Thompson, and gang members James Townsley and Theodore Weiner. Together, the terrorists headed for the section of Pottawatomie Creek where two German immigrants, Henry and William Sherman, ran a store. There settlers of the Southern culture lived. "But it's killing men in cold blood," Townsley protested. Brown replied, "It has been ordained by the Almighty God, ordained from eternity, that I should make an example of these men." It was about 11:00 pm when the Doyle household, just getting ready to go to bed, was startled by a knock on the door. Upon entering the house, with the heavily armed gang following, Brown demanded that the father, James Doyle, surrender "in the name of the Army of the North." James did the only thing he could do. He obeyed orders and stepped outside to meet whatever was in store for him, while 2 men of the "Army of the North" stood guard over his family. After a few minutes of dead silence, Brown came back and ordered two boys, William and Drury, to step outside. At daybreak Mahala Doyle found, in scattered places her husband, shot dead and pierced in the side, and her two

sons dead, their heads split open, their sides pierced, and William's fingers chopped off. Also killed in similar fashion that night were Allen Wilkinson, a member of the Kansas Territory Legislature, and William Sherman, "whose skull was split with the brains spilled out but still holding in the waters of Mosquito Creek." News of these terrorist murders did not receive attention in Northern newspapers, except for a few that briefly mentioned some attacks blamed on Native Americans. This was typical, for Republican newspapers were focused on demeaning Southerners and Democrats in general to win fall elections for the sectional Republican Party. Later, to forget memory of terrorist John Brown, residents of Dutch Henry's Crossing would rename the place "Lane" in honor of James Henry Lane (Google James Henery Lane of Kansas fame).

In 1859, as political excitement over the upcoming 1860 elections mounted, the terrorist John Brown enlarged his gang and launched a foolish raid on the Federal armory at Harper's Ferry, near the northern boundary of Virginia. That is another story, not much more than a doomed criminal assault on a poorly defended Federal facility, but a story that won amazing praise across the Northern states, eventually elevating John Brown to a Christ-like being in the original version of America's patriotic song, "The Battle Hymn of the Republic."

The sectional Republicans ran a candidate for President in the 1856 elections. Although their candidate for President, John Fremont, lost, he carried 11 Northern states, Republican strength in Congress would reduce Democrats to 50 percent of House seats and 56 percent of Senate seats. All 16 Northern states had vigorous Republican parties and, by early 1857, 12 governors were Republicans. The sectional Republican Party was clearly politically powerful, even though limited to the Northern states. Furthermore, it was apparent that propaganda over Bleeding Kansas was a potent political tool for gathering additional votes, looking forward to 1860.

After the secession of several Southern states, Republicans, no longer needing Bleeding Kansas propaganda, granted statehood to Kansas.

I have insufficient space for full coverage of Kansas terrorism, the killings, the arson, threats against settlers of the opposite culture. Southerners did resort to violence in retaliation, but Northerners instigated the vast majority of the incidents.

Summation

It was not so much the terrorism taking place in Kansas Territory as the twisted Northern states newspaper coverage. The terrorists were from the North, but the blame was directed at the settlers from the South. Kansas Territory and John Brown is a study in political demagoguery – a big word, worthy of looking up – more than any other word, characterizing political sectionalism in the Northern States.

Topic for Class Discussion

Why should Americans be always searching for the truth, inspecting with questioning minds messages that smell like political deception, political demagoguery, and so forth?

Recommended Reading

- ***Bleeding Kansas*** by Alice Nichols, pub. 1954.
- ***The Secret Six, John Brown and the Abolitionist Movement***, Otto Scott, pub. 1979.

Chapter 16* – The Rise of Political Sectionalism in the Northern States.

By Howard Ray White of N. C., S.I.S.H.

Let's talk about how to properly study history. Trained as a chemical engineer, the Scientific Method of study is a firmly ingrained habit. I always select "scientifically correct" truth over "politically correct" truth, even when that feels harsh. I seek proof of accusations and claims, for "it is the victors who write the history of military and political conquests."

I mentally transport myself to the time period being studied, to take on the life of those people, for only then can I truly understand history from their perspective. I follow events chronologically to ensure correct matching of actions, reactions, actions, reactions, etc., all in the proper sequence. I look at actions, not words, because politicians often claim to advocate a certain policy to win votes, but make no effort to implement that policy once elected. I focus on the means because "the ends do not justify the means."

It is important to name a political movement for what Activists say they were **for**, never for what they say they were **against**. So, the three different political movements that are normally grouped under the single term "Anti-slavery," I rename: **"Exclusionism," "Deportationism"** and **"Abolitionism."** And I call slaves by a different name to emphasize both their bonded status and their race, because race was far more at issue in the 1800s than it is today. Instead of calling them "slaves," I call them "bonded African Americans."

With that said, let us together "live" the history of America's political sectionalism. Let us enhance your understanding by naming a few leaders of these political movements. I will mention Stephen Douglas, Jefferson Davis, Abraham Lincoln, Thad Stevens, and Charles Sumner.

First, I will discuss the dominant political party of the 1830s, 1840s and early 1850s – the **Democratic Party**. It seems that the contentious nature of the Administration of John Quincy Adams of Massachusetts re-ignited party politics, giving rise in 1828 to the Democratic Party under the leadership of Andrew Jackson of Tennessee and Martin Van Buren of New York. The two most important Democrats during the 1850s, during the rise of Political Sectionalism, were Stephen Douglas and Jefferson Davis.

Stephen Douglas was a great admirer of Andrew Jackson and an amazingly successful politician at a very young age. Born in Vermont and schooled in upper New York State, he arrived in central Illinois in 1833 at the age of 20, became a lawyer in 1834 and quickly became an influential leader of the Illinois Democratic Party. He was elected Federal Congressman in 1843 and Federal Senator in 1847, where he chaired the Committee on National Territories. Douglas was the leader of the Democratic Party in the northern States by the early 1850s.

Jefferson Davis of Mississippi was also a Democrat, but his early years were spent in military service and farming, for he did not enter politics until 1845 at the age of 37, when he became a Federal Congressman. Commander of a Mississippi regiment in the Mexican War and a wounded hero, he became a Federal Senator in 1848. Between Senate terms he was a very able Secretary of War in President Pierce's cabinet.

Davis believed firmly in limiting the power of the Federal Government to only that clearly stipulated in the Federal Constitution. He was a great admirer of John Calhoun of South Carolina, and, when Calhoun died in 1850, Davis became the leader of the Democratic Party in the South.

What about the Democratic Party platform? Democrats typically advocated **for** a Federal Government limited in power as clearly defined in the Federal Constitution; **for** Nation Building regardless of sectional jealousies; **for** limiting import tax rates to only what was needed for Federal revenue; **for** ensuring that bank and capitalistic business influences did not become too powerful, and **for** ensuring that government was attentive to the welfare and interests of the farmer and the working man. The Democratic Party platform had wide appeal everywhere, and forced the political opposition to contrive devious methods for winning elections. Yes: "devious methods for winning elections." Does that sound familiar?

Now let us look at the several parties that were opposed to the Democratic Party.

The first opposition party was the **Whig Party**, which advocated **for** a more powerful Federal Government than intended by the Federal Constitution; **for** divergent attitudes about Nation Building while often exploiting sectional jealousies to gain political advantage; **for** high import tax rates that were designed to choke off imports and maximize the profits of American manufacturers; **for** helping banks and capitalist business expand influence and profitability, and **for** being often more attentive to them than to the welfare and interests of the farmer and the working man. Since the majority of voting men were not naturally attracted to the Whig Party, Whig politicians were often exploiting jealousies of all sorts in attempts to deflect voter attention away from naturally important issues and toward sideshow issues. Whigs were prone to be demagogues.

Abe Lincoln became an important Whig leader in central Illinois, but not beyond that region. He was raised on various farms in Kentucky and Indiana. Grown by the time the family moved to a new farm in central Illinois, he became a lawyer and a State Legislator. For two years, beginning in 1847, he was a Federal Congressman. But Whigs did not nominate him for a second term because his opposition to the Mexican War had destroyed his popularity back home. Although Lincoln would rise again with the Republican Party, he would never again hold elective office prior to becoming President. Not a very impressive record. Suggest you compare Lincoln's and Davis's record of military and government service.

In the 1830s and 1840s Democrats were also opposed by the **Anti-Mason Party**, which was based on an amazing sideshow campaign against members of Masonic Lodges. The Anti-Mason Party arose in 1827 in New York State in reaction to the alleged murder of a man who was reportedly about to expose to public view alleged evil and secret pseudo-religious initiation "rites and oaths" conducted within Masonic Lodges. Have you ever heard of a more fitting cover for a political Demagogue?

Thad Stevens became the most important leader of the Pennsylvania Anti-Mason Party, and for a time the most powerful member of the Pennsylvania House. Born and raised in Vermont, he graduated from Dartmouth and moved to south-central Pennsylvania, where he became a lawyer, and a bit later the owner of a sizable iron smelting business, which employed about 200 workers. Through a coalition of Anti-Masons and Whigs, he won election to the Federal House in 1848 and was reelected in 1850. But he failed to win re-election in 1852. Yet, Stevens would rise again with the Republican Party and become the most powerful leader in the Federal House during the war years and Political Reconstruction, at times more powerful than Presidents Lincoln and Johnson.

The Democratic Party was also opposed by the **Know-Nothing Party**. Don't you love these crazy names? That Party was established in 1850 in New York City to oppose Catholic influence in schools and government. This was a political movement to obstruct religious, social and political influence by recent immigrants, most of them being Catholic, and many of them being from western Ireland and the Germanic countries, who were arriving in the northeastern States in huge numbers, and, upon acquiring the right to vote, usually siding with the Democratic Party. Know-Nothing's were of the Order of the Star Spangled Banner, a Secret Fraternal Order of political Activists that opponents dubbed, "The Know-Nothing Party," to publicize the fact that no member would admit that he knew anything about the Order or its secret slate of candidates. By 1854 the Order had become very powerful, especially in Massachusetts. Many former Whig and Anti-Mason politicians were attracted to the Order, including Thad Stevens of Pennsylvania. A temporary home for Whigs, Know-Nothings ran former President Fillmore for President in 1856 and polled 22 percent of the vote. They enjoyed limited support in Kentucky, Maryland and a few Southern states.

Democrats were also opposed by the **Free Soil Party**. Instead of excluding recent immigrants, especially Catholics, from local schools and political influence, the Free Soil Party was aimed at excluding southern States farmers and their bonded African Americans from the National Territories. It was always a minority party that sought coalitions to share power. Through a coalition of Democrats and Free Soilers, Salmon Chase was elected Federal Senator from Ohio in 1848 and **Charles Sumner** was elected Federal Senator from Massachusetts in 1851.

Democrats were also opposed by the **Liberty Party**. In addition to excluding bonded African Americans from the National Territories and all future States, the Liberty Party wished to do everything possible, within the constraints of a liberally interpreted Federal Constitution, to make bonded African Americans independent in the southern States. The core Activists in this Party were Abolitionists at heart, and Exclusionism was their pragmatic beginning. But very few northern States voters supported Abolitionism for the southern States. So this party never gained significant power.

Finally, I come to something that merely resembled a party – the **Prohibition Movement**, which began in Maine. It aimed to outlaw alcoholic beverages. This movement was also motivated by Exclusion passions, for, as intended, it fell hardest upon recent immigrants, who loved their beer and ale and gathering at taverns to drink and socialize.

That was a long list of parties opposed to Democrats? Too many. Too factious. Too much vote splitting. Well, by 1855

a struggle was climaxing in the northern States for the <u>soul</u> of the party that would become the dominant opposition to the Democrats, most importantly in Massachusetts. It is hard to believe, but in 1855 the Massachusetts Know Nothing Party was so completely victorious that it controlled all but 3 of 378 House seats, every Senate seat, and the Governor's office. The Know Nothing Party would try to step out of its Secret Order hiding place and go nation-wide, calling itself the **American Party**, but that would fail. It would not become the dominant opposition to the Democrats.

Instead a new party emerged and swallowed up all the other opposition parties. This was the sectional **Republican Party**, which held its first successful state election campaign in Michigan in 1854. During 1854, '55 and early '56 it spread throughout the northern States. The top plank in the Republican Party Platform was Exclusionism. It would not seek to make bonded African Americans independent. It would not agitate against immigrants and Catholic influence in government or schools. It would not advocate prohibition of alcoholic beverages. Behind closed doors, it would be very friendly toward bankers, capitalists, railroad tycoons and tariff-seeking manufacturers, because these wealthy men would provide important political support. But publicly it would seek to identify with farmers, tradesmen and factory workers as Republicans persistently called for Exclusion of bonded African Americans from the National Territories and all new States. The Party would be purely sectional, have no presence in the southern States, and, after 1856, be the only opposition to the Democrats in the northern States.

Free Soilers Charles Sumner and Salmon Chase were quick to switch to the Republican Party and Anti-Mason Thad Stevens joined in 1856. That same crucial year, under the leadership of former Whig Abe Lincoln, a powerful Republican Party was organized in Illinois.

How could a sectional party succeed? Because rapid population growth in the northern States made it theoretically possible, without any southern States support whatsoever, to take control of the Federal Government in 1856 and 1860, and it would be even easier when new census data would apportion voting in 1864. But how was Republican control of the Federal Government to be attained? By persistently agitating for Exclusion, and not much else. But how could excitement about Exclusionism be sustained for so many years? By exploiting Bleeding Kansas, about which you read earlier.

The Republican campaign strategy included often lying to voters, like in the amazing deception known as "Bleeding Sumner." What was, Charles Sumner, like? Well Charles Sumner of Massachusetts was born and raised in Boston, schooled at Harvard, and worked some as a lawyer. He was brilliant and literary, but quite short on common sense. Except for a few months in a failed marriage, he was a bachelor. In May 1856, Sumner rose before the Federal Senate and delivered a long and hateful speech, titled "The Crime Against Kansas," in which he damned the people of the southern States as evil and unfit to live in Kansas Territory, and pronounced ugly personal attacks on specific Senators, including Andrew Butler of South Carolina. Two days later Butler's nephew, Congressman Preston Brooks, entered the almost vacant Senate Chamber and punished Sumner by whipping him about the head with a hard rubber walking cane. Although Sumner bled a lot he was not seriously injured. But Republicans were so successful at martyring Sumner in news reports, that he eagerly began a three-year martyrdom in which he pretended to be seriously injured and unable to attend sessions of the Federal Senate, while secretly enjoying paid vacation trips about Europe. Republicans newspapermen persistently told northern States people that Brooks' caning of Sumner was proof that men from the southern States were evil, bullying "ruffians." Sumner went along for three years while enjoying European vacations.

Were Abolition Activists concerned about being helpful to bonded African Americans? They were not. Their objective was fighting the perceived sinfulness associated with owning bonded African Americans and enforcing Exclusionism, which most expected would conclude with Deportation. Widespread approval of John Brown's gang by northern States preachers, intellectuals and newspapermen, was amazing to behold. Nothing troubled southern States people more than widespread and intense glorification of Brown's mindless terrorist attack.

Compared to the excitement in the northern States, the southern States response to Exclusion propaganda was rather muted. Edmund Ruffin, a very successful and widely respected Virginia farmer and soil scientist, was one of the most effective in asserting, through published essays, that owning bonded African Americans was not evil in itself. He submitted that people of African descent had benefited in many ways by living on American farms: that many had accepted Christ; that most owners were kind to and protective of them, and, with few exceptions, that they were much better off in America than were their cousins in Africa. Southern clergymen knew that Abolitionism was not supported by the Bible, and they worked to promote Christianity and stable marriages among the bonded people.

By the summer of 1860 the Republican steamroller seemed to be unstoppable. Throughout the northern States, election victories between 1854 and 1859 put Republicans in control of almost all the State governments, including Governors, as well as a large portion of Federal House and Senate seats. This swift domination of State governments in the northern States was severely marginalizing the Democratic Party in those States. Republican exploitation of Bleeding Kansas propaganda forced northern States Democrats, including their leader Stephen Douglas, to cave in and embrace Exclusionism as well.

This infuriated southern States Democrats and resulted in a split at the 1860 Democratic National Convention. They refused to support the national Party unless it approved of letting bonded African Americans live in the National Territories until a vote by settlers to include or exclude when statehood was achieved. But almost all northern States Delegates insisted on exclusion throughout the National Territories from the outset. So, southern States Delegates withdrew and nominated their own slate of candidates.

Since the Republican Party was not national, it held a convention of only the northern States in Chicago. Delegates decided not to risk nominating an experienced office holder, such as William Seward of New York. Abe Lincoln was only considered because of the seven debates Stephen Douglas had granted him in 1858, which had received wide newspaper coverage all over the northern States. Furthermore, Illinois

Republican Party workers packed the galleries and engaged in "dirty tricks." That got Lincoln nominated. As candidate, he made no public speeches and issued no public letters, while Republican campaigners across the northern States emphasized Exclusionism in attacks against Democrats. Republicans easily won all the northern States in the four-way race for President.

Republican Party leaders had not wanted to be listed on ballots in the Southern states, because that would have compromised the purity of their crusade. Republican candidates had been listed on only 23 of the 33 State ballots. Of the election results Wendell Phillips wrote, "with defiant satisfaction: 'No man has a right to be surprised at this state of things. It is the first sectional Party ever organized in this [country] . . . it is not national – it is sectional. The Republican Party is a Party of the [northern States] pledged against the [southern States].'"

1860 election results for the next Congress gave Republicans 29 of 66 Senate seats and 108 of 237 House seats, plus the support of others from the northern States. And Abe Lincoln was elected President with 40 percent of the vote. The final numbers appear below:

Popular Vote: Lincoln, 1,833,352 (40%); Douglas, 1,375,157 (29%); Breckinridge, 845,763 (18%); Bell, 589,581 (13%).

Electoral Vote: Lincoln, 180 (59%); Breckinridge, 72 (24%); Bell, 39 (13%); Douglas, 12 (4%).

States Carried: Lincoln carried all 16 northern States and the 2 Pacific States (from east to west they were: ME, RI, MA, NH, VT, CT, NY, NJ, PA, OH, IN, IL, MI, IA, WI, MN, OR, CA); Breckinridge carried 11 southern States (from east to west they were: DE, MD, NC, SC, GA, FL, AL, MS, LA, AR, TX). Bell carried 3 southern States (VA, KY, TN). Douglas carried 1 southern State (MO).

The Republican Party completed its profound sweep of Northern States Governor jobs. With the additions won in the 1860 elections, Republican Governors controlled, or would by early 1861 control, the State Militia of the following northern States. Please remember you are studying the War Between the States, and when Lincoln requested state militia, each governor was empowered to say yes or no. That State power is a key to your understanding of the WBTS, a war between political parties. Here are the details. Find your state.

Maine: Israel Washburn, Jr., Republican Governor from 1861 to 1863; a lawyer and Republican Federal Representative from 1855 to 1860. He was preceded by Governor Lot Myrick Morrill, Republican Governor from 1858 to 1860, also a lawyer. By the way, in Congress in 1861, Morrill would give his name to that year's exorbitant Republican tariff.

Rhode Island: William Sprague, Republican Governor from 1860 to 1863, a very wealthy industrialist.

Massachusetts: John Andrew, Republican Governor from 1861 to 1866, a lawyer.

New Hampshire: Nathaniel Berry; Republican Governor from 1861 to 1863. Preceded by Ichabod Goodwin, Republican Governor from 1859 to 1861.

Vermont: Frederick Holbrook, Republican Governor from 1861 to 1863; preceded by Erastus Fairbanks, Republican Governor from 1860 to 1861.

Connecticut: William Buckingham; Republican Governor from 1858 to 1866, an industrialist.

New York: Edwin Morgan; Republican Governor from 1859 to 1863; Republican Party State Chairman from 1856 to 1858; Republican Party Northern States Chairman from 1856 to 1864, a wholesale merchant, banker and broker.

New Jersey: Charles Olden; Republican Governor from 1860 to 1863, merchant.

Pennsylvania: Andrew Curtin; Republican Governor from 1861 to 1867, a lawyer. Preceded by William Packer, Democrat Governor from 1858 to 1861.

Ohio: William Dennison, Jr.; Republican Governor from 1860 to 1862, law, railroads, banking. Preceded by Salmon Chase; Free Soil and Republican Governor from 1856 to 1860, lawyer.

Indiana: Oliver Morton; Republican Governor from 1861 to 1867, a lawyer (During wartime Morton ignored the legislature and ruled as a dictator). Preceded by Abram Adams Hammond; Republican Governor from 1860 to 1861.

Illinois: Richard Yates; Republican Governor from 1861 to 1865, a lawyer. Preceded by John Wood; Republican Governor from 1860 to 1861.

Michigan: Austin Blair; Republican Governor from 1861 to 1865, a lawyer. Preceded by Moses Wisner, Republican Governor from 1859 to 1861.

Iowa: Samuel Kirkwood; Republican Governor from 1860 to 1864, a lawyer.

Wisconsin: Alexander Randall; Republican Governor from 1858 to 1862, a lawyer.

Minnesota: Alexander Ramsey; Republican Governor from 1860 to 1863; a lawyer who spent early career in Pennsylvania. Preceded by Henry Sibley; Democrat Governor from 1858 to 1860, a businessman and politician.

By early 1861 the above Republican-dominated northern States contained an unbroken and unified majority of politically galvanized people (in spite of notable opposition). Four States were placed in immediate harm's way, since a Federal invasion force, which could only be launched from the Republican States, would first have to march southward through their land. The Republican Party had no significant influence in these four States. Their governors were:

Delaware: William Burton; Democrat Governor from 1859 to 1863, a physician.

Maryland: Thomas Hicks; Know Nothing Governor from 1858 to 1862, a politician and a sheriff.

Kentucky: Beriah Magoffin; Democrat Governor from 1859 to 1862, a lawyer.

Missouri: Claiborne Jackson; Democrat Governor in 1861; forced to flee Missouri by Republican revolutionaries and died few months later. Preceded by Governor Robert Stewart; Democrat Governor from 1857 to 1861.

Four southern States were positioned immediately south of the above 4 States. Except for a faction in the Appalachian Mountain region, most of the people in these States would surely fight any attempt by the Lincoln Administration to draft their men and force them to join in a Federal invasion of States positioned further south. The governors of these four States were as follows:

Virginia (Including present-day West Virginia): John Letcher; Democrat Governor of Virginia from 1860 to 1863, a lawyer.

North Carolina: John Ellis; Democrat Governor from 1859 to June 1861, at which time illness would force him to pass authority to Henry Toole Clark, also a Democrat. Clark would hold the office until 1862.

Tennessee: Isham Harris; Democrat Governor from 1857 to 1862; Federal Representative from 1849 to 1853, a lawyer.

Arkansas: Henry Rector; Democrat Governor from 1860 to 1862; State Supreme Court Justice from 1859 to 1860, a lawyer.

Since 1856, southern States politicians and their constituents had viewed the Republican Party in the northern States as terrifying and dangerous. They hoped the President-elect would issue an encouraging message. But, once elected, Abe Lincoln remained quiet, giving no assurances whatsoever that he would respect State Rights and ameliorate Southern fears of Federal subjugation. Consequently the State secession movement in the Deep South became unstoppable.

Close

You are often asked, "What caused the war?"

Never be drawn into looking for the answer among deep South politicians – they only encouraged a vote to peacefully secede; they did not start the war or have a hostile agenda.

Never be drawn into looking for it in State secession – that was legal, peaceful and non-aggressive. It did not start the war.

Never be embroiled in allegations that it was started to make bonded African Americans independent – Lincoln made every effort in 1860 and 1861 to insist otherwise.

Never allow anyone to blame Confederates because they fired on Fort Sumter – they did not kill anybody.

You must always make sure the question is this: "Why did Federals invade the Confederacy?" That is the question! Win the argument to define the question and you will surely win the argument to define the answer.

Suggestions for Class Discussion

How was it possible for political opposition to the national Democratic Party to unite so quickly under a Northern Sectional Party and take over all of the northern States and the Federal Government in only six (6) years?

Recommended Reading

- *The Origins of the Republican Party, 1852-1856*, by William E. Gienapp, pub. 1987.
- *Nativism and Slavery, The Northern Know Nothings, and the Politics of the 1850s*, by Tyler Anbinder, pub. 1994.
- *The Story of the Democratic Party*, by Henry Minor, pub. 1928.

Chapter 17 – The Nature of the Union and the Right of State Secession

By Clyde N. Wilson of S. C., Ph.D., S. I. S. H.

Introduction

In the early 1900s, a famous professor of languages, who had been a Confederate soldier as a young man, wrote that after long contemplation he at last understood what the great WBTS had been about. The war, he said, was fought over grammar. The issue was which was correct: "the United States *are*" or "the United States *is.*" While he was not entirely serious he was pointing to an important truth. The **nature** of the Union, established 70 years before the war by the Constitution, was central. Were Confederates merely "rebels," as Lincoln contended, who could be made to obey his government by force? Or were they, as Confederates believed, exercising a right of self-government in a manner that had always been understood as legitimate for Americans? It is worth noting that before the WBTS every law, speech, and publication referred to "United States" in the plural, as does the Constitution itself. (I bet you didn't know that.) Americans had a good deal of fellow feeling from their common experiences and values and they understood that they were one people compared to other countries. So they sometimes called themselves a "nation." But they usually referred to their government arrangements as "the Union," a "confederacy," or a "compact" among the States.

Sovereignty

We can perhaps advance our understanding here by using a concept that political philosophers find useful – sovereignty. Groups of humans always have institutions to govern themselves, whether it be a tribe or an empire. Officials – governors, judges, generals – have powers and responsibilities. But where does their power come from? Setting aside that all legitimate authority comes from God, let us consider the earthly aspect. Power must come from the "sovereign," the final authority. Almost all Americans agree that our sovereign is "the people" – not a king or a dictator, a nobility or a party soviet. But who are the people? How does one measure their will? We have elections by which the majority is said to rule. But that may not be as definitive as it seems. Elections and majorities are useful but temporary things. They can change overnight for flimsy reasons. Abraham Lincoln in the 1860 election was opposed by more than 60% of the voters. Was he exercising the sovereign will of the people when, while ignoring the Supreme Court, he expanded the powers of the Presidency beyond the Constitution to make an unprecedented war of conquest against the people of nearly half of the States?

James Madison, often considered the "Father of the Constitution," wrote that the Constitution was created by the people of the States and that its meaning can be found only "in the opinions and intentions of the State conventions where it received all … authority which it possesses." The Constitution was not decreed from above by all wise Founding Fathers as many seem to think today. Nobody had the power to do that among free American States. It was not established by the group at Philadelphia that wrote it – they merely presented a proposal to be considered by the States. It was established by the people of each State for that State, acting for themselves. The Constitution and the Union did not exist otherwise. Nobody could force the people of a State to accept the Constitution. In fact, two States rejected it until certain amendments were passed. Before the Revolution each colony had a separate constitutional existence within the British Empire. During the Revolution the people of each colony declared and defended its independence. Each new State exercised every right of a sovereign nation – before and after the Articles of Confederation that united the 13 for carrying on their war of independence. In concluding the war, Great Britain recognized thirteen "free and independent States." Lincoln was clearly incorrect when he claimed that the "Union" came before and created the States.

Confederates found their sovereign in the people of the States. The Constitution had been ratified by a special convention elected fresh from the people to exercise their sovereignty in accepting or rejecting the new Constitution. The Southern States seceded in exactly the same way – a sovereign convention of the people to express their will. To repeal their people's former ratification of the Constitution was to secede.

Historians like to say that State Rights was only a phony "theory" invented by Southerners for the sole purpose of defending their evil institution of slavery. This is simply not true. Two years before he was elected President, Thomas Jefferson wrote the "Kentucky Resolutions." Here he very plainly stated that the Federal Government was not sovereign. It was merely an instrument that had been created by agreement among the States. In this arrangement the States had specified exactly defined and limited powers that they were delegating to Federal officials to be exercised for the common good of the States. The States, having made the Constitution as a contract among themselves, were the judges of interpretation. When the Federal Government exercised more power than it was allowed, a State could "interpose" its sovereignty to prevent unconstitutional Federal actions. State sovereignty was not a subversive "theory," it was intrinsic to the Constitution from the beginning. One can discount State rights and agree with Lincoln only by ignoring an overwhelming weight of evidence. And ignoring the Tenth Amendment which Madison said was "the cornerstone of the Constitution."

The Right of State Secession

The understanding that the Federal Government had limited powers given it by the people of the States, and that the Union was an agreement among the States, was widespread before the WBTS, accepted in the North as well as the South. William Rawle, a Philadelphia judge, wrote a book on American government that clearly stated that States could secede from the Union – a book used as a text in West Point classes for years. The first systematic study of the Constitution, by St. George Tucker, which was long used as a lawyer's handbook, said the same thing. Several States stated in their ratifications that they had the right to withdraw if the Union did not work out as they hoped. New Englanders seriously raised the possibility of seceding at the time of the Louisiana Purchase and during the War of 1812. In 1794 Senator Rufus King of New York asked Senator John Taylor of Virginia to join with him in a proposal to divide up the Union into Northern and Southern confederacies because "we never had and never would think alike." The Frenchman Alexis de Tocqueville spent much time in the U.S. in the 1830s and is widely regarded as an insightful foreign observer. In his famous book, *Democracy in America,* he wrote: "The Union was formed by the voluntary agreement of the States; and these, in uniting together, have not forfeited their nationality . . . If one of the States chose to withdraw its name from the contract, it would be difficult to disprove its right to do so."

Thousands of other facts might be shown to prove that a State in the last resort might withdraw from the Union. The Constitution requires that new States founded after the original 13 have all the rights of the old States. The U.S. government might own the real estate and admit new States to the Union, or not. But only a sovereign people could create a state by adopting their constitution and ratifying that of the U.S. The extent to which the right of secession was recognized outside the South is demonstrated by the North's curious flip-flop in early 1861. At first even Republicans and abolitionists accepted secession. Abolitionists pointed to the Declaration's consent of the governed and the famed Republican editor Horace Greeley said, "Let the erring sisters go in peace." But within a few weeks it was realized that without the South the North's economy would nose-dive and both groups became enthusiastic for war. Lincoln had understood this all along.

Not only did the American majority of Jeffersonians understand that State sovereignty was the true interpretation of the Constitution and an indispensable protection against threats to freedom, they were also philosophically opposed to centralization of power. They called such undesirable centralization "consolidation" and considered it far more threatening to the people than secession. History taught, they believed, that centralization of power in a government with no effective limits, especially in a land as large and diverse as America, would inevitably lead to an empire with a tyrant at the center. Were they prophetic?

Nationalism vs. Patriotism

Nationalism won the WBTS and colors our thinking about the past. Today we imagine President Jefferson sitting in the White House glorying at how the Louisiana Purchase had added power to the mighty new nation. But that was not how he saw it at all. He saw that new sovereign States would be formed by the people in the new territory. They might want to secede and form a different Union of their own. That was perfectly OK. It would be just like an older and younger brother separating. They would still be Americans exercising the right of self-government. The Union was not eternal but consent of the governed should be.

Old-fashioned patriots love their people and their land. That is why Confederates rallied enthusiastically to defend against Federal invasion. But they lost their struggle against nationalism. Nationalists connect their patriotism to their government – they love the government's flag and armed forces and are proud when their government stands up to other governments. Nationalism was a major historic force in the 19th century. It is very relevant that Italy and Germany, previously composed of many different states, were being centralized by force at the very time that Lincoln was doing the same to the American States – North and South.

Nationalism rests on two strong pillars: the belief that a country controlled as one economy is highly desirable, and a mass emotional attachment to that country. Secession was sound Constitutionally, historically, and philosophically, but it could not survive the North's desire for economic control and attachment to "the grand old flag."

At his inauguration in 1861, Lincoln refused to acknowledge the reality of secession or to negotiate with the seceded States. He said that seceded States were only temporarily under the control of "a combination" of criminals who refused to obey him. The lawbreakers were too numerous for the U.S. marshals to re-establish his control in those areas, so the army would be used if necessary. Lincoln did not argue as a statesman or a philosopher. He argued as a lawyer putting the best spin on a weak case.

Lincoln's career success had been as a "jury lawyer," – one who won cases by emotional appeals rather than legal wisdom. He knew he could arouse the economic interests and the emotional nationalism of Northerners to support war. After all, Northerners for the previous 30 years had been subjected to endless hate propaganda against Southerners. His position was not Constitutionally or historically accurate and it violated the central meaning of the Declaration of Independence – consent of the governed. The acts of secession were not conspiratorial. They had been long debated and openly voted in the light of long-standing Constitutional understandings. They clearly expressed the will of the people of those States. Many in the South doubted the wisdom of secession but nobody doubted the right. The Southern States that were not among the first seven to secede did not want to secede. But when Lincoln violated the nature of the Union by launching war against other Americans, they had no choice.

Summary

Americans tend to forget a very simple fact. Counting the Border States (DE, MD, KY, MO), Lincoln invaded 15 States for the purpose of overthrowing their legal, democratically-elected governments and depriving their citizens of self-government. This did not "preserve the Union," but changed it into something new and different.

Suggestions for Class Discussion

Is it immoral or unpatriotic to think about how Americans might better govern themselves by institutions other than an all-powerful central government? Does democracy require centralized power? We oppose monopolies in business; why not government?

It surprises many people to learn that the Constitution defines treason not as being against the U.S. government but as "levying war against them" – "them" meaning the States. Is that what Lincoln did? Levy war against the states?

Recommended Readings

- *The Webster-Hayne Debates on the Nature of the Union*, Herman E. Belz, editor, pub. 2000.
- *Is Jefferson Davis a Traitor?*, by Albert T. Bledsoe, pub. 1866.
- *The Politics of Dissolution, Quest for A National Identity and the American Civil War*, Marshall L. DeRosa, editor, pub. 1997.

Chapter 18* – The Secession of South Carolina, Georgia, Florida, Alabama, Mississippi, Louisiana and Texas, the Birth of the Confederate States of America, and the Election of Jefferson Davis.

By Howard Ray White of N. C., S.I.S.H

Introduction

The purely sectional, six-year campaign by the new Republican Party – full of rhetoric demonizing and punishing the Southern states, their political leaders and their slave holders – had produced numerous advocates of State Secession. Although a Republican attempt to emancipate slaves was of little immediate concern, high import taxation, restrictions on moving slaves into the National Territories and a general punitive attitude toward the Southern culture was viewed as impossible to endure any longer. Although State Secession was viewed as a legal remedy, a Republican-launched War Between the States was certainly viewed as a horrible, although real, possibility.

Relevant History

President James Buchanan's Cabinet lost three Southerners during December and January. Secretary of the Treasury Howell Cobb of Georgia resigned to help lead his state in secession. Secretary of War John Floyd of Virginia was forced out of office by intense Republican pressure. The day before Mississippi seceded, Secretary of Interior Jacob Thompson resigned to return home. Although a Democrat, Buchanan of Pennsylvania was giving in to Republican pressure.

South Carolina Secession, December 20, 1860, by a 169 versus 0 vote. On November 8, the South Carolina Legislature began debating a bill to call for a Secession Convention, which passed a few days later. South Carolinians elected delegates who gathered at Charleston. The final secession vote was taken on December 20. The tally was 169 in favor, none opposed. South Carolina – of a rich colonial history, heroic in gaining victory in the Revolutionary War, and a founder of the Federal Government – was the South's secession leader and unanimously committed. The Ordinance of Secession said:

> "We, the people of the State of South Carolina, in convention assembled, do declare and ordain, and it is hereby declared and ordained, That the ordinance adopted by us in convention on [May 23,1788], whereby the Constitution of the United States of America was ratified, and also all acts and parts of acts of the General Assembly of this State ratifying amendments of the said Constitution, are hereby repealed; and that the union now subsisting between South Carolina and other States, under the name of the "United States of America," is hereby dissolved."

On December 24 delegates approved a carefully worded, legal and comprehensive secession justification document (see Google link at end). Students should study this document on a computer or tablet. Careful study and legal analysis will show that secession is defended but slavery is not the cause of it.

Mississippi Secession, January 9, by a 84 versus 15 vote. Two important events occurred on January 9. An "unlawful" attempt by Federals to reinforce Fort Sumter with 200 soldiers and supplies failed when South Carolina artillery turned back the merchant ship *Star of the West* while the escorting warship *Brooklyn* declined to engage its guns. (Attorney General, Jeremiah S. Black of PA, had advised President Buchanan that he could defend the government but had no right to use offensive force against a State.) Meanwhile, Mississippi seceded, declaring "That all the laws and ordinances by which the said State of Mississippi became a member of the Federal Union [are . . .] repealed, and that all obligations . . . be withdrawn, and that the said State doth hereby resume all the rights, functions, and powers . . . and shall from henceforth be a free, sovereign, and independent State."

The Farewell Address of Senator Jefferson Davis. Upon his state's secession, Senator Jefferson Davis, of Mississippi, addressed the US Senate, saying in part:

> "Then, Senators, we recur to the compact which binds us together; we recur to the principles upon which our Government was founded; and when you deny them, and when you deny to us the right to withdraw from a Government which thus perverted threatens to be destructive of our rights, we but tread in the path of our fathers when we proclaim our independence, and take the hazard. This is done not in hostility to others, not to injure any section of the country, not even for our own pecuniary benefit; but from the high and solemn motive of defending and protecting the rights we inherited, and which it is our sacred duty to transmit unshorn to our children."

Also resigning from the Senate that day were Democrats David Yulee and Stephen Mallory of FL, and Clement Clay and Benjamin Fitzpatrick of AL. Republicans would soon admit Kansas to statehood to gain two more Republican Senate seats.

Florida Secession, January 10, by a 62 versus 7 vote. "We, the people of the State of Florida in Convention assembled, do solemnly ordain, publish and declare: That the State of Florida hereby withdraws herself from the . . . United States of America, and from the existing Government of said States . . . and the State of Florida is hereby declared a Sovereign and Independent Nation . . . ."

Alabama Secession, January 11, by a 61 versus 39 vote. "Be it declared and ordained by the people of the State of Alabama, in Convention assembled, That the State of Alabama now withdraws . . . from the Union known as 'the United States of America,' and henceforth ceases to be one of said United States, and is, and of right ought to be a Sovereign and Independent State."

Georgia Secession, January 19, by a 208 versus 89 vote. "We the people of the State of Georgia in Convention assembled do declare and ordain and it is hereby declared and ordained that the ordinance adopted by the State of Georgia in Convention on [January 2, 1788], whereby the constitution of the United States of America was assented to, ratified and adopted, and also all acts and parts of acts of the general assembly of this State, ratifying and adopting amendments to said constitution, are hereby repealed, rescinded and abrogated.

"We do further declare and ordain that the union now existing between the State of Georgia and other States under the name of the United States of America is hereby dissolved, and that the State of Georgia is in full possession and exercise of all those rights of sovereignty which belong and appertain to a free and independent State."

Louisiana Secession, January 26, by a 113 versus 17 vote. "We, the people of the State of Louisiana, in Convention assembled, do declare and ordain, and it is hereby declared and ordained, That the ordinance passed by us in Convention on [November 22, 1811], whereby the Constitution of the United States of America and the amendments of the said Constitution were adopted, and all laws and ordinances by which the State of Louisiana became a member of the Federal Union, be, and the same are hereby, repealed and abrogated; and that the union now subsisting between Louisiana and other States under the name of "The United States of America" is hereby dissolved. We do further declare and ordain, That the State of Louisiana hereby resumes all rights and powers . . . which appertain to a free and independent State."

Texas Secession, February 1, by a 166 versus 8 vote. "We, the people of the State of Texas, by Delegates in Convention assembled, do declare and ordain that the ordinance adopted by our Convention of Delegates on [July 4, 1845], and afterwards ratified by us, under which the Republic of Texas was admitted into the Union with other States, and became a party to the compact styled "The Constitution of the United States of America," be, and is hereby, repealed and annulled; that all the powers which, by the said compact, were delegated by Texas to the Federal Government are revoked and resumed; that Texas is of right absolved from all restraints and obligations incurred by said compact, and is a separate sovereign State . ."

The Birth of the Confederate States of America.

With few exceptions, those mentioned above who voted against secession accepted the will of the majority and became dedicated Confederates. They had not doubted the right of secession, only its prudence or timing. A section of the Alabama Ordinance of Secession invited delegates to come to Montgomery to discuss founding a constitution for the Confederate States of America.

"Be it resolved by the people of Alabama in Convention assembled, That the people of the States of Delaware, Maryland, Virginia, North Carolina, South Carolina, Florida, Georgia, Mississippi, Louisiana, Texas, Arkansas, Tennessee, Kentucky and Missouri, be and are hereby invited to meet the people of the State of Alabama, by their Delegates, in Convention, on [February 4, 1861], at the city of Montgomery, in the State of Alabama, for the purpose of consulting with each other as to the most effectual mode of securing concerted and harmonious action in whatever measures may be deemed most desirable for our common peace and security."

These seceded states sent delegates who quickly created a Confederate Government limited in power by a provisional Constitution approved four days later. The preamble stated:

"We the People of the Confederate States, each acting in its sovereign and independent character, in order to form a permanent Federal Government, establish justice, insure domestic tranquility, and secure the blessings of liberty to ourselves and our posterity – invoking the favor and guidance of Almighty God – do ordain and establish this Constitution for the Confederate States of America."

It limited tax rates on imports to only that needed for revenue and prohibited Confederate financing of construction projects (harbors, canals, railroads) for they were to be state projects. It prohibited the importation of bonded African Americans unless accompanied by an immigrant owner (say, a Kentuckian immigrates to Alabama and brings his bonded people). Any three states could propose an amendment to the Confederate Constitution which would be approved if agreed to by two thirds of the states. The President and Vice President would serve for six years and could not seek re-election.

For Provisional President, Delegates elected resigned U.S. Senator Jefferson Davis of Mississippi and for Provisional Vice President, Alexander Stephens of Georgia. Davis had graduated from the U.S. Military Academy at West Point, had fought in the Mexican War and had been U.S. Secretary of War from 1853 to 1857. Both were sworn in on February 18. A portion of Davis's inaugural address is given below:

"We have entered upon the career of independence, and it must be inflexibly pursued. . . . As a necessity, not a choice, we have resorted to the remedy of separation; and henceforth our energies must he directed to the conduct of our own affairs, and the perpetuity of the Confederacy which we have formed. If a just perception of mutual interest shall permit us peaceably to pursue our separate political career, my most earnest desire will have been fulfilled. But, if this be denied to us, and the integrity of our territory and jurisdiction be assailed, it will but remain for us, with firm resolve, to appeal to arms and invoke the blessings of Providence on a just cause.

"Reverently let us invoke the God of our fathers to guide and protect us in our efforts to perpetuate the principles which, by his blessing, they were able to vindicate, establish and transmit to their posterity, and with a continuance of His favor, ever gratefully acknowledged, we may hopefully look forward to success, to peace, and to prosperity."

Organizing the Confederate Government.

The next day Davis dispatched Major Caleb Huse to Europe to purchase ships and arms, appointed General Josiah Gorgas Chief of Ordinance, and directed Raphael Semmes to go north to purchase ships and arms and to hire mechanics. Six days later he dispatched a three-man commission to Washington to seek peaceful relations with Abraham Lincoln.

Davis soon had a functioning Cabinet – Sect. of State, Robert Toombs of GA; Sect. of the Treasury, Christopher Memminger of SC; Sect. of War, LeRoy Pope Walker of AL; Attorney General, Judah Benjamin, of LA; Sect. of the Navy, Stephen Mallory of FL, and Postmaster General, John Reagan of TX.

Suggestions for Class Discussion

You have learned much about the secession of 7 states and the political organization of the Confederate government. But 8 Democrat Southern states declined to secede. Imagine that you are Republican President Lincoln, just entering the White House. How would you deal with the Davis government?

Recommended Reading

- Google this and read: "Declaration of the Immediate Causes Which Induce and Justify the Secession of South Carolina . . ."

Chapter 19* – The Response to Secession by President Lincoln and the Republican Governors of the Northern States: Their Fort Sumter "First Shot" Strategy to Launch the Subjugation of Democrat Border States and Proceed with the Invasion.

By Howard Ray White of N. C., S. I. S. H.

Introduction

In seeking to understand a military conflict, nothing is more important than figuring out how it got started. We present evidence in this chapter that provides that understanding. Howard Ray White takes the history forward to the Fort Sumter incident and President Lincoln's demand for state militia to enforce Federal subjugation and conquest.

The History

During November, December and January, President-elect Abraham Lincoln declined to publicly reveal his intentions for dealing with state secession, remaining in Springfield, Illinois, at his home and law office, limiting his communications to Republican governors and political leaders. Meanwhile, wife Mary, of the politically influential Todd family of Lexington, Kentucky, traveled to New York to shop for new clothes. But 7 states had seceded by the time the Lincolns hosted a good-bye reception at their home, with 700 attending. Yet no public word. Mary burned records and letters in the back alley, to wipe the slate clean one would suppose, and Abe said "good-bye" to law partner Billy Herndon. Remember, the Lincoln-Herndon law office was the biggest outfit in which Abe had ever worked. Next job: Commander in Chief over the War Between the States.

Plans were complete to parade Lincoln in a slow-moving special train routed through Republican states – a 12-day trip covering 1,904 miles over tracks of 18 railroad companies, ending in Washington. This author calls the trip the "Republican Railroad Rally," for the intent was to "rally" the people of the Republican states to support Lincoln's tough stand against seceded states.

The railroad rally left Springfield on February 11, routed to Indianapolis; to Cincinnati; to Columbus; to Pittsburgh; to Cleveland; to Buffalo; to Albany, to New York; to Philadelphia; to Harrisburg, to (wait and see). Republican flagmen stood along the track every half-mile, inferring that danger was lurking about. At every significant town it stopped so Lincoln could be seen and speak to the crowd from the last car. Also, he got off and addressed state legislatures in Indiana, Ohio, New York, New Jersey and Pennsylvania. Never speaking of the Confederate States or President Davis, Lincoln deceptively referred to misguided citizens who had mistakenly supported a conspiracy by rebellious politicians that intended violent injury to the northern States. Despite Lincoln's vagueness, it was apparent that he firmly opposed permitting the seceded States to live in peace. There was never a hint of a willingness to negotiate, to even speak to a Confederate emissary, to recognize his existence.

February 18 was an exciting day in Montgomery, Alabama, for Jefferson Davis was sworn in as provisional President of the Confederate States of America, complete with a celebratory brass band playing a new tune, "*I Wish I Was in Dixie's Land.*" President Davis advised the crowd:

> "Our present political position has been achieved in a manner unprecedented in the history of nations. It illustrates the American idea that governments rest on the consent of the governed, and that it is the right of all those to whom we would sell, and from whom we would buy, that there should be the fewest practicable restrictions upon the interchange of these commodities. . . . As a necessity, not a choice, we have resorted to the remedy of separation, and henceforth our energies must be directed to the conduct of our own affairs, and the perpetuity of the Confederacy, which we have formed. . . ." But if the Republican governors and the Lincoln Administration should make war, "The suffering of millions will bear testimony to the folly and wickedness of our aggressors."

> "Reverently let us invoke the God of our fathers to guide and protect us in our efforts to perpetuate the principles which by His blessing they were able to vindicate, establish, and transmit to their posterity. With the continuation of His favor ever gratefully acknowledged, we may hopefully look forward to success, to peace, and to prosperity."

President Davis went to work the following day – dispatching Major Caleb Huse to Europe to purchase available inventory of ships and arms and contract for future production – instructing Raphael Semmes, just resigned from the U. S. Navy, to travel north to buy guns, hire mechanics, and purchase available, serviceable ships – appointing to the office of Chief of Ordinance, General Josias Gorgas, a Pennsylvanian married to the Alabama Governor's daughter – directing Col. George Rains to set up a Georgia gunpowder factory – yet President Davis only sought peace. The next day he wrote wife Varina: "I was inaugurated on Monday, having reached here on Saturday night. The audience was large and brilliant. Upon my weary heart was showered smiles, plaudits, and flowers; but beyond them I saw troubles and thorns innumerable."

Two days later the Republican Railroad Rally secretly concluded in Harrisburg, Pennsylvania. Next destination: Washington. Since Marylanders would not be cheering this new Republican president, Allan Pinkerton, of the famous Chicago detective agency, threw a large overcoat across Lincoln's shoulders, concealing his long arms, topped his head with a low felt hat and spirited him aboard a special night train. In disguise Abe arrived in Washington in the morning. Mary and the others followed according to the published schedule.

On February 25, Jeff Davis appointed three men to travel to Washington City and attempt to negotiate friendly relations with the Lincoln Administration: Martin Crawford of Georgia; A. B. Roman of Louisiana, and John Forsyth of Alabama. Seeking friendly relations, the Confederate House and Senate also approved a law establishing "free navigation of the Mississippi River without any duty or hindrance except light-money, pilotage, and other like customary charges."

At noon, on March 4, President James Buchanan, Democrat, and Republican Abraham Lincoln rode side-by-side down Pennsylvania Avenue to the Capitol, while sharpshooters looked on from rooftops, soldiers secured intersections and artillery stood at the ready, giving the impression of a military exercise, not a government ceremony. Chief Justice Roger Taney, 84 and frail, administered the oath of office. Then Lincoln stepped forward to deliver his inaugural address. In part he said, "I have no purpose, directly or indirectly, to interfere with slavery in the States where it exists. I believe I have no lawful right to do so, and I have no inclination to do so." But he warned, "The power confided in me will be used to hold, occupy, and possess the property and places belonging to the [Federal] Government, and to collect the [Federal taxes]; but beyond what may be necessary for these objects, there will be no invasion – no using of force against or among the people anywhere. . . . In your hands, my dis-satisfied countrymen and not in mine, is the momentous issue of civil war. The [Federal] Government will not assail you. You can have no conflict, without being yourselves the aggressors." That is what he said, but he meant, "I shall maneuver events to incite you to fire the coveted 'first shot'." We now tell the story of President Lincoln's "First Shot Strategy."

Lincoln's Cabinet was soon in place: William Seward of New York, State; Simon Cameron of Pennsylvania, War; Gideon Welles of Connecticut, Navy; Salmon Chase of Ohio, Treasury; Caleb Smith of Indiana, Interior; Edward Bates of Missouri, Attorney General; and Montgomery Blair of Maryland, Postmaster General, the latter two being new-found Republicans from Democrat states. On his eleventh day in office Lincoln consulted his Cabinet about sending the Navy into Charleston harbor, where a small garrison of U. S. troops was occupying Fort Sumter. That was where Lincoln wanted to elicit the coveted "first shot." His Postmaster General had an idea: his wife's brother-in-law, a former Navy man, already had a proposal to do just that. But the rest of the Cabinet opposed the Navy plan and Army Chief Winfield Scott favored giving up the fort. On the other hand, recognition of the existence of the Confederate Government or chatting with Confederate commissioners was strongly opposed.

Republican leaders had no passion for freeing slaves, but they were passionate about ensuring high taxes on imports, scheduled to soon triple on average. The March 18 issue of the Boston *Transcript* advised, "It is apparent that the people of the principal seceding states are now for commercial independence." The Confederacy would be a free-trade area, tempting many Northern smugglers to evade high U.S. tariffs.

Lacking support from his Cabinet or Army Chief, President Lincoln dispatched three spies to Charleston to snoop around, for he had scant personal knowledge of the Southern states. To Charleston he sent the previously mentioned brother-in-law, Gustavus Fox, plus Stephen Hurlbut and Ward Lamon. All three reported back, giving Lincoln greater confidence that navy ships would draw the coveted "first shot." He called another Cabinet meeting on March 29, seeking approval of his navy mission to Charleston. Three approved, but the Army Chief and four opposed. Lincoln proceeded anyway, authorizing Gustavus Fox to direct the outfitting at New York of a fleet of warships and transports to steam south, some to enter Charleston harbor, the remainder to proceed on and re-inforce Fort Pickens at Pensacola, Florida. The Fort Sumter fleet consisted of the warships, *Powhatan, Pawnee, Pocahontas* and *Harriet Lane*; steam-tugs *Uncle Ben, Yankee and Freeborn*, and merchant ship *Baltic*. A mission of this size was no secret; Confederate leaders soon knew the fleet was coming to Fort Sumter and Fort Pickens.

Confederate Commissioners Roman, Crawford and Forsyth, never gaining an audience, wrote Lincoln a final letter: "Your refusal to entertain these overtures for a peaceful solution, the active naval and military preparations . . . can only be received by the world as a declaration of war . . ."

Now, about the small garrison of Federal troops occupying Fort Sumter? Why didn't they agree to come ashore as demanded by Confederates? Because they remained loyal to former President Buchanan's orders to stay put, which Lincoln endorsed. Time was running out. Confederates preferred firing on the fort to firing on incoming navy ships. That they did. As the navy ships gathered offshore cannon bombardment of Fort Sumter began. Federals returned fire. It was quite an artillery show, but no one on either side was hurt. Federal ships remained offshore, their commanders seeing the coveted "first shot" achieved. The garrison then agreed to come ashore and leave for Washington by railroad. Lincoln did not draw blood, but he incited fire. Oh, I almost forgot – the garrison got permission to fire cannon in salute to their flag prior to coming ashore. Fifty firings were planned. But on the 49th the barrel exploded killing a soldier. The body went to Washington for display. In a way Lincoln did draw blood.

The very next day President Lincoln, acting as Commander-in-chief, issued an Executive Order directing his 15,000 Federal troops and 75,000 state militiamen to subjugate the Democrat states and conquer the states he alleged to be controlled by "combinations too powerful to be suppressed by the ordinary course of judicial proceedings" – an allegation drawn from President George Washington's "1795 Act for Calling forth the Militia," which he had felt necessary to stop backwoodsmen from selling untaxed whiskey. If Lincoln had recognized secession, he could have sought to conquer a foreign nation. Instead, he was violating his Constitution. But he had the guns and the Supreme Court had none.

Federals were prepared when Virginia quickly seceded, burning the large armory at Harper's Ferry and the ships and shipyard at Norfolk. Democrat governors lambasted Lincoln and refused to send militia. The Know-Nothing governor of Maryland refused as well. First blood was drawn on the streets of Baltimore as Massschusetts militiamen crossed town while changing trains. Dead were 9 Baltimore protestors and 4 militiamen. Lincoln's response: a Federal blockade of the 3,600-mile Confederate coast. He blockaded his own people, lawyers would argue. All this by April 19, 1861.

Summary

President Lincoln refused to recognize secession or negotiate peaceful accommodation, instead personally leading his Republican Party to war.

Class Discussion

Historians admire Lincoln's cleverness in rallying Republican militia to go to war, but can we admire his refusal to negotiate? Hint: 400,000 dead Federal troops!

Recommended Reading

- *Understanding Abe Lincoln's First Shot Strategy (Inciting Confederates to Fire First at Fort Sumter)*, by Howard Ray White, pub. 2014.
- *Lincoln*, by David Herbert Donald, pub. 1995.

Chapter 20* – In Response to Lincoln's War Proclamation, Virginia, North Carolina, Tennessee and Arkansas Secede, and the Civilized Native American Nations Choose Sides.

By Howard Ray White of N. C., S. I. S. H.

You should not be surprised that the people and governments of Virginia, North Carolina, Tennessee and Arkansas refused to support a military invasion of sister states to their south. Below, read about President Lincoln's request for state militia, and, in response, the refusals and secessions of Virginia, North Carolina, Tennessee and Arkansas, which expanded the Confederacy to 11 states and doubled the white population. Earlier, all four states had experienced votes against secession.

President Lincoln only had access to about 16,000 U.S. troops to stop further secession and to force seceded states back under the Federal Government. But there was a 1799 law that allowed him to ask governors for state militia on short notice, but it limited the total requested to 75,000. So, on April 15, 1861, President Lincoln asked the governor of each US state to send militia to reinforce the US Army – submitting the following justification to each governor and to the population:

> "Whereas the laws of the United States have been, for some time past, and now are opposed, and the execution thereof obstructed, in the States of South Carolina, Georgia, Alabama, Florida, Mississippi, Louisiana, and Texas, by combinations too powerful to be suppressed by the ordinary course of judicial proceedings, or by the powers vested in the marshals by law. Now, therefore, I, Abraham Lincoln, President of the United States, in virtue of the power in me vested by the Constitution and the laws, have thought fit to call forth, and hereby do call forth, the militia of the several States of the Union, to the aggregate number of 75,000, in order to suppress said combinations, and to cause the laws to be duly executed. . . . And I hereby command the persons composing the combinations aforesaid to disperse, and retire peaceably to their respective abodes within 20 days from this date. . . ."

At the same time Secretary of War Simon Cameron sent each governor the following telegraphed request for militia:

> "Sir: Under the act of Congress for calling out the militia to execute the laws of the Union to suppress insurrection, repel invasion, &c., approved February 28th, 1795, I have the honor to request your Excellency to cause to be immediately detached from the militia of your state, the **quota** designated in the table below to serve as infantry or riflemen for three months, or sooner, if discharged."

The quota for states with Republican governors totaled 72 regiments (56,160 troops) – 17 regiments from NY, 16 from PA, 13 from OH; 6 each from IL and IN; 4 from NJ, 2 from MA, 1 each from: ME, NH, VT, RI, CT, MI, WI, IA, and MN, and less than one from DC. The quota for states with Democrat governors totaled 21 regiments (16,380 troops) – 4 each from MD, KY, and MO; 3 from VA, 2 each from NC and TN; 1 each from DE and AR. There was to be 37 officers and 743 men in each regiment. The defiant response from the following Democrat governors helps the student understand why state secession quickly followed.

Virginia Governor John Letcher refused to send Lincoln any militia. On the same day, April 17, the Virginia Convention adopted an Ordinance of Secession by a final vote of 103 versus 46. On May 23, Virginians would ratify secession by 78% versus 22%. Most of the no votes were from Virginia's western counties (now in West Virginia), which were economically tied to the Ohio River Valley. Immediately, the commander of the Federal arsenal at Harper's Ferry directed the destruction by fire of all the buildings, armaments and arms manufacturing and repair machinery. Likewise, the commander of the Federal shipyard at Norfolk directed the torching of all buildings, destroying valuable steam engines and other machinery, and the burning of the large warship *Pennsylvania* and the sinking of six, including the *Merrimac*.

North Carolina Governor John Ellis told Lincoln, "I can be no party to this wicked violation of the laws of the United States, and to this war upon the liberties of a free people. You can get no troops from North Carolina." Anticipating Federal destruction of NC armaments, Ellis shrewdly ordered the State Militia to immediately seize the arsenal at Fayetteville and the 3 Federal forts located within the State. On May 20 the North Carolina Convention would vote, 120 versus 0, to secede.

Tennessee Governor Isham Harris refused to send militia, telegraphing Lincoln he would not send even one man for the purpose of invading the Confederacy, "but 50,000, if necessary, for the defense of our rights, and those of our Southern brothers." The Tennessee State Legislature would approve an Ordinance of Session on May 6, which Tennesseans would vote, 69% versus 31%, to ratify on June 8.

Arkansas Governor Henry Rector refused to send the Federal Government any militia. Rector informed Lincoln, "The people of this Commonwealth are freemen, not slaves, and will defend to the last extremity, their honor, lives and property against Northern mendacity and usurpation." Rector ordered the state militia to immediately seize the Federal military stores at Napoleon, Arkansas. On May 6 the Arkansas Convention would vote, 69 versus 1, to secede.

Virginia, North Carolina, Tennessee and Arkansas joined the Confederate States of America and the Confederate capital would soon be moved from Montgomery, Alabama to Richmond, Virginia. The addition of these 4 states greatly increased the Confederate economic and military capacity.

For the most part, Cherokees, Creeks, Seminoles, Choctaws and Chickasaws supported the Confederacy. To learn why, Google "Cherokee Declaration of Causes, October 28, 1861." Cherokee brigadier general Stand Watie would be the last to surrender. But Confederate faithfulness would severely punish these Native Americans: never to have a state of their own.

In the next chapter you will learn how the Democrat states of Delaware, Maryland, Kentucky and Missouri responded to the request for militia to reinforce the Republican military campaign to conquer seceded states.

Suggestions for Class Discussion

S.I.S.H. member Gene Kizer, Jr. asks, "Since 52.4% of white Southerners, a majority, lived in Virginia, Arkansas, Tennessee and North Carolina, and since those states clearly seceded over the issue of Federal coercion (use of military force), isn't it fair to say that Federal coercion is the major cause of the war?"

Chapter 21* – Federal Military Occupation of the Border States, 1861 – 1865

By Clyde N. Wilson of S. C., Ph.D., S.I.S.H.

Introduction

As the crisis caused by Republican control of the Federal Government deepened, everyone realized that the Border States of MD, KY, and MO were critical from their geographic location and population and resources. The border area was mostly of the Southern Culture. Most people were reluctant to secede from a beloved old Union but had no sympathy with the Republican regime. Lincoln had received 2.5 per cent of the vote in MD and 0.09 per cent in his native KY. He received somewhat more in MO – there were many Northern-leaning Democrats and, in St. Louis, a large Republican group of New England businessmen and militaristic recent German immigrants. To secede and join the Confederacy required public debate and discussion, elections, and constitutional proceedings. To control these States for "the Union" Lincoln needed only quick and decisive military action. Lincoln realized the vital importance of the Border States to Union victory and, significantly, would exempt them from the Emancipation Proclamation.

Maryland, Delaware, and the District of Columbia

When Lincoln demanded troops to suppress the "rebellion," the governor of MD, the only non-Democratic governor in the South, temporized, although the legislature rejected the demand. On April 19, 1861, Massachusetts troops marching through Baltimore fired on a protesting crowd, killing a number of citizens and increasing Southern sentiment. Mayor George Brown said: "Our people viewed the passage of armed troops to another State as an invasion of our soil, and could not be restrained." James Ryder Randall, a Marylander who had moved to LA, wrote a song that is one of the best produced by the war: "Maryland, My Maryland! Avenge the patriotic gore that flecked the streets of Baltimore . . . ."

Lincoln moved swiftly. The army seized the mayor, city council, and police chief of Baltimore, a congressman, and many members of the MD legislature, which had a strong secessionist minority and a large anti-Lincoln majority. A prominent Baltimore railroad man and military veteran, Isaac R. Trimble, on orders of the mayor, blew up the bridges that facilitated Union entry into the city before departing for the Confederate army. (He would lose a leg and be captured fighting for the South at Gettysburg.) These arrests created a strange irony. The grandson of Francis Scott Key, writer of "The Star-Spangled Banner," was imprisoned in the same fort where his grandfather had been inspired to write the National Anthem. From Lincoln's prison the grandson wrote of his grandfather: "The flag which he then so proudly hailed, I saw waving at the same place over the victims of as vulgar and brutal a despotism as modern times have witnessed."

MD was thereafter officially declared to be for "the Union" although it remained under army occupation for the rest of the war and the Lincoln administration treated its people with great suspicion as Confederate sympathizers and controlled the voting polls. A similar situation prevailed in the little State of DE where there was much Southern sentiment, although the Dupont industrial empire in the North provided strong Union support. (Breckinridge carried DE in the 1860 election.) The District of Columbia was also treated as a potentially "disloyal" part of the Border because its permanent, pre-Republican residents were mostly Southern. Republicans saw "traitors" under every bed in this area and one editor demanded that Baltimore be obliterated, man, woman, and child.

During the war, the Senators from MD and DE, elected before Union army control of the polls, were a determined and eloquent though tiny minority opposition in the Republican Congress. The "Unionism" of Maryland has perhaps been over-stated. As soon as the military occupation was lifted, both MD and DE elected Southern Democrats to office and opposed Republican Reconstruction. Maryland's state song and state flag have Confederate origins.

Kentucky

KY was, after VA, perhaps the most prestigious State in the Union, noted for its patriotism and efforts to keep the peace between Northern and Southern Cultures. It was the birthplace of both Abraham Lincoln and Jefferson Davis. Lincoln was determined to keep control of KY. He once said, "I think to lose Kentucky is nearly the same as to lose the whole game. Kentucky gone, we cannot hold Missouri, nor Maryland. These all against us, and the job on our hands is too large for us. We would as well consent to separation at once, including the surrender of this capital." (Who did Lincoln mean by "us"?)

The governor of KY vehemently refused Lincoln's demand for troops to suppress the South and he and many Kentuckians hoped to avoid war and promote peace by a policy of armed neutrality, which was proclaimed on May 20, 1861. However, the entrance of Confederate and then Union forces motivated by military concerns ended that hope. Many prominent Kentuckians, including several congressmen and former governors, recent Vice-President John C. Breckinridge, and Simon B. Buckner, commander of the State army, to avoid arrest by the Union army, left to become Confederates. Probably a majority of Kentuckians opposed breaking up the Union, but they also opposed Republican policies and continually protested the heavy-handed Union occupation of the State and violation of the rights of citizens. It truly felt to them like a civil war – families were divided and some followed the old Irish tradition of having members on both sides so their property would be safe whoever might win.

Lincoln appointed the ruthless Stephen Burbridge to be a general and commander at Louisville. Interestingly, Burbridge was one of the largest slave-owners in the State but hated his fellow citizens who had repeatedly voted against his attempts to achieve public office. He did not hesitate at summary executions of suspected Confederates. The Louisville Military Prison was known as "the Killing Pen." Kentuckians were "loyal" to the Union but felt like an occupied people. Whenever Confederate cavalry raided into KY they were received enthusiastically and departed with recruits and supplies. There were two State governments, neither of which was entirely perfect constitutionally. It has often been remarked that KY joined the Confederacy after the war.

Missouri

The governor of Missouri, like those of KY and the upper South States, vehemently refused Lincoln's call for troops to suppress "the rebellion." Governor Claiborne F. Jackson called Lincoln's demand "illegal, unconstitutional, and revolutionary . . . inhuman and diabolical." On April 26, a Union officer, Nathaniel Lyon, organized a military force of 6,000 volunteers in St. Louis, 80 per cent of them recent, mostly German, immigrants. In response, Governor Jackson called out the State militia. Citizens of St. Louis protested the Union military force, resulting in an altercation which left 28 dead, including women and children. At this point MO still had a vain hope of maintaining neutrality. The legislature created a Missouri State Guard under the command of Sterling Price, a former governor and perhaps the most respected man in the State. On May 12 Price and U.S. General William S. Harney agreed to a truce. However, on June 12 Lyon marched on the state government at Jefferson City, forcing it to flee.

Price's Missouri Guard joined with Confederate forces under General Ben McCulloch and defeated U.S. forces at Wilson's Creek. On October 31, 1861, in the town of Neosho, Jackson and the exiled state legislators enacted a secession ordinance, and the next month MO was admitted to the Confederate States of America. Following indecisive battles at Pea Ridge and Prairie Grove in northwest Arkansas, the Confederate state government of Missouri was exiled. The State was now considered "Unionist," with a government supported by the army and part of the people.

If it felt like a civil war to Kentuckians, that went double for Missouri, where violence continued even after the war. Unable to suppress bold and skillful Confederate partisan fighters, the Republicans resorted to ethnic cleansing. In the infamous Order 11, U.S. General Thomas Ewing, a step-brother of William T. Sherman, ordered four western MO counties where he thought the civilians supported the partisans, to be cleared of population. The resulting hardships are depicted in a famous painting by Missourian George Caleb Bingham, one of the foremost American artists of the time. Women relatives of some of the partisans were jailed in a rickety building in Kansas City which collapsed, killing a number of the prisoners.

The guerilla war in MO is conventionally pictured as carried on by brutal Confederates against hapless civilians. The truth is more nearly the opposite. "Jayhawkers" from KS before and during the war plundered, burned out, and killed Southern-leaning civilians in MO, as pictured in the films "The Outlaw Josey Wales," and "Ride with the Devil." The postwar banditry of former guerillas like Frank and Jesse James has attracted much attention, resulting in mostly inaccurate if not absurd portrayals. The guerilla leader "Bloody Bill" Anderson, not surprisingly, raised the black flag after his sister was killed in the Kansas City incident. The most famous of the guerilla leaders, William C. Quantrill, is an interesting case. He was from OH and came to KS as an antislavery man. He was so disgusted with the stealing and plundering of his associates that he joined the other side and became a Confederate guerilla when war broke out. The Confederate government did not approve of his activities, notably the sacking of the Republican town of Lawrence KS. Historians generally fail to notice that this raid was in retaliation for Union atrocities against Southerners. During the raid not a single woman was harmed.

Ex-Confederates who tried to return to peaceful pursuits were harassed by "Unionists" and forced to turn outlaw, like the James and Younger brothers who became sensational for robbing Yankee banks and trains. Frank and Jesse James were the sons of a prosperous Baptist minister. In 1874 agents of Allen Pinkerton, the immigrant head of Lincoln's secret police, who after the war turned to strike breaking, attacked the James family home, although knowing the "outlaws" were not there. After killing the James' half-brother and torturing their step-father, the Pinkerton's blew up the house, destroying their mother's arm. It is little wonder that Missourians honoured and protected their "outlaws."

The Strange Case of West Virginia

The voters of VA approved secession on April 17, 1861, by a vote of 132,201 to 37,451. Ninety per cent of the no vote came from the northwestern area of isolated mountain people and towns economically tied to the Ohio River Valley. In June about 100 self-appointed delegates from the area, claiming to represent the people, met at Wheeling. They announced that a rump government appointed by Lincoln in Alexandria was the government of VA. The Constitution requires that no State can be divided without its consent. The rump, which represented nobody, granted the Wheeling group its consent to form a State. The next year the U.S. Congress admitted the new slave of West Virginia, consisting of 50 counties, to the Union. While this area contained more "Unionists" than other parts of the South, it seems that not all the people approved of this. It is estimated that West Virginia supplied about an equal number of soldiers (around 20,000) to the Union and Confederate armies.

Summary

The Border States are said to have furnished 120,000 Union soldiers and 86,000 Confederate soldiers. Many of the Union soldiers resembled those in Northern regiments – immigrants and unemployed labourers, conscripted or enlisted for large cash bounties. The Confederates were volunteers who risked much to join the War for Southern Independence. Historians have rather too easily assumed that the Border States were "Unionist" and rather too easily overlooked the role played by military force. The devices used by Lincoln to quash dissent in the Northern States – suppression of newspapers, control of the mails and telegraph, and warrantless detention of civilians by the army – were carried out in the Border States and other occupied areas and then some. There was hostage taking and executions of civilians. Clergymen who refused to pray for Lincoln and persons named in anonymous complaints disappeared into distant military prisons. These prisoners included women and African Americans. It is perhaps significant that the people of the Border States (including WV) welcomed their Confederates home and had no hesitation in electing them to public office when U.S. troops departed.

Recommended Readings

- *Civil War and Readjustment in Kentucky* by E. Merton Coulter, pub. 1926.
- *Maryland: The South's First Casualty* by Bart R Talbert, pub. 1995.
- *Turbulent Partnership, Missouri and the Union, 1861-1865*, by William E. Parrish, pub. 1963.

Chapter 22* – Fourteen Battles in Four Years of War

By Howard Ray White of N. C., S. I. S. H

Introduction

Let me first explain what the WBTS meant to me as a 10-year-old boy in 1948 when my family lived at my grandfather's farm near Murfreesboro, TN. My brother and I slept in an upstairs room. The Battle of Murfreesboro (Stone's River) had been fought on this farm and others nearby as 1862 ended and 1863 began. It was one of the war's major battles. In that upstairs room, 85 years before, a Federal surgeon had amputated arms and legs on scores of wounded soldiers, tossing body parts out the window into a wagon below, the blood soaking into the wooden floor. We slept amid those bloodstains. A huge graveyard just down the road displayed 6,000 Federal tombstones as far as the eye could see. Now the political nightmare called the WBTS became personal. This boy had to understand the politics that had caused it. Soon, as a voter, you will need to make political choices. So understand America's greatest tragedy to help you choose more wisely.

Examples of Relevant History

These four pages present brief histories of 14 major battles: Manassas, VA (July 1861); Western Virginia (Oct. 1861); Forts Donelson and Henry, TN (February 1862); Pittsburg Landing and Island #10, TN (April 1862); New Orleans, LA (April 1862); Seven Days' before Richmond, VA (June 1862); Sharpsburg, MD (Sept. 1862); Chancellorsville, VA (May 1863); Gettysburg, PA (July 1863); Vicksburg, MS (July 1863); Chattanooga, TN (Oct. 1863); Cold Harbor, VA (June 1864); Atlanta, GA (Aug. 1864), and Petersburg, VA (1865).

July 1861: Manassas Junction, northern Virginia.

By mid-July the Federal invasion force amassed just south of Washington, D. C. was the largest army ever gathered at one spot in American history, consisting of 40,000 well-armed men and the best field artillery the world had ever seen. Commanded by Irvin McDowell of Ohio, it intended to fight all the way to Richmond and crush the Confederate Government. Important Republican political leaders were gathering not far behind their army to enjoy a picnic and to witness the invasion's historic launch. At Manassas Junction, an important Virginia railroad hub, Confederates under Pierre Beauregard of Louisiana, prepared to meet the attack. On the 17th Beauregard telegraphed Richmond, "The enemy has assailed my outposts in heavy force," prompting President Davis to order Confederate troops then west of the Blue Ridge Mountains, to cross over and reinforce Manassas. Intense fighting erupted on the 21st; a Confederate defeat seemed likely. But, Thomas Jackson's tough troops had crossed over the Blue Ridge and arrived by noon. Joe Johnston's troops arrived by train from Winchester at mid-afternoon. Now re-enforced, with Jackson's men firing in support, many other Confederates charged forward like furies and drove the Federals from the field in disorganized panic. Abandoning cannon, firearms and most everything, the Federals scampered back to Washington in disarray, struggling with Republican picnickers to get across congested bridges. After a few miles of pursuit, Confederates pressed no farther. President Davis arrived by railroad at the climax of the victory. He and his generals agreed their orders were to defend Virginia, not invade Washington. And many wounded needed attention.

This was where Thomas Jackson gained the name "Stonewall." His troop's protective fire was an important part of the victory.

October 1861: Western Virginia.

The Virginia counties located in the Appalachian Mountains proved impossible to defend with available resources. Steep ridges greatly impeded travel from the east; access to and from the Ohio River was much easier – from the north a simple ride down valley roads. And many of the people were more tied economically to the north and west than to the east. The Kanawha Valley was an industrial region (annual capacity of 1,500,000 bushels of salt; almost 2,000,000 gallons of coal oil; valuable niter deposits for making gunpowder, and more). By early September, Federals controlled it, unopposed. By October Confederates under Robert E. Lee had retreated to make a defensive stand at Sewell Mountain. Rosecrans' Federals chose not to attack since bad weather would prevent Confederates from wintering over in the mountains. Lee ordered a retreat out of western Virginia as Federals organized a rigged voting process to allegedly justify the secession of 39 western Virginia counties.

February 1862: Forts Donelson and Henry, Tennessee.

The Federal defeat of Forts Donelson and Henry in February can be credited to James Eads of St. Louis, who had received a contract for 7 iron-clad river gunboats. In one of the war's greatest feats, Eads, an engineer and river wrecks salvager, completed his designs, hired crews and supplied the powerful craft in time to lead the capture of Fort Henry on the Tennessee River and Fort Donelson on the Cumberland River. The gunboats were named *Carondelet, Louisville, Pittsburg, St. Louis, Cairo, Mound City* and *Cincinnati*. The fall of the Confederate forts was a disaster, resulting in the capture and imprisonment at Chicago of 4,459 Confederates. Indefensible, Nashville surrendered without a fight. Tennessee lay exposed.

April 1862: Pittsburg Landing and Island #10, Tennessee.

Corinth, MS was the junction of the Mobile and Ohio and the Memphis and Charleston railroads and its defense was vital. But not far away was the Tennessee River, which steamboats could access from the Ohio River. By late March, Confederates under Albert Sidney Johnston were concentrated into an army of 40,000 troops. But, by this time Federals under Ulysses Grant had landed 40,000 troops at the Tennessee River port town of Pittsburg Landing and would soon be reinforced by 20,000 more. On the morning of April 6 Johnston decided to attack before those reinforcements arrived. The surprise attack drove many Federals back toward the river bank in panic, and many prisoners and weapons were captured, but the eventual arrival of reinforcements forced a Confederate retreat the next day. Federals suffered 13,047 casualties, Confederates suffered 10,694. It was the bloodiest battle ever fought on either American continent. Johnston, the Confederate army's most valuable leader, was killed leading a charge. That same day Federals captured over 6,000 Confederates who had been defending the Mississippi River at Island Number 10. James Eads' gunboats, with larger, longer range artillery, had been decisive by blocking retreat, and would give the Federals a great advantage on the western rivers.

April 1862: New Orleans, Louisiana.

The Federal navy also held a major advantage over Confederates. In 1814 Andrew Jackson's army of Southern volunteers, mostly from Tennessee and Kentucky, had driven off a large British invasion force, saving New Orleans. But this time efforts to defend against attack failed. On April 24 the Federal invasion fleet gathered into formation and ran past the two Confederate forts, most surviving to reach the city. Confederate forces under Mansfield Lovell burned the warehoused cotton and withdrew with their arms. Benjamin Butler of Massachusetts accepted the surrender of Mayor John Monroe.

June 1862: Seven Days' before Richmond, Virginia. By June 23, a 105,000, well-equipped Federal army under George McClellan was in position to lay siege on Richmond. Robert E. Lee, realizing a siege could not be withstood, gathered his top commanders and planned a fierce attack to drive the Federals away. They knew a lot about the enemy since Jeb Stuart had led 1,200 Confederate cavalry in a "ride around" McClellan's approaching Federals, viewing enemy strengths and capturing significant troops and war materiel. The attack was to include Stonewall Jackson's Confederates, who had been in the Valley, keeping Federals there occupied and defeated. The bold attack was planned for 3 am, June 26. Would Jackson's men arrive in time to reinforce troops under A. P. Hill, D. H. Hill and James Longstreet? Heroic and tough as they had persistently been, Jackson's troops did not arrive until 11 am, long after the attack had begun. Nevertheless, Confederates forced the Federals at Mechanicsville to retreat to Gaines' Mill. On the 27th, Confederates drove them back further. On the 28th, Federals began withdrawing from around Richmond toward Savage's Station. On the 29th, Confederates drove them back to Frayser's Farm. On the 30th, they drove them back to Malvern Hill. But there Federals were protected by artillery on the hill and on warships in the James River. It looked like surviving Federals would make a total escape. Should Confederates charge again considering the artillery they now faced? Hard decision! Although the victory was won and Richmond was saved, forcing a Federal surrender would help Peace Democrats defeat Republicans in Congressional elections only 4 months away, perhaps advancing peace talks. General Lee made the decision: attack up Malvern Hill. His troops charged forth. The death toll was awful. But the Lincoln Administration learned that Confederates were determined and fearless. Richmond would be successfully defended for 34 more months. Confederates captured 52 artillery pieces and 35,000 muskets, but suffered 20,141 casualties versus 15,849 for the Federals.

September 1862: Sharpsburg, Maryland. Confederates under Robert E. Lee defeated Federals under John Pope in the second battle of Manassas Junction, again forcing Federals to abandon supplies and retreat to Washington, the 75,000-man army suffering 16,054 casualties. As follow-up, with mid-term elections less than two months off, Lee advocated a counter-offensive into Federal territory in hopes of bruising Northern morale and encouraging votes for Peace Democrat candidates. Davis agreed. The invasion began with troops singing "*My Maryland.*" Bad luck: a copy of Lee's battle plan was lost and found by a Federal. Lee's effort climaxed near Sharpsburg along Antietam Creek. At most 40,000 Confederates faced 87,000 Federals under McClellan. Federals suffered 12,469 casualties, Confederates, 13,724, the latter retreating in order to Virginia. Bad idea: Democrats elected the NY Governor and gained a few Congressional seats, but too few to matter.

May 1863: Fredericksburg and Chancellorsville, Virginia. You recall that it was at Pittsburg Landing that Confederates

lost Albert Sidney Johnston. Well, it was at Chancellorsville that they lost Stonewall Jackson. Federals under Joe Hooker, a force of 133,868 men, advanced southward toward Richmond. First stop Fredericksburg. Hooker spit his army, leaving 64,000 behind and leading 70,000 westward to the vicinity of Mr. Chancellor's house, where he set up headquarters. Making an audacious decision, Robert E. Lee dispatched Stonewall Jackson with 26,000 of his 60,000-man army to attack Hooker's 70,000. Jackson's men caught Hookers' men by surprise and overwhelmed the far larger army, which retreated back toward Fredericksburg. There was more fighting at Fredericksburg before Federals withdrew toward Washington. Again, a huge Federal offensive toward Richmond had failed. Overall, Federal casualties were 17,287; Confederate were 12,764. But Stonewall Jackson would soon to die of a bullet wound. The loss would be greatly felt.

July 1863: Gettysburg, Pennsylvania. In Richmond on May 16, President Davis and his Cabinet debated seriously two military proposals. Davis, of Mississippi, and John Reagan, of Texas, advocated sending 25,000 troops from Robert E. Lee's army to help break the siege of Vicksburg. The rest of the Cabinet supported Lee's proposal to retain his entire army and use it to counterattack into Pennsylvania, hoping that would strengthen Peace Democrats in the northern states. Lee was desperate. A war of attrition would surely give eventual victory to Lincoln, who had an inexhaustible supply of draftees. A bold stroke might force negotiations. All but Reagan sided with Lee. Davis felt he could not object. Lee was going on the counterattack a second time. On June 25, with Confederate cavalry already in Gettysburg and York, PA, Lee led his troops into Maryland. From its post in northern Virginia the huge Federal army headed north to defend PA and Washington. On July 1 Federals under Oliver Howard attempted to take the town but were driven out, taking the high ground upon Cemetery Ridge. The main Federal army, under George Meade, arrived during the night and the Confederate advantage was lost. There was a massive battle just outside Gettysburg on and around Cemetery Ridge. Federals occupied the high ground. There was bloody fighting on July 2 and if there was a winner it was the Confederate side. But both armies held their ground. Determined to strike a decisive blow, Lee ordered a frontal attack against the Federals for July 3. After a massive artillery attack, Confederates under George Pickett, James Pettigrew and Isaac Trimble ran the one-mile gauntlet up the hillside. It was deadly. That night Lee's Confederates began their retreat into Virginia, taking wounded as they could. Meade's Federals were slow to pursue. Lee's men returned to Virginia to fight another 22 months. Rethinking that Cabinet debate in Richmond – Lee's counterattack into Pennsylvania versus Davis's proposal to send 25,000 of Lee's men to help Vicksburg – you probably agree that neither should have been attempted. Of 85,000 Federals engaged, casualties totaled 23,049; of 65,000 Confederates it was 20,451. Peace Democrats got no boost.

July 1863: Vicksburg and Port Hudson, Mississippi. It had been a long siege of these two last remaining impediments to total Federal control of the Mississippi River. At Vicksburg artillery defended a narrow spot in the big river and John Pemberton commanded 31,000 troops in fortifications surrounding it. Civilians and others dug caves into the banks to elude exploding artillery. Beyond were far more Federals under Ulysses Grant. The Siege of Vicksburg had begun on May 23, following an ill-advised frontal attack by 45,000 Federals, which had resulted in 3,199 casualties. Further down the river, the Siege of fortified Port Hudson had begun two days earlier with up to 13,000 Federals under Nathaniel Banks surrounding 4,500 Confederates under Franklin Gardner. Banks ordered frontal attacks on May 27 and on June 14, together resulting in 3,787 Federal casualties. But by five weeks, troops at Port Hudson and citizens and troops in Vicksburg were suffering starvation. At Vicksburg, Pemberton negotiated surrender terms with Grant which were unusually generous. On July 4, his 29,000 soldiers were allowed to lay down their arms and walk out of Vicksburg with nothing more than a personal promise to not rejoin the fight until exchanged. Officers were allowed to leave with their horse and side-arm with a promise of exchange for Federal officers imprisoned elsewhere. Four days later Gardner surrendered Port Hudson; 405 officers were sent to Federal Prisons and troops and support crews, numbering 5,935 men, were allowed to go home if they promised to not rejoin the fight until exchanged.

October and November 1863: Chattanooga TN and Chickamauga GA. Following the surrender of Nashville, Confederates under Braxton Bragg had held Murfreesboro until January 1, and held Tullahoma until June. By July 7 they were in Chattanooga building defensive works. They had been retreating down the railroad that ran from Nashville to Chattanooga to Atlanta to Savannah, striving to prevent a Federal takeover. But, on September 9 Federals under William Rosecrans forced Bragg's Confederates to give up Chattanooga and retreat down the railroad into Georgia, where they set up their defense at Chickamauga Creek Valley. The same day 11,000 Confederates under James Longstreet left their defensive lines north of Richmond and crowded into rail cars for a 900 mile, rickety journey to reinforce Bragg. Many of them were on hand when, on September 19, Rosecrans's Federals attacked the Confederates with great force. This was the horrific Battle of Chickamauga, which resulted in a Federal withdrawal back into Chattanooga. But Confederates had suffered great losses in their determined defense of the railroad line. The 58,000 Federals engaged suffered 16,170 casualties; the 66,000 Confederates suffered 18,454. Among the Confederate dead was Brig. General Ben Helm of Kentucky, Mary Lincoln's sister's husband. Confederates advanced to Chattanooga and set up a siege around the city containing Rosecrans's army, now reduced to 50,000 men. Federals then sent 23,000 soldiers, 3,000 horses and mules, and ample artillery, weaponry and supplies from northern Virginia to Chattanooga over 1,233 miles of railroad. It took only 12 days. Federals also replaced Rosecrans with George Thomas, who was to report to Ulysses Grant. Grant managed to get into Chattanooga on October 23 and laid plans for getting his reinforcements into attack position. Federals were reinforced and the Battle of Chattanooga ensued on November 23. The 56,000 Federals engaged suffered 5,824 casualties, the 46,000 Confederates suffered 6,667. Confederates retreated southward toward Atlanta. Bragg resigned, soon to be replaced by Joe Johnson..

June 1864: Cold Harbor, Virginia. Of 14 battles presented here, none reeked more of politics than Cold Harbor. Desperate to retain political control, Republicans rebranded themselves as the Union Party, selected Democrat stronghold Baltimore for their nominating convention and aimed to choose for VP former Democrat Andrew Johnson of Tennessee. But Republicans sought another re-election boost four days before the Convention was to open: a major victory at Cold Harbor, only 9 miles from Richmond. Lee's Confederates, 25,000 strong, were ready and protected behind earthworks. Ulysses Grant, with a force of 50,000, ordered the charge. It was a slaughter. Federals were mowed down. Don't take a body count. Don't tell newspapermen. For four days Grant allowed Federal wounded to suffer, unattended on the battlefield, crying out for "water," many dying of non-fatal wounds. The convention opened on June 6. On June 7, Grant told Lee he wanted to gather his dead and wounded. That day Republicans nominated the Lincoln-Johnson ticket. Federal dead and wounded at Cold Harbor was about 13,000. Since Grant had begun his advance toward Richmond on May 5, his troops had suffered 54,929 killed, wounded and missing, a number almost equaling Robert E. Lee's total army. Grant was called "The Butcher." Richmond remained free.

August 1864: Atlanta, Georgia. Although Richmond remained unconquered, the conquest of Atlanta was to give Republicans a significant re-election boost. By late August it was obvious to John Hood that his Confederates were unable to counter the encirclement of Atlanta by William Sherman's large army. He must give up Atlanta and save his army. On September 1 Hood's army evacuated to the south. Sherman's Federals moved into the city and ordered all African Americans to remain and all whites to evacuate with little more than the clothes on their backs. He would be preparing a "March to the Sea" after the November elections.

April 1865: Petersburg, Virginia. We now come to the climatic end: the conquest of Petersburg and nearby Richmond. The effort to conquer Petersburg had begun 11 months earlier, on May 5, 1864, when 30,000 Federals under Benjamin Butler landed at City Point on the south bank of the James River, aiming to get to Richmond by way of Petersburg. Reinforced two weeks later by Grant's Cold Harbor troops, Federals repeatedly attacked, suffering 8,150 killed and wounded. On June 18 Grant decided to lay siege and attempt to cut railroad connections. It would be a long campaign. Federal miners dug a 586-foot tunnel under the Confederate earthworks and detonated a huge explosion. Federals rushed into the resulting crater, bogged down and suffered under intense Confederate fire, resulting in 4,000 killed and wounded, many being African American troops. The siege continued into 1865. On March 25 a surprise attack from the Fort Stedman section of the defensive works failed. Finally, on April 1, at the Battle of Five Forks, Federals cut railroad access and Confederates retreated west, giving up Petersburg and Richmond. Three days later Lincoln toured Richmond.

Summary

War is Hell!

Suggestions for Class Discussion

Why were Confederates so difficult to conquer?

Recommended Reading

- *The Civil War, Day by Day*, by E. B. and Barbara Long, pub. 1971.

Chapter 23 – Abraham Lincoln: Fact and Fiction

By Vance Caswell of N. C., S.I.S.H.

Introduction

In 1939 American moviegoers enjoyed *Young Mr. Lincoln.* A handsome, youthful Henry Fonda portrayed Abraham Lincoln's early life. The next year Raymond Massey was Lincoln in a similar story, *Abe Lincoln in Illinois.* These films, along with a highly fictionalized "biography" by Carl Sandburg, encapsulate what most Americans believe about their most revered symbol and hero. A young man of humble circumstances, he strived hard for an education. He was so honest that he would walk miles to pay a small debt. He was admired by his associates for his sterling qualities. He was not above hard outdoor work – in fact, was known for his prowess as a rail-splitter. His heart was broken when his love Ann Rutledge died in youth. He took a raft trip down the Mississippi, viewing slavery first-hand, and vowed he would some day strike a blow at the evil institution. Finally, a groundswell of popular admiration swept him into the White House, and he departed Springfield for a divine mission – to save the Union and free the slaves, and to achieve martyrdom. (Nobody seemed to notice that the Union would not have been in any danger if Lincoln had not been elected and that more than 60% of American voters rejected him.)

Henry Fonda's Lincoln is embraced by Americans as a sacred national myth – perhaps because it represents what Americans like to believe about themselves – a people down-to-earth, open, and practical, but capable of righteous wrath and action against injustice. Generations of Southerners have accepted the Lincoln mythology because it helped to reconcile them to the Union and because it was useful to believe in a generous Lincoln who would have presided over a mild Reconstruction if he had not been killed. Yet almost everything "known" about "Honest Abe" is highly questionable. As historians we ought to make an effort to evaluate Lincoln like any other important person in history and separate fact from myth and propaganda.

Obstacles to Knowledge

Important parts of Lincoln's life – his birth and parentage and his assassination – are involved in so many doubts and contradictions that the truth will never be certain. Howard Ray White in *Bloodstains,* vol. 1, discusses thoroughly the tangled question of Lincoln's origins. A number of writers have argued that the conventional story of the assassination leaves out important facts. Strangely, Lincoln's son Robert destroyed a large amount of his father's papers. You would think that every scrap relating to such a figure would have been preserved with reverence. If you had a small piece of paper with an authentic "A. Lincoln" signature today, you could sell it for enough for a year's vacation on the French Riviera. Professor Thomas DiLorenzo, in his book *Lincoln Unmasked,* shows that an incredible number of statements have been attributed to Lincoln that he never uttered. It seems that anyone who had an idea or a product to sell made up a Lincoln quotation endorsing it. For generations Republican orators and pious writers embellished the story of a saintly, benevolent President. A letter quoted a thousand times, in which Lincoln supposedly said that he would accept as voters African American men who were educated or who had been

soldiers, has been shown to be inauthentic. It is contradicted by reliable testimony that he still was hopeful for colonization of blacks outside the U.S. days before he died.

Herndon and Lamon

The writings of two men who knew Lincoln up close for long periods are perhaps one of our best sources on the real Lincoln. Their writings have been suppressed and denigrated ever since they appeared. William Henry Herndon was closely associated with Lincoln for 31 years. They were roommates for four years and worked in the same law office for 18 years. Herndon did much of Lincoln's legal work, was his researcher and personal contact with abolitionists and eastern Republicans. Lamon was a junior law partner who went with Lincoln to Washington, lived in the White House, saw the President almost every day during the war, and carried out confidential missions. Both men were younger than Lincoln, admired him, and supported his cause. Both were rather more antislavery than Lincoln himself. But the Lincoln they admired was not the saint created after his death. It was a tough, relentlessly ambitious and clever politician who had done whatever was necessary to save the Union. They were realists who had contempt for pious mythmaking that distorted what they considered Lincoln's true greatness.

Early Life and Family

Lincoln did not attend his father's funeral, perhaps because he believed that Thomas Lincoln was not his real father. It is interesting that all of Lincoln's relatives except one voted against him. That was also true of his immediate neighbours. Votes for him were always a bit lower in nearby areas where he was known than in areas a little further away. As a young man Lincoln courted popularity as a story-teller around the cracker barrel in every country store and tavern he visited in his law circuit. He was notorious for his obscene anecdotes, a fact well-known at the time that has since disappeared down a memory hole. It was said that when Lincoln came to town, you put the women, children, and preachers to bed. He also had jokes ridiculing "Yankees" (New Englanders) to amuse his neighbours, most of whom came from the South.

There is absolutely no substantial evidence for the Ann Rutledge story. We do know that he rather churlishly dumped a lady, Mary Owen, with whom he apparently had an understanding, and that he left Mary Todd at the altar the first time their wedding was scheduled. His early associations in IL were with prominent slaveholding families from KY, who treated him kindly and nurtured his career. He shared in his slaveholding father-in-law's estate and took at least one legal case regarding the recovery of a runaway slave.

Family life in the Springfield Lincoln mansion was not happy. Herndon recorded instances in which Abe was driven from home by his wife's rages. In Washington he would take her to the window and show her the insane asylum in the distance where he was going to send her, and indeed she ended her life in an asylum. In Washington she was morbidly jealous and greatly over-spent the White House accounts, which might, uncharitably, be called embezzlement. By contrast, Varina Howell Davis, the wife of Jefferson Davis, is one of the true heroines of American history. An intelligent woman who wrote books and could hold her own in discussion with the greatest statesmen of the day, she endured privation, danger, and detention without loss of faith in her husband and the Confederate cause. When she died in New York City in the early 1900s she was given a royal funeral as a national treasure.

Mary Todd Lincoln, of course, had much to be sorrowful about. Even before the assassination of her husband she had lost her little son "Tad." This poignant story is somewhat modified by another uncharitable fact. Many visitors to the White House thought of "Tad" as an obnoxious, undisciplined brat. The Davises also lost a young son during the war. Outsiders have erected in Richmond a pious statue of Abe and "Tad," but there is no memorial for young Joe Davis, dead at 5 from a fall. While every relative of Southern leaders was in the thick of the fighting, Lincoln's grown son Robert spent most of the war as a student at Harvard, his father having purchased for him a substitute. When the war was almost over he was given a safe commission on Grant's staff. Things were very different among the leaders of the Confederacy.

Lincoln, alas, was no Henry Fonda. One side of his face was disfigured and his arms were abnormally long. This caused many of his close allies to call him, behind his back, "the Gorilla." His close allies also complained bitterly that when approached with a serious matter he would, instead of giving an answer, tell an irrelevant humourous story. He had been kicked in the head by a horse or mule as a young man and had momentary blackouts that disconcerted some people. He suffered from severe depressive spells and is thought to have had a degenerative disease that eventually would have incapacitated him.

Lincoln as Christian

It seems reasonable to say that for many Americans Lincoln is a kind of saint – wise, merciful, and sorrowful for the terrible war that had befallen his country. After his death Republicans created such a image. It did not exist while he was alive. Generations of Sunday School children and magazine readers were inundated with Lincoln-centered sermons and pictures of the holy martyr being wafted to Heaven by flights of angels. As a young man he wrote an atheist treatise which friends destroyed as harmful to his reputation. Those who knew him best said he was a non-believer. He was adept at couching his speeches in language reflective of the King James Bible, for which his hearers had familiarity and reverence. Imagine the Gettysburg Address saying "87 years ago" instead of "four score and seven years ago" and "founded" rather than "brought forth." There is no evidence that he ever had any serious faith. A Confederate wit said that Lincoln was the only person who became a Christian *after* he died. He supported and rewarded the war crimes committed by his generals against Southern civilians. There is no evidence that he suffered any serious regret for the immense suffering of his war. He always treated the war as a political goal to be accomplished. In his strange 2nd Inaugural Address he suggested that God had deliberately brought about the war to punish sins. It was not his fault.

Lincoln the Statesman

No one elected President before Lincoln and very few after were as completely a single-minded politician as Lincoln. He never had any vision or agenda of doing good. As law partner Herndon said, Lincoln's primary drive and motivation was always ambition, an ambition which gave him no rest. He spent most of his career as a follower of Henry Clay, spokesman for the Whig program of tariff, national bank, and internal improvements. Clay was also a slaveholder and a severe critic of abolitionists, and his program at bottom was a selfish one of limited appeal. Lincoln had never been senator, governor, Secretary of State, or a successful military officer, unlike every previously elected President. In 1853-1854, when the Kansas/Nebraska question ignited Northern public opinion, Lincoln was a wealthy corporation lawyer, living in one of the biggest mansions in Springfield. His political career had consisted of one term in the U.S. House of Representatives almost a decade previously for which his Whig party had not even re-nominated him. His political ambitions seemed to have no future. He spent much time on the couch in his law office, reading the political news while Herndon carried on the business. The 1854 Kansas-Nebraska Act gave him his opportunity. Very cautiously at first and somewhat secretly he began making contacts with "free soil" leaders and groups that were rising into becoming the Republican Party. From then on, still relatively unknown, he was a tireless presidential candidate, quietly buying up newspapers and networking.

Several lucky advantages came Lincoln's way. He was invited east to speak at NY's Cooper Union. (His gofer Herndon had already been on quiet connection-making missions to Republicans and anti-slavery men in the East.) There and elsewhere Lincoln used his considerable rhetorical skills to position himself as an enemy of slavery but not associated with the unpopular abolitionists. His chief rivals for the Republican leadership, William H. Seward of NY and Salmon P. Chase of OH, were already on record with statements offensive to the South and many moderate Northerners. He got the Republican nomination for U.S. Senator from IL, to run against Stephen A. Douglas, the likely next Democratic presidential nominee. Douglas generously and unwisely agreed to a series of debates with Lincoln across the State. Lincoln changed around his speeches so as to be agreeable to Republicans in the northern part of IL and not give ammunition to Southern-origin Democrats in the southern part of the State. He lost the election but got big media exposure and managed to trap the forthright Douglas into a position on slavery in the territories that raised doubts among his Southern supporters. The notion that a great surge of popular admiration swept Lincoln into the White House is a joke. There was never a campaign that was more intensely plotted and unscrupulously carried on. A high mark was the 1860 Northern States nominating convention in Chicago, where Lincoln's men engaged in various dirty tricks and physical intimidation to enhance their candidate's appearance of popularity. Lincoln's step-brother, Dennis Hanks, appeared on stage with rails which he claimed the candidate had split as a young man – a bit of demagoguery that would have sickened the Founding Fathers. Cynical neighbours later reported that Lincoln was not fond of hard work and had split fewer rails than any man in the county.

Lincoln, the President

It seems compulsory for historians to say not only that Lincoln won the war but that he was a supreme genius in everything he did as President. But Lincoln's performance was far from outstanding. He had no government experience and had never managed anything bigger than a small law office. His entire being was political. After the election and after his inauguration he spent his time filling offices with greedy

Republican supporters and said nothing about the secession crisis that his election had caused. Given that he was a minority candidate, a statesman would have made every possible move to preserve peace. The Founding Fathers would have wept. The Republicans gloried in their seizure of power and were not about to make any concessions, although an overwhelming majority of Americans hoped for peace. Stephen Douglas said that Lincoln faced a choice – he could please his party or he could save the country. He chose the first alternative by his maneuvering at Fort Sumter. When he had the incident he wanted, he declared war on the Confederacy. The Upper South repudiated him and doubled the size of the Confederacy. Was this the greatest blunder in U.S. history?

As President, Lincoln did not often get involved in details other than maintaining his and his party's control. At times his hands-off attitude was excessive. His admiring secretaries Nicolay and Hay said he never wrote more than one letter a day. He allowed his subordinates to run separate empires. Vast corruption flourished in Union army contracting. Many Northerners treated the war as a money-making opportunity. The oft repeated assertion that Lincoln was a military genius is an absurdity. He time and again forced unwise decisions on his generals and appointed them for political reasons. Confederate President Davis made one great mistake in supporting General Braxton Bragg, but most of his appointments were good and made for military rather than political reasons. It took the North four very bloody years to defeat a country with one-fourth its manpower and wealth.

Lincoln's great achievement was as a politician. He held together a coalition that finally won. He kept together elements that agreed on very little – Radical Republicans, the Border States, vast numbers of Northerners who did not agree with Republican rule. Lincoln entered office with little respect. His associates in his cabinet and Republican leaders in Congress thought of him as incompetent and opportunistic, certainly lacking their zeal. He gathered respect in some quarters as the war went on, but most of the leaders that later canonized him despised him when he was alive. They especially feared the hints that he was giving toward the end of a more lenient Reconstruction approach than they wanted. There have always been observers who see more to his assassination than the official story. Who profited from Lincoln's death? The Radical Republicans who assumed real power when he was gone. Why was John Wilkes Booth, cornered and injured, killed instead of captured and questioned? Why were pages missing from Booth's diary? Why were the "conspirators" held nearly incommunicado by the army and swiftly executed without ever being allowed to tell their story in open court? We will probably never know. We do know that assassinations were not in the repertoire of Confederate leaders but that Radical Republicans like Edwin Stanton and Thaddeus Stevens were fully capable of such.

The Lincoln Legacy

Few historians would dispute that the period after the WBTS was one of immense government corruption. But somehow this seems to have mysteriously come about after Lincoln was off the scene. But corruption was implicit in Lincoln's program from the beginning. The expected favours to Big Business were exponentially increased by war expenditures.

There is no question that a great many fortunes, bigger than had existed before in the U.S., were made by the war and that many Northerners regarded the war primarily as a money-making opportunity. Visiting foreigners in the North noted that they hardly noticed that a war was going on except for those busily seeking government contracts. Northern soldiers complained often about shoddy shoes and bad food. There was a great deal of currency manipulation. Lincoln himself enraged his Secretary of War by personally giving favoured businessmen exemptions from the rule against trading with the enemy, which allowed them to get cotton on the Texas coast in exchange for materiel needed by the Confederacy.

Lincoln is remembered for "emancipation." His emancipation is rather tainted by expediency and white supremacy. But emancipation would have come sooner or later anyway – in a far less destructive way. Lincoln's more lasting legacy was the establishment of the virtual rule of Big Business which lasts till this day. By "capitalism" Republicans meant not "free enterprise" but private ownership and profit with government subsidy and support.

In the "Gettysburg Address" Lincoln justified, and even glorified, his war. Americans have made this a sacred document. But a close look raises all sorts of questions. The Confederacy was never a threat to "government of the people," as Lincoln claimed. It could be argued that his government was a greater threat. The essential "proposition" of the Declaration of Independence was not Equality but the Consent of the Governed. The Declaration did not establish a "nation," but was a manifesto of 13 colonies struggling to become "free and independent States." The Constitution did not establish a "nation" but a confederacy, a Union. Lincoln himself did not often use the term "nation" until the war was well underway. Edgar Lee Masters, a great poet from Lincoln's home region of central Illinois, wrote that the Address only works if one does not inquire into its truth and reads it apart from the facts. A "refusal of the truth" of Lincoln's brutal war is written all over it, Masters said. The popular gadfly writer H. L. Mencken wrote this about the Address in the 1920s:

> It is genuinely stupendous. But let us not forget that it is poetry, not logic; beauty, not sense. . . . The doctrine is simply this: that the Union soldiers who died at Gettysburg sacrificed their lives to the cause of self-determination – "that government of the people, by the people, for the people" should not perish from the earth. It is difficult to imagine anything more untrue. The Union soldiers in that battle actually fought against self-determination; it was the Confederates who fought for the right of their people to govern themselves.

Suggestions for Class Discussion

How does the Lincoln mythology affect American public affairs today?

Recommended Readings

- *The Real Lincoln, A New Look at Abraham Lincoln, His Agenda, and an Unnecessary War*, by Thomas J. DiLorenzo, pub. 2002.
- *Lincoln, the Man*, by Edgar Lee Masters, pub. 1931.
- *Mr. Lincoln Goes to War*, by William Marvel, 4 vols., pub. 2006-2011.

Chapter 24 – Comparing the Two Armies with Regard to Size, Leadership, Resourcefulness, Materiel, Commitment, etc.

By Steve Litteral of Illinois, S.I.S.H.

Introduction

Maryland, Kentucky and Missouri were more of a burden than an asset for the Republican governors and the Lincoln Administration. And the Pacific west was too far away to provide much military support. So we can ignore those regions when comparing the Confederate States to the Federal States. The Confederates had a lot more land. But the Federals had a lot more men of fighting age and bringing in more men from Europe was destined to swell their ranks. Confederates had superior leadership, although Republicans certainly had no problem pressing on in spite of huge casualties, eventually escalating the fight to include "total war" against civilians. Confederates were more resourceful, but Federals had a far, far greater industrial base, useful in supplying weaponry. Comparing ocean vessels and armed riverboats, Federals were clearly superior and that was most effective in taking the Tennessee and Mississippi rivers. Federals were the invaders; Confederates were the defenders, and that explained much of the difference in commitment. Confederates troops and cavalry were more effective, suffering 50,000 fewer military deaths. Steve Litteral tells the story.

History Relevant To Understanding the WBTS

When President Lincoln announced the military invasion of the Confederacy, the United States did not have a large professional military like today. Many states had militias, and the Federal military was relatively small compared to the size of the country. Traditionally, militia in the Southern states were much more organized, usually commanded by men who had some form of military education. Although the U.S. Military Academy (West Point) is located in New York, the Southern states had several military academies, like the Virginia Military Institute (VMI). But the Southern states were disadvantaged in other ways.

The Union had a white population of 20 million, where the Confederate states had a mere 6 million. Also, roughly 800,000 immigrants arrived in the North during the war, and many of them were inducted into the Federal army. In total, the Federal forces had over 2 million men in its military and the Confederacy had approximately 750,000.

The Northern states also had a large industrial base to make their weapons and equipment, whereas the Southern states were largely an agrarian society lacking capacity to produce large amounts of military armaments. Confederates had to become very creative in the manufacture of military equipment. Many Confederate troops brought their own weapons from home to offset a shortage of arms. The Confederacy also engaged in blockade running and purchasing equipment from countries like Great Britain, which did have a large industrial base. Throughout the war, the Confederates resupplied their soldiers with Federal equipment taken in numerous battlefield victories. In 1862 over 250 artillery pieces were captured and used by the Confederates. Eventually, the Southern states started to produce larger amounts of weapons, but they were never able to compete with the 110,000 manufacturing companies in the Northern states.

Although disadvantage in manpower and industrial capacity, Confederate forces benefitted from brilliant leaders like Robert E. Lee and Thomas "Stonewall" Jackson. Although Federals had several effective leaders, it was took men of heroic battlefield prowess to fight a war against the Federal Government for four long years.

Concerning government leadership we shall look at the two presidents. Jefferson Davis (1808-1889) was a graduate of the U.S. Military Academy and served as the President of the Confederate States of America. He had served on the frontier as an officer in the U.S. Army for many years and had later fought gallantly in the Mexican-American War. He also served as a member of the House of Representatives, Senate, and as Secretary of War. This military and political experience enabled Davis to keep the Confederacy together during four years of brutal warfare on Southern soil.

Abraham Lincoln (1809-1865) served as the President of the United States from 1861 to 1865. He had little formal education or military experience (he served in the Illinois militia for a short, insignificant, time during the Black Hawk War of 1832, but never participated in a battle). Of noteworthy intelligence and savvy, he eventually became a lawyer, and served in the U.S. House of Representatives one two-year term. In 1856 he rose as a leader of the new Illinois Republican Party and became well known during the well-publicized Lincoln-Douglas debates of 1858.

The Confederate Army had 425 General officers in total. Out of this number, 146 were West Point graduates, 17 were VMI graduates, 4 were South Carolina Military Academy graduates, and 19 had previous military experience. Besides having a number of officers with a great military education, many of these Southern leaders were also veterans of the Mexican-American War (1846-1848).

Being much larger, the Federal Army supported many more General officers. There were 583 regular General officers and 1,367 Generals by brevet, which served as a temporary rank. The Federal Army also had veterans of the Mexican-American War within their ranks, such as U.S. Grant. Politics were involved in the promotion of generals in both armies, but the Federal Army suffered from a large amount of officers who were called 'political generals.' They won promotion because of political friends in Washington, D.C., instead of demonstrated military expertise. A good example is Daniel Sickles, a former New York politician and army general, whose lack of military knowledge cost the lives of many of his men when he unnecessarily exposed them to withering fire at the Battle of Gettysburg in 1863.

When we look at the common soldiers, they came from many different backgrounds, and cultures. Television and Hollywood movies suggest that all Confederate soldiers were white, Southern-born Christian men. The truth is much more complicated. The Confederate Army was also home to many foreign-born men who decided to fight for the Southern states. There were also Native-Americans, African-American, Latinos, and Jewish soldiers fighting as Confederates. The same can be said of the Federal forces, although the Federal forces had many more foreign-born soldiers. Over 20% of the soldiers that fought for the Federal forces were not born in the United States. Many of them came from European countries like Ireland and Germany.

As far as organization goes, the two armies were basically the same since they came out of the same American military tradition. The main branches of the military were the infantry, cavalry, and artillery, with numerous other support units. The infantry was the main fighting force that fought on foot. They used tactics to maneuver across the battlefield and shock the enemy into either surrender or retreat through the use of superior fire power and face-to-face combat.

The cavalry was a force that fought on horseback and they could be used for various missions including reconnaissance, flanking maneuvers, and swift attacks against enemy units.

The artillery used large caliber weapons (i.e. cannons) to fire munitions on enemy soldiers that are far beyond the range of infantry small arms. The artillery would fire direct and indirect rounds into enemy formations to cause mass casualties. The Confederate Army needed as many men in the combat branches as possible, especially in the infantry which did the brunt of the fighting on the battlefield.

Since the Federal forces were better supplied, they had better logistical support. They had large supply units that would be able to move huge numbers of men from one place to another with their tents, food, ammunition, and other supplies. Many of the Confederate units did not have extensive supply units to follow them, so many of them carried everything they owned on their back. The Southern cavalry units proved to be very effective against the larger and slower Federal units. Some daring tactics by Confederate commanders are still studied by the military men today, such as those of J.E.B. Stuart and Nathan Bedford Forrest. There were great artillery units on both sides of the conflict, but the Confederate units should be commended since they would accomplish their mission with very limited supplies compared to the gunners on the Federal side who usually had an abundance of shells and powder.

Throughout the conflict, Federal forces dominated on the water. At the start of the conflict, the U.S. Navy was able to create a naval blockade that severely restricted maritime trade off the coast of the Southern states. The goal was to stop the trade of cotton to countries like Great Britain that needed Southern cotton for their textile manufacturing. The Federal Navy also purchased a fleet of ironclad gunboats that would steam up and down large interior rivers like the Mississippi and transport troops, supplies, and also fire on fortifications along the rivers. The war did spawn the creation of a new kind of ship called the ironclads. The most famous naval battles involving ironclads was the Battle of Hampton Roads where the *C.S.S. Virginia* and the *U.S.S. Monitor* clashed off the coast of Virginia. These were basically ships that were covered in armor and had large caliber guns installed to fire against other naval vessels. Although the Federal forces dominated the surface, the Confederate Navy was able to create the first submarine, the *H.L. Hunley*. Although it was lost at sea, it was able to sink the *U.S.S. Housatonic,* making it the first combat submarine to successfully sink a surface ship.

One of the things that cannot be measured with mathematics is the will to fight. Many of the things that have been discussed so far can be compared by using statistics and percentages.

The commitment to a cause is not so easy to compare. What we can do is simply look at a map and see that the Federal forces obviously invaded the Southern states. If you look at the major battles of the war, they stretch like a snake from the state of Virginia, down to Georgia, and across the Southern states to Texas. The men who joined the Confederate Army did so for many different reasons, but if you read the letters and diaries of the soldiers who fought, the common theme is the defense of their family and homes. By the latter years they were greatly worried about their families since Federal forces were marching over much of the South, burning down farms, taking livestock, and stealing food from the civilian population. Imagine your family and home today. If a neighboring state invaded your state tomorrow, would you simply surrender or fight to protect your family and land? The soldiers who fought for the Confederacy decided that they did not want an over-reaching Federal Government destroying their hearth and home for any reason—including under a false notion of 'saving the Union.' Once you force people into subservience at the point of a bayonet, the 'Union' is essentially dead since citizens are no longer there under their own free will. By 1865, the states that made up the United States were forced into an agreement where they were to be dominated by the Federal government, and therefore killing the experiment that the Founding Fathers fought so hard to create.

Again and again outnumbered Confederates defeated much larger forces. It was almost never the other way. In 1862 in the Shenandoah Valley Stonewall Jackson's small force, in a campaign that is still studied in every military academy, defeated 4 different Federal forces and then slipped away to join the Richmond defenses. Gen. Richard Taylor's small army repulsed a large federal army/navy invasion up the Red River in LA. Bedford Forrest's cavalry raids behind enemy lines tied down great numbers of bluecoats in defensive positions. Both Lee and Sherman said after the war that Forrest was the greatest soldier the war had produced. From a light industrial base, Confederates created miracles of production in weapons, gunpowder, steam driven ironclad ships. The armies suffered less from the unavailability of supplies than from the ongoing deterioration of the railroads, which were difficult to replace. Confederate sea raiders covered the world and interfered with Northern commerce to a degree that nearly d¬estroyed it – and without ever harming a single merchant sailor.

Summation

Although the Federal forces had a large and well-supplied Army and Navy, the Southern forces were very motivated, resourceful, and fortunate to have many successful military leaders throughout the conflict.

Suggestions for Class Discussion

Imagine the kind of stresses that the Southern citizens faced on the battlefield and on the home front. Would you endure the same kind of hardships to protect your family and property?

Recommended Reading

- *The Life of Johnny Reb: The Common Soldier of the Confederacy*, by Bell Irvin Wiley, pub. 1943.
- *Bloodstains, An Epic History of the Politics that Produced and Sustained the American Civil War*, vol. 3: *The Bleeding*, by Howard Ray White, pub. 2007.

Chapter 25* – The Federal War Against Southern Civilians.

By Karen Stokes of S. C., S. I. S. H.

Introduction

During the first year of the Federal invasion of the Confederacy – largely following the subjugation of the Democrat states of Maryland, Kentucky and Missouri – the Federal army and navy focused on defeating the Confederate armies in the field and tearing up railroad tracks and destroying weaponry, ships and riverboats. But the Confederate defense persisted and deaths among Federal troops mounted to alarming numbers. President Lincoln therefore escalated the conflict through his Emancipation Proclamation, a "war measure" he expected would disrupt Confederate supportive relationships. Even then defenses persisted. His final escalation was the massive destruction of civilian property, a total war policy. South Carolina author Karen Stokes tells the story of these devastators – men attempting to return wayward Southerners to their rightful seat in the democratic central government at Washington, D. C.

History Relevant To Understanding the WBTS

When Americans think of the "Civil War," they usually picture deadly struggles fought on battlefields between opposing armies – soldier against soldier – but in the conflict that raged in America from 1861 to 1865, another kind of warfare frequently occurred which has not been given enough attention in "mainstream" histories, perhaps because it reflects so badly on those who carried it out. This other kind of warfare has been called *total war*, because it involves civilians.

When wrongs committed against civilians by the Federal armies are presented, some are quick to protest that there were "atrocities" committed by both sides. However, from what we know, excesses perpetrated by the Federals were much more pervasive and *systematic* than those committed by the Confederate Army. Thomas Bland Keys, who cataloged many of the Union Army's outrages in his book *The Uncivil War*, noted: "Excesses by Confederates were limited in number and ferocity as contrasted with irregularities by Federals. The majority of such Southern excesses occurred in Missouri, where fire was being fought with fire."

Historian Walter Brian Cisco wrote that "warring against noncombatants came to be the stated and deliberate practice of the United States" during the war, adding, "Shelling and burning of cities, systematic destruction of entire districts, wholesale plundering of personal property, even murder became routine." Cisco also pointed out that "there was from the beginning a widespread conviction [among Federal authorities] that the crushing of secession justified the severest of measures."

It would be understandable that a country might be forced to wage a fierce, even ruthless war against an aggressive, malevolent foe, resorting to any means necessary to prevail and thus save itself. However, the United States had no such foe in the Confederacy. The United States was in no danger, under no threat, from the Confederate States, whose citizens had only wished to peacefully and lawfully secede and govern themselves as they saw fit. The invading North had no justification of self-defense, and therefore no just cause to go to war. And what made all of this unjust and ruthless warfare by the United States even more terrible and, almost incomprehensibly, it was carried out, not against some foreign invader bent on conquest and slaughter, but against *fellow Americans* – fellow countrymen whose forefathers had fought in the Revolution for the cause of self-government. Many Northern Radicals demonized the South, calling for harsh measures against the Confederacy with bloodthirsty and sometimes even genocidal rhetoric. In his book *When in the Course of Human Events,* Charles Adams argued that the Radicals' hatred "found expression in the devastation of civilians and civilian property by Sherman, Grant and Sheridan." The following examples of the "hard war" waged against the South by these and other Union generals are only a sampling.

In May 1861, the Federal Government instituted a military occupation and dictatorship in Missouri, where many of the state's people were sympathetic to the Confederacy. In what came to be known as the St. Louis massacre, 28 protesting civilians, including women and children, were shot in the streets by troops and militia under Federal command, more than half recent German immigrants. Later, in 1863, there was a Federal decree that forced 20,000 Missouri civilians into exile, causing them immense suffering and hardship.

On December 11, 1862, after U.S. forces drove back the defending Confederate troops from Fredericksburg, Virginia, the town was thoroughly pillaged and vandalized. Even churches were defaced and looted, and valuables were stolen from the Masonic lodge in which George Washington had once been a member. Confederate soldiers contributed money for the relief of the destitute civilians of Fredericksburg, "pitiable refugees" whose homes and been plundered by the Federal soldiers who occupied the town.

From May through early July 1863, Vicksburg, Mississippi, a strategically important city on the Mississippi River, was besieged by Federal forces under the command of General Ulysses S. Grant, and by a flotilla of gunboats in the river commanded by Admiral David Porter. The city was surrounded by outlying Confederate lines of defense, but the Union forces also shelled the city itself, which was full of civilians, who dug caves into the clay hills of Vicksburg for protection from the artillery bombardment. The siege lasted 47 days, until the city and its Confederate defenders were at last starved into submission. In his book *Vicksburg 1863,* Winston Groom noted the following: "From the river, Porter's mortar boats kept up a regular bombardment of the city's environs, while from landward Grant's artillery relentlessly threw barrages of shells into the town. The shocking part of it was that much of the naval firing was *deliberately aimed at the civilians.*" (emphasis added) Mary Longborough, a resident of Vicksburg, kept a diary (published as *My Cave Life in Vicksburg*) which recounts the deaths of some civilians resulting from the shelling.

Since 1861, the city of Charleston, South Carolina had been blockaded and besieged by the Federal navy and army, and in the third year of the war, the siege intensified when General Quincy A. Gillmore took command. He demanded the immediate evacuation of Confederate troops from Morris Island and Fort Sumter in Charleston harbor, and when the Confederate commander General P.G.T. Beauregard refused,

Gillmore opened fire on the city of Charleston in the middle of the night on August 22, 1863. The bombardment of Charleston continued in varying degrees of intensity until the end of the war. Confederate General Samuel Jones angrily protested to one of the Union generals that the indiscriminate shelling of houses, stores, churches and other buildings was not accomplishing any military purpose, but was simply being carried out to destroy the city. Though most of the civilians had evacuated Charleston, some remained, and a number were killed or wounded by the shelling.

In Virginia, Federal infantry and cavalry under the command of General Philip Sheridan devastated the Shenandoah Valley beginning in September 1864, burning crops and other properties under orders of General Grant that the area "cease to be a granary and a sanctuary for the enemy." A Confederate cavalryman from Virginia described the expedition thus: "Sheridan . . . was disgracing the humanity of any age and visiting the Valley with a baptism of fire, in which was swept away the bread of the old men and women and children of that weeping land. On every side, from mountain to mountain, the flames from all the barns, mills, grain and hay stacks, and in very many instances from dwellings, too, were blazing skyward, leaving a smoky trail of desolation."

General William T. Sherman also employed a "total war" policy when his army ravaged the state of Georgia in 1864. His strategy was to cruelly break the morale of the Confederate Army and Southern civilians, and to destroy military supplies and the railroad lines transporting them. Contemporary official military correspondence and reports document the fact that Sherman shelled Atlanta without notice, deliberately aiming his guns over the Confederate lines of defense and firing into the residential and business areas of the city, killing civilians there. Mrs. Robert Campbell, who fled her home in Bolton, Georgia to take refuge in Atlanta, recalled that during the shelling, "A shell killed a newborn baby and its mother in a house adjoining mine. I hastened into a bomb-proof, as fast as possible. As I entered the door to this shelter a six-pounder fell almost at my feet. Suppose it had burst, where would I have been?" Sherman's 62,000 troops, many of them recent German immigrants, devastated a region averaging 50 miles wide by 250 miles long. During its so-called "March to the Sea," his army left a path of misery "as great as it was unnecessary" as one historian described it – pillaging and impoverishing civilians (black and white), destroying their food supplies, crops, homes, and railways. Historian John B. Walters wrote: "[H]ardened, undisciplined men were loosed on a country inhabited largely by women, children and old men." Sherman estimated the damage done by his army "at $100,000,000; at least $20,000,000 of which has inured to our advantage, and the remainder is simple waste and destruction."

Sherman took possession of Savannah, Georgia, in December 1864. He then turned his eyes toward his next objective, South Carolina. In his report concerning the fall of Savannah, General Sherman informed General Grant that he intended to "smash South Carolina—all to pieces." Sherman himself regarded secessionists as traitors, and wrote that the state "deserves all that seems in store for her." In a letter to Major R. M. Sawyer dated January 31, 1864, the general declared his belief that the war was the result of a "false political doctrine," namely, "that any and every people have a right to self-government." In the same letter (published in *The Rebellion Record* in 1865), Sherman contended that the Federal government could rightfully take the property, and even the life, of *anyone* who did not submit to its authority, and he complained that it was the "political nonsense of slave rights, State rights, freedom of conscience, freedom of press, and other such trash" which had, as he untruthfully put it, "deluded the Southern people into war."

In January 1865, many of Sherman's forces gathered at Beaufort, South Carolina, and during that month a few of his brigades moved a little farther inland. By the first of February, the main advance was underway. Divided into two wings, the army began to cut a wide path of destruction across South Carolina from the coast to the North Carolina border, burning farms, plantations, and towns, demolishing railroad lines, destroying or confiscating crops and livestock, and plundering and abusing civilians, reducing them to hopelessness and destitution. The soldiers sent out as foragers, usually in advance of the main army, were some of the worst offenders in terms of pillaging and other wrongdoing. These men were called "bummers." In his book *Merchant of Terror,* author John B. Walters described them as "brigands and desperadoes," who operated virtually free of any military discipline or restraint.

His army burned the capital city of Columbia, and many of Sherman's soldiers admitted that they had. The Columbia correspondent for the *New York Herald* newspaper reported in an article of June 21, 1865, "There can be but little doubt that the destruction of Columbia was the work of our army."

Arson and plundering were not the only outrages committed against the civilian population in South Carolina. Murders, rapes and other serious offenses also occurred. African Americans, especially female ones, were often the victims of mistreatment by the Federal soldiers, black women being viewed by them as "the legitimate prey of lust" (as one of their own generals described it). In addition to houses, churches, crops, railroads, farms and plantations, the irreplaceable public records of many South Carolina counties were destroyed. Courthouses were burned, and many private libraries were also stolen or destroyed, as well as a large number of important collections of great artistic, scientific, and literary value.

Summation

In the operations of the Union Army, the practices of wanton destruction, pillage and abuse of civilians were widespread and often systematic from beginning to end, increasing in ferocity each year, and carried out with a ruthlessness that was all the more monstrous because it was directed at fellow Americans.

Suggestions for Class Discussion

Why is it that many popular histories of the war (in print and film) omit, minimize, or try to justify or excuse the Republican North's "hard war" against the non-Republican South?

Recommended Reading

- *War Crimes Against Southern Civilians,* by Walter Brian Cisco, pub. 2007.
- *Merchant of Terror: General Sherman and Total War,* by John B. Walters, pub. 1973.
- *South Carolina Civilians in Sherman's Path,* by Karen Stokes, pub. 2012.

Chapter 26 – Pondering Why Slaves Refrained from Attacking Owners' Families

By Patrick J. Kealey of California, S. I. S. H.

Introduction

By late 1862, it had become obvious to President Lincoln and the Republican governors that the conquest of the Confederate States was far from accomplished and another year or two would be required to complete the mission, with the death toll probably doubling. Proclaim immediately emancipated those slaves living in regions controlled by the Republican-led Federals? Out of the question! Proclaim immediately emancipated those slaves living in regions controlled by the Confederates? Yes. Republican dreams of deportation, considered by many the ultimate solution to anti-slavery concerns, had been seriously discussed and actually experimented with during 1861 and 1862, but was finally abandoned by the end of 1863. Furthermore, the mounting death toll among Federals required a more noble goal than the conquest of State Secessionists. So President Lincoln, in search of justification, decided on the "Emancipation Proclamation" – a "war measure" that held out hopes for inciting a rebellion among the slaves living on farms all across the Confederacy. Republicans reasoned that, if slaves were killing whites, nothing would stop Confederate troops from deserting the ranks and rushing home to defend their families. And Republicans further reasoned that, if the race war became wide-spread and really horrific, that would resurrect the stalled deportation solution, for attacks on whites by slaves would justify that final solution. But the Emancipation Proclamation did not produce a race war as anticipated. Why no race war? This chapter by Patrick J. Kealey provides evidence and ponders why, for the most part, slaves remained faithful to the families with whom they were living.

The History

The Emancipation Proclamation which officially went into effect January 1863 was described by Lincoln as a "war measure." The Proclamation rather than granting freedom to all the slaves was very selective as to where freedom was supposedly granted. William Seward, Lincoln's Secretary of State, cynically said of it, "We show our sympathy with slavery by emancipating slaves where we cannot reach them and holding them in bondage where we can set them free."

1862 had been a difficult year for the Northern Armies trying to defeat the Army of Northern Virginia and capture Richmond. Jackson's Valley Campaign, the Seven Days Battles and Second Manassas had been costly losses. Lincoln feared Britain and France would recognize and support the Confederacy if reverses on the battlefield continued despite their official positions against slavery. Not only would the Emancipation Proclamation present the Northern invasion as a noble cause, but it had the potential to provide the North with a military advantage that would remove Confederate soldiers from the battlefield. A servile insurrection would force thousands of soldiers to flee Southern armies to defend the women, children and elderly that had been left defenseless back home on the farms and plantations.

In fact in January of 1862, Thaddeus Stevens of Pennsylvania made an impassioned speech in the House of Representatives calling for just such a race war that was anticipated by Lincoln when he later issued the Emancipation Proclamation. Stevens reasoned it was better for the slaves to fight against their masters than for the North to send forth its "sons and brothers . . . to reach the same end." Republicans hoped the African Americans left back home would imitate the servile insurrection that had been led by Nat Turner in 1831. Then, slaves led by Nat Turner, armed mostly with farm implements such as axes, scythes, hammers, hoes and knives, had embarked on a killing spree in which 58 whites were murdered, the majority being children. Turner's plan to induce other slaves to overthrow slavery met with failure after a few days, and he was ultimately captured and executed. In 1863 families left back home would be easy targets even if slaves were only armed with farm tools.

But the insurrections hoped for by Lincoln and other Republicans never materialized, primarily because they had little understanding of the South's society and culture to which African Americans had contributed. At the time of the Northern invasion more than one half of the free African Americans in the country made the South their home. While they may not have enjoyed the same social or political status of whites, many owned property and were engaged in diverse enterprises throughout the region. Marie Thereze Coincoin, a former slave who purchased her own freedom, and later that of her children; owned slaves and a large plantation at Brevelle Isle, Louisiana. It was renowned for the quality of the tobacco produced which was actually imported by Cuba to make fine cigars. Her Franco-Creole family was prominent for generations in the area, and even outfitted Confederate militia during the war.

While there were large plantations, most southern farms were small to medium in size. The number of slaves might number from two or three to eight or nine depending on the acreage and crops involved. This meant both whites and African Americans often worked next to each other in the fields and shared the work and responsibility to make the farm profitable and self-sustaining, including raising most of its own food. Slaves not only planted and harvested crops but performed a variety of other tasks: buying and selling provisions, animal husbandry, herding livestock, raising chickens and geese, repairing equipment and constructing outbuildings, to name just a few. What is now called "multi-tasking" was a daily occurrence on southern farms. In the evenings women would work with fabrics, spin wool, weave cloth and sew. Adeline Willis, a former slave in Georgia, in the *Slave Narratives* collected by the government in the 1930s, related how her mother was skilled at dyeing fabric and could produce a "lilac" color from maple and pine bark for dresses the women and children would wear. Fogel and Engerman in their book, *Time on the Cross: The Economics of American Negro Slavery,* note that these farms were thirty-five percent more productive than Northern farms of the same size and equivalent resources. Southern farms were not the stereotype characterized in *Uncle Tom's Cabin* by Harriet Beecher Stowe, who had never visited the South. Despite all the literature about evil overseers, most plantation overseers were trusted black men.

While agriculture was the economic engine of the South, it also fostered an environment of close relationships and community that often transcended the boundaries imposed by slavery. It was common on both farms and large plantations for the older slaves to be addressed with family titles such as "uncle" or "aunt" by their peers as well as the families they served. This form of respect came from African culture and became part of the fabric of Southern life. Often these elderly slaves had a great deal of influence on the farms and plantations. Edmund Kirke, in his book *Among the Pines,* describes an incident whereby the master of a large turpentine plantation considers taking revenge against an overseer who committed a crime. His (the master's) former nurse, Aunty Lucy makes it known that the master's enemies would use the revenge as a pretext to harm him due to his political views, and she would feel badly if that were to happen. The master acknowledges her feelings, reflects how he was raised by her, and decides on another course of action. The Northern visitor who chronicled the event was astounded by the outcome and by the relationships developed on a large plantation with 270 slaves. The Northern visitor is even more astounded to discover that this large and complex operation was actually being run by a charming female slave.

Large plantations required skilled workers such as masons, carpenters, coopers and blacksmiths. Skilled workers would be in ever greater demand as the fledgling industries of the Confederacy produced pig iron, munitions, arms, tents and uniforms for the army. It was not uncommon for slaves to do contract work whereby they would divide the wages with masters. Lincoln would have been shocked to discover the country would not yet have the same percentage of skilled workers in 1870 that the South had in 1850. On the large farms and plantations African Americans were typically foremen and managers responsible for critical operations. The planting and harvesting of crops on large tracts of land required organization and teamwork to insure crops like tobacco, sugar cane, indigo and cotton were planted and harvested under the best conditions of the growing season. While African Americans were not in bondage in the North, even those who were educated and skilled struggled to find employment sufficient to meet their basic needs. Discrimination and laws even forbade them to reside in certain states such as Lincoln's own Illinois. They weren't welcome in the North, nor was their culture. This was not lost on the African Americans of the South where their culture and contributions could be acknowledged and respected.

It would be naïve to assume the slaves on farms and plantations not yet under Northern military control were not aware of the status of the war. An informal, yet effective communications network known as the "grapevine" existed whereby news was spread from farm to farm in the South among African Americans. The news was spread in a variety of ways. Often traveling preachers or slaves contracted to other farms or the cities were instrumental in bringing information to the rural areas. Literate African Americans of course would pass on information they read in newspapers or flyers. Confederate soldiers returning home on furloughs or to recover from wounds were also sources of new information. Even on the largest plantations news spread quickly about the war, secession, abolitionists, and Lincoln. The Northern blockade made them aware that many goods were now in short supply, and it was increasingly more difficult to get goods to market for sale in Europe. In the *Slave Narratives* many of the interviewees describe the hardships that the war brought to those left back home on the farms of the South. In 1863 and beyond, the hardships they experienced would escalate much further up to the war's conclusion.

In March of 1863, General Ulysses Grant wrote: "Rebellion has assumed the shape now that it can only terminate by the complete subjugation of the South. It is our duty to weaken the enemy, by destroying their means of subsistence, withdrawing their means of cultivating their fields, and in every other way possible." In short, Grant was talking about not only making war against Confederate armies but also against the Southern people, their food and shelter.

It did not take long for news of the destructive results of this new "total war" policy against civilians to reach the farms and plantations not yet under Northern control. Many slaves were now entrusted with helping to hide family heirlooms and valuables, as well as their own property from marauding Northern armies. What was even more disturbing to hear was that homes and outbuildings were being set afire, livestock was being slaughtered and crops destroyed by the invaders. Everyone knew this was a recipe for impending starvation.

While slaves suspected that an eventual Northern victory would bring about their independence, they still had strong feelings of loyalty to the families they served. In his autobiography, *Up from Slavery*, famous educator and former slave, Booker T. Washington stated, "In order to defend and protect the women and children who were left behind on the plantations when the white males went to war, the slaves would have laid down their lives. The slave who was selected to sleep in the 'big house' during the absence of males was considered to have a place of honor. Anyone attempting to harm 'young Mistress' or 'old Mistress' during the night would have to cross the dead body of a slave to do so." Washington relates that the death of one of the young masters in the war, 'Mars' Billy, brought sadness to slaves who had nursed him and those who had played with him as a child. In the South, under the most trying conditions, Booker T. Washington was correct when he wrote, "I think it will be found to be true that there are few instances, either in slavery or freedom, in which a member of my race has been known to betray a specific trust."

Summation

While slaves did yearn for peaceful independence, their contributions within their environment, relationships and loyalty were a far cry from the stereotypical behavior the Republicans believed would foster servile insurrections.

- Stereotype is defined thusly: a standardized mental picture that is held in common by members of a group and that represents an oversimplified opinion, prejudiced attitude, or uncritical judgment. Merriam-Webster.

Topic for Class Discussion

Are there still stereotypes about the South today? Who promotes them? Hint: Entertainment industry.

Recommended Reading

- *Up from Slavery* by Booker T. Washington, pub. 1901.
- *North of Slavery: The Negro in the Free States, 1790-1860*, by Leon F. Litwack, pub. 1965.

Chapter 27 – The Story of African American Support of Confederate Forces and, during 1863-1865, of those Inducted into Federal African American Regiments.

By Earl L. Ijames of N. C., S.I.S.H.

Introduction

Students will be surprised to learn of the extent to which African Americans supported the Confederate army and navy. That will be covered in some detail in this chapter. Also covered with be the more familiar story of African Americans fighting in Federal regiments, but fewer words are devoted to that subject, for it is covered well in histories you already have. You probably know that President Lincoln's January 1863 Emancipation Proclamation was also aimed at inducting into the Federal army many African American men living in regions of the Confederacy occupied by Federal forces. By that time Federals controlled much of Tennessee, Arkansas, southern Louisiana and certain coastal Atlantic islands, where large African American populations existed. They could also be inducted out of Maryland, Kentucky and Missouri in addition to the Republican states – all taken into regiments reserved for African American soldiers, led by white officers. Here, Earl L. Ijames presents the history of African American participation on the battlefields of the War Between the States and explains why they were there – south and north.

The History

The War Between the States was more like The Revolutionary War than a Civil War. The Rebel Army of 1776 allowed and encouraged enslaved men like Toby Gilmore of Massachusetts and free persons of color like John Chavis who served from Virginia to enlist in their colony's defense and earn their freedom and citizenship in a new America. After the British Army encountered the Patriots' guerilla tactics and their employment of these men in various capacities, Gen. Corwallis similarly declared freedom to encourage those men to join the British. After Independence, the 1792 Militia Act disallowed future service by African Americans in the U.S. Army and in fact paved the way for Veterans of Color like James Newby of North Carolina to be re-enslaved.

Four score after gaining freedom from Great Britain, America faced an internal war that threatened her existence. The Civil War would be waged between the states in the Union and the states and territories sympathetic to the more autonomous Confederate States. Initially, the Federal government fought the war to keep these states that still allowed slavery from leaving the Union. But the Federal Militia Act prohibited enslaved and free men of color from fighting for the Union. "When the Civil War started there went up a cry for volunteers, white or Negro. Daniel and Milford Brooks were free men of color from Cleveland County, NC who would have been conscripted into the Confederate Army. The Brooks brothers preferred to volunteer and walked 17 miles to Shelby, NC and did so."

With the 1861 capture of New Orleans, Union Gen. Benjamin Butler encountered the Louisiana Native Guard, a militia comprised of free men of color for the defense of the economic and cultural hub of the Gulf Coast. After the fall of the Crescent City, Gen. Butler attempted to recruit the Confederates of Color into the Union ranks. But Pres. Lincoln prohibited the gesture with a reminder of the Federal prohibition of troops of color in the Union Army.

After nearly two years of Civil War, the Confederate Army, with the aid of people of color, had been defeating the Union army in battle. Formerly enslaved men like John Parker of Virginia served at First Manassas. Weary Clyburn escaped slavery to serve as a body servant in the Co. E, 12th S.C. Regiment and free persons of color like Pvt. Miles Reed manned one of the artillery regiments, the Co. D, 40th NC Troops, at the fall of Ft. Fisher. These men fought for their individual freedom and defense of their country (now referred as states) before the Emancipation Proclamation.

The July 1862 Confederate Victory at the Second Battle of Bull Run at Manassas, VA, prompted the United States Congress to pass the Second Confiscation Act, which called for the seizure of property, or contraband, from supporters of the Confederacy in the South. Additionally, Great Britain and France moved closer to recognizing the Confederacy with each Union defeat.

Seeking a way to reverse the tide of war, President Abraham Lincoln wrote a draft floating the idea of emancipation, or freedom, to his cabinet. Secretary of State William Seward warned Lincoln that the Union needed a victory before the President's idea could be made public. In 1862, formerly enslaved Frederick Douglass observed "There are at the present moment, many Colored men in the Confederate Army doing duty not only as cooks, laborers and servants but as real soldiers having muskets on their shoulders and bullets in their pockets ready to shoot down… and do what soldiers may do to destroy the Federal Government."

On September 17, 1862 the Union and Confederate Armies converged on a large corn field in Sharpsburg, MD with a single dirt road winding through it. What ensued was the bloodiest day in American history- The Battle of Antietam. One of those casualties was Capt. Walter Bryson of Henderson, NC. Capt. Bryson's remains were brought home to western North Carolina by his body servant, George Mills.

President Lincoln, being a masterful politician and psychological operative, declared victory over the 23,000 American casualties and then issued the Preliminary Emancipation Proclamation. Lincoln changed the course of the WBTS from saving the Union to include emancipation of more than 4 million men, women and children of African descent. The Preliminary Emancipation Proclamation (PEP) is a handwritten, seven-page, ribbon-bound document signed by President Abraham Lincoln and Secretary of State William Seward and affixed with the seal of the United States. This document warns the Confederate States that if the South did not end the war by January 1, 1863, he would free the men, women and children they held in chattel slavery.

January 1, 1863 marked a turning point for the nation. The PEP had served notice to the Confederate States to return to the Union by New Year's Day 1863 or their enslaved persons would be declared free. Enslaved persons in Union-held territory were omitted from the freedom document. The masterful psychological operative transformed New Year's Day – a day historically designated to buy, sell and hire slaves – into Emancipation Day. Men like Sam Ashe served as a body servant to Capt. Richard Ashe at the 1861 Battle of Big Bethel, VA Sam Ashe fired the fatal shot killing Union Major Theodore Winthrop thus deciding the first battle of the war in the Confederate's favor. After January 1862, Sam Ashe was hired out to the North Carolina Railroad to serve the Confederacy.

New Year's Eve has been known as First Night Watch in the African American community since 1863. It is still observed in many African American churches and organizations. The Emancipation Proclamation (EP) went into effect New Year's Day 1863.

The Emancipation Proclamation facilitated the enlistment of enslaved and free people of color into the Union Army. As Commander in Chief, President Lincoln called the EP a "fit and necessary war measure." The First Confiscation Act allowed the Union to employ "persons of African descent" in the war effort in supporting roles. But the Second Confiscation Act repealed the 1792 Militia Act that barred men of color from serving in the United States Army. Under the Second Act, the U.S. War Department authorized raising the African Brigade, later renamed the United States Colored Troops (USCT).

Confederates of Color served and died on the battlefields of America before and after the formation of the United States Colored Troops. Some of these soldiers of color were also Indians like Thomas' Legion, the 23rd Reg. NC Troops. Confederates of Color like Pvt. Hawkins Wesley Carter of the 46th NC Troops served for the entire war in various capacities. According to Carter's 1927 Confederate pension application, he "threw up breast works, worked on the railroad, cooked, waited on white soldiers, and fought seven days at the 1864 Wilderness Campaign in Virginia."

Unlike the Confederates of Color, however, the United States Colored Troops served in segregated units under the command of President Lincoln's handpicked white abolitionists. Gen. Edward A. Wild was appointed by Pres. Lincoln in North Carolina. Gen. Wild recruited in the heavily concentrated black counties across eastern North Carolina. The USCT was stationed in New Bern, NC where men, women and children sought freedom under the protection of the USCT in nearby James City. More than 200,000 formerly enslaved and free persons of color enlisted in the Union Army and Navy beginning in 1863.

Men like Abraham Galloway, son of an Irish seaman and an African American woman, was born enslaved in Wilmington, NC. During the War Between the States, Galloway was a spy who later met with President Lincoln to help raise the USCT, especially in the South. Robert Smalls commandeered a Confederate vessel into the hands of the Union Navy. Smalls also helped to raise the first Colored Union Regiment in the South, the 33rd USCT in South Carolina.

Other men like William Henry Singleton left the 7th NC Cavalry after the 1862 Battle of Kinston to enlist in the USCT in nearby New Bern. The Union army first thought that Singleton was a spy until the Colonel from the NC Cavalry sought him at New Bern. And Luke Martin left his plantation in Washington Co., NC and swam three rivers during the winter of 1863 to earn the title as Pvt. Luke Martin, 35th USCT.

A few USCT earned rank as Sergeant Major. Sgt. Parker D. Robbins enlisted in the 2nd US Colored Cavalry in Virginia in 1863. The 2nd USCC was among the first four regiments (all USCT) at the April 1865 fall of the Confederate Capital at Richmond, VA. The 36th USCT raised in northeastern NC was the first regiment at the fall of Richmond.

The Emancipation Proclamation needed to be secured with a military victory and unconditional surrender of the Confederate Army. Otherwise, the EP had no constitutional merit. The ultimate military victory would entail conquering Fort Fisher, the largest earthen fortress in the history of the world constructed by free persons of color like Enos Jacobs of Sampson County, NC. The fort was largely constructed by enslaved men like Aaron Perry of Union Co., NC who also served in the 37th NC Troops as a body servant. Many Indians from Robeson County, NC also worked on the fort. General Robert E. Lee declared that if Fort Fisher fell, then the Confederacy would follow suit.

After an initial failure to take the fort in December 1864, Union forces mounted the largest amphibious attack in the history of the world (World War II D-Day June 6, 1944 would later surpass Ft. Fisher). On January 20, 1865 the fort fell and was surrendered to the 27th USCT, raised in Ohio. Confederates of Color like Pvt. Richard Dempsey in the 36th NC Troops and Pvt. Reed in the 40th NCT were captured by the Federals as Prisoners of War. After the fall of Fort Fisher, the US Congress passed the 13th Amendment to the Constitution on January 31, 1865. The amendment stated that slavery nor involuntary servitude could not exist in the United States "or any place subject to their jurisdiction."

President Lincoln praised the USCT: "Without the help of the black freedmen, the war against the South could not have been won." The U. S. Colored Troops fought for their freedom and helped to save the Union.

Summary

The history of African Americans of the Southern Culture during the era of the War Between the States is complex. After early 1863, many were inducted into regiments of Colored Troops, under white officers. And many of those suffered horrific fighting. But a great number were helpful to the defense of the Confederacy, and that is the important lesson to be learned. It takes some digging, for most of the evidence of Confederate support is obscured. But learning the Confederate part of the story is a worthwhile adventure.

Suggestions for Class Discussion

Why did many African Americans of the Southern Culture help in the defense of the Confederacy? Were they also defending "hearth and home" and defending their families against the ravages of Total War? Perhaps they understood that people of the Northern Culture did not want to be their friends. Consider the evidence: few African Americans of the Southern Culture ever attacked owners or neighbors in support of the Federal invasion.

Chapter 28* – The Sufferings of the Prisoners of War and Why it Happened.

By Karen Stokes of S. C., S. I. S. H.

Introduction

This is the saddest chapter of them all. To think that Republican-led officers and soldiers would intentionally starve captured Confederates and encourage disease within prison camps is hard for Americans today to understand. Early in the war, in addition to blockading Southern ports, the Lincoln administration took the harsh and unprecedented measure of declaring medical supplies, including surgical equipment and medicines, contraband, and their scarcity caused great suffering among Confederate soldiers as well as Federals imprisoned in the South. As the Federals continued to conquer and occupy more and more Confederate territory and to wage war on civilians – their property and their ability to produce food – everyone living within Confederate-controlled territory suffered, including POWS. But the North had ample food, clothing and shelter. From 1863 on, the Lincoln Administration resorted to denying prisoner exchanges as a war measure: making imprisoned federals suffer to avoid freeing imprisoned Confederates in humane exchanges. We, the authors of *Understanding the War Between the States*, wish we could have avoided writing this chapter, but write we must.

History Relevant To Understanding the WBTS

When the war began, the governments of the United States and the Confederate States were not well prepared to hold and care for large numbers of prisoners of war. As hundreds of POWs turned into thousands, more military prisons were created, as well as bureaucracies to administer them. The Dix-Hill Cartel, an agreement between the two governments defining procedures for the parole and exchange of prisoners, was enacted in July 1862. About a year afterward, the U.S. government put a stop to most prisoner exchanges for a considerable period. Later, limited exchanges were resumed, but in the meantime, many thousands of men held in prisons in the north and south languished and died in captivity.

In 1864, in response to questionable allegations of deliberate mistreatment of Union prisoners by their Confederate captors, Union authorities instituted a policy of systematic retaliation against prisoners of war in their hands. "Retaliatory" measures included reducing the food rations of Confederate prisoners, and restricting their receipt of food and other comforts sent into prisons from family and friends. As a result, there was a rise in malnourishment, as well as all the sufferings and afflictions that went along with it, among the prisoners held by the North.

In March 1864, George H. Moffett, a Confederate POW at Fort Delaware, recalled seeing a printed order posted in the prison "from the War Department at Washington," announcing this "retaliatory measure." Moffett commented: "Was it possible that there was a civilized government on earth willing to place itself on record in practicing such an enormous barbarity? But there it was in legible characters posted up against the outside wall of the mess hall…in full view of all who cared to stop and read it."

The "retaliatory" policy approved by U.S. Secretary of War Edwin M. Stanton had been justified in part by a pamphlet produced by the Committee on the Conduct of the War, a powerful U.S. congressional committee dominated by the radical faction of the Republican Party. In May 1864, investigating reports of intentional mistreatment of Union prisoners in the south, members of this committee visited some ex-prisoners (Federals) who were being treated for illness and wounds. The result of their visit was a 30 page report which the U.S. government printed and distributed by the thousands, purporting to offer evidence that the Confederate authorities were maliciously and systematically starving and abusing prisoners of war in their hands. Several months later, it was followed by a similar publication produced by the United States Sanitary Commission, a relief agency providing medical care for the sick and wounded soldiers of the U.S. Army. Its report also concluded that there was "a predetermined plan, originating somewhere in the rebel counsels, for destroying and disabling the soldiers of their enemy." The authors of this report disputed notions that the Confederate government was unable to provide sufficient rations and supplies for its army and prisoners of war, and documented at length and in glowing terms the humane and sanitary conditions in United States prison camps., claiming, among other things, that rations were of good quality and quantity in all northern facilities.

In response to these two reports, a joint committee of the Confederate Congress presented its own report, near war's end, March 1865, emphatically denying northern accusations of a diabolical "predetermined plan" to destroy helpless prisoners of war, and asserting that the Northern report was only a "false and slanderous charge against the South." In its report, the Confederate committee admitted that there was "a vast amount of suffering and fearful mortality among the Federal prisoners at the South," but they placed the blame for these conditions on "the authorities at Washington" and their "settled policy in conducting the war not to exchange prisoners." Confederate legislators also claimed that their prison system was as humane as possible under the circumstances. Some historians contend otherwise, and have written that there was in both of the prison systems, north and south, a considerable degree of mismanagement, neglect, and even deliberate mistreatment of prisoners. However, the resumption of exchange, "the obviously humane solution," as historian William B. Hesseltine put it, would have alleviated much suffering, especially for the men held in the Confederate prison system, overwhelmed as it was, especially later in the war, with enormous numbers of prisoners to feed and manage.

The most singular and unconscionable manifestation of the North's retaliatory policy occurred when six hundred Confederate POWs were taken out of Fort Delaware in August 1864 and sent into harsh, sometimes hellish conditions at Union prisons in South Carolina and Georgia. Known as "The Immortal 600," most of these men were deliberately subjected to an ordeal of insufficient food rations and medicines at Fort Pulaski, Georgia.

In early 1864, the Confederates constructed a 20-acre camp at **Andersonville**, Georgia. Meant to contain 10,000 prisoners, it was soon overwhelmed by many thousands more, and enlarged to 30 acres. Though the site had been chosen for humane reasons, including a pure water supply, conditions there became terrible. Sanitation was a major problem, medicines were scarce, and the POWs were dying of diarrhea, dysentery, scurvy and gangrene at a fearful rate. Louis Manigault, a Confederate medical officer, observed that many of the Andersonville prisoners were malnourished because they were not accustomed to "our corn hominy…the Confederate Government not having it in their power to furnish them with wheat." The Confederacy urgently pressed for the resumption of prisoner exchanges, proposed sending home sick and wounded prisoners without the equivalent exchange of Confederate POWs, and offered to buy medicines for the prisoners in the South; but the U.S. government made little response to these proposals.

Andersonville is often singled out as one of the worst atrocities of the war, but there were a number of Northern prison camps that were just as horrible or worse in many ways. **Elmira** prison camp in New York, and Camp **Douglas** in Chicago, Illinois, were two of the worst examples. At Elmira, as rations were progressively reduced under the "retaliatory regime," many Confederates died in an epidemic of scurvy, a disease of malnourishment. They also perished because of filthy conditions and for want of sufficient shelter in the brutally cold northern winters. After the war, a northern medical officer who served at Elmira wrote that out of about 11,000 Confederate prisoners there, over 3,000 "now lie buried in the cemetery near the camp … a mortality equal, of not greater than that of any prison in the South." He added about Elmira: "The sick in hospitals were curtailed in every respect (fresh vegetables and other anti-scorbutics were dropped from the list); the food scant, crude, and unfit; medicine so badly dispensed that it was a farce for the medical man to prescribe. At large, in the camp, the prisoner fared still worse; a slice of bread and salt meat was given him for his breakfast; a poor, hatched-up concocted cup of soup, so called, and a slice of miserable bread, was all he could obtain for his coming meal; and hundreds of sick, who could in nowise obtain medical aid, died 'unknelled, un-coffined, and unknown.'"

Similarly, at **Camp Douglas** in Chicago, large numbers of Confederate prisoners died from a lack of shelter, clothing and nutritious food. Smallpox also killed many POWs there. Two physicians working for the U.S. Sanitary Commission, reported: "From January 27, 1863, when the prisoners (in number about 3,800) arrived at Camp Douglas, to February 18, the day of our visit, 385 patients have been admitted to the hospitals, of whom 130 had died. This mortality of 33 per cent does not express the whole truth, for of the 148 patients then remaining in hospital a large number must have since died. Besides this, about 130 prisoners had died in barracks, not having been able to gain admission even to the miserable accommodations of the hospital, and at the time of our visit 150 persons were sick in barracks waiting for room in [the] hospital." This report, which was sent to the U.S. Secretary of War Edwin Stanton, further stated that the deplorable condition of Camp Douglas was "disgraceful to us as a Christian people." One of the Camp Douglas guards wrote of the fearful winter of 1863-64 that "the mercury often fell to 20 degrees below zero. The sight of 4 sallow [Confederates], clad in butternut, bearing the corpse of a comrade to the dead house was an almost hourly spectacle." The exact number of Confederate POWs who died at Camp Douglas is not known,

but long after the war, a monument built on the site of the prison graveyard bore the inscription: "Erected to the memory of the six thousand southern soldiers here buried who died in Camp Douglas Prison, 1862-5." George Levy's book about Camp Douglas, *To Die in Chicago,* describes a period from August to December 1863 as a particularly cruel one overseen by a commandant named Charles De Land. A Federal inspector criticized De Land for taking blankets and clothing from prisoners to discourage escapes, and for punishing insubordinate prisoners by confining them in a small, grossly overcrowded room known as the "White Oak Dungeon." De Land also tortured prisoners for information by hanging them by their thumbs.

In Jefferson Davis's two-volume history, *The Rise and Fall of the Confederate Government,* written in the 1880's, the former Confederate president stated, "The report of the Secretary of War E. M. Stanton, made on July 19, 1866, shows that, of all the prisoners in our hands during the war, only 22,576 died, while, of the prisoners in our opponent's hands, 26,246 died; second, the official report of Surgeon General Barnes, an officer of the United States government, states that, in round numbers, the numbers of Confederate States prisoners in their hands amounted to 220,000, the number of United States prisoners in our hands amounted to 270,000. Thus 12% of the prisoners in our opponent's hands died, and less than 9% of the prisoners in our hands died. When, in this connection, it is remembered that our resources were greatly reduced, that our supply of medicines required in summer diseases was exhausted, and that Northern men when first residing at the South must undergo acclimation, and that those conditions in the Northern states were the reverse in each particular – the fact that greater mortality existed in the Northern than in Southern prisons can be accounted for only by the kinder treatment received in the latter." (Volume 2, page 513)

Summation

The U.S. government had it in its power to exchange prisoners, yet generally refused to do so in the last half of the conflict, and though other motives for this policy were publicly given out to the people of the north, General Ulysses S. Grant made the carefully calculated decision to put an end to most exchanges as a matter of military strategy: keeping southern prisoners in captivity helped to deplete the manpower of the Confederate Army.

Suggestions for Class Discussion

How could the sufferings of the prisoners of war in the North and South have been avoided or reduced?

Recommended Reading

- *Portals to Hell: Military Prisons of the Civil War,* by Lonnie R. Speer, pub. 1997.
- *Civil War Prisons: A Study in War Psychology,* by William B. Hesseltine, pub. 1964.
- *The Immortal 600: Surviving Civil War Charleston and Savannah,* by Karen Stokes, pub. 2013.
- *Elmira, Death Camp of the North,* by Michael Horigan, pub. 2002.

Section Six: After the Conquest – Consequences of Political Sectionalism and Horrific War

Chapter 29* – The Cost of the War in Lives Lost and Families Shattered.

By William Cawthon of Alabama, S.I.S.H.

Introduction

The War Between the States was the most horrific conflict ever fought by United States troops. Of those Federals who fought, 400,000 died. That is a huge number. If you went to your computer and took an image of each one of these 400,000 dead Federal soldiers and sailors, stretched his arms up high, put a tall bouquet of carnations in his right hand and laid him down on the highway that runs from the White House in Washington, D. C. to the harbor at Charleston, South Carolina – If you kept laying down those dead bodies, the toes of one touching the flowers of the next; one after the other; until you laid down the last of the 400,000 – then the flowers in the right hand of the last soldier would dip into the seawater in Charleston harbor, within sight of Fort Sumter. That is the image of the WBTS that we hope you always remember, for those Federal dead had been duped into going to war to enable political domination by a Sectional Republican Party – a sad cause for which to die. The Confederates lost 350,000 in their defensive effort. Their bodies, when laid out with carnations in a similar fashion would reach well into North Carolina. Author William Cawthon tells the story of lives shattered and lost, including a range of estimates of deaths suffered by Southern civilians, Black and White.

History Relevant

The War between North and South between the years 1861 and 1865 was the epic war of American history and one of the epic wars of world history. This is so for any number of reasons, the most searingly brutal the magnitude of the loss of life. Modern Americans cannot even begin to truly comprehend the extent of the slaughter and wholesale and widespread destruction in every facet of life, uprooting people from their homes, the wholesale destruction of property, a violent and brutal tearing apart of the society of the South from which the South has in truth never recovered.

Historian Drew Gilpin Faust in her book, *This Republic Of Suffering: Death and the American Civil War* (2008), presents the horror of the hand of death "everywhere in the land" in a manner that makes it feel palpable to us today, yet her work, by combining the suffering of North and South, cannot begin to reveal the many times greater death and devastation wrought upon the South.

The long-standing "official" death tolls, with which anyone who is interested in the war is familiar, are 360,000 Union dead and 260,000 Confederate dead, or a total of 620,000 soldier deaths. These figures, however, were approximations which two Union veterans developed in the late 19th century. They recognized that their figures were not final and were based on incomplete records, particularly on the Southern side. The last year of the war was very catastrophic to the South and many records were lost. Records on the Northern side also were inadequate. Evidence for the lack of knowledge about the deaths is the remarkable statistic that only 54% of Northern men who lost their lives in this terrible war were identified.

A new estimate of the number of soldiers who died based on U. S. Census data analysis estimates that 750,000 soldier deaths would be a more accurate figure than the ones cited. The author of the Census analysis, J. David Hacker, believes that the Confederate deaths from disease and accidents are particularly undercounted. He notes that Confederates hailed from rural areas to a much greater degree than Northern soldiers, and were therefore less likely to have been exposed to infectious diseases than Union soldiers. The Union blockade of Southern ports contributed greatly to the hardships of life in the Confederate armies. Food and clothing were often in short supply, increasing the rate of death from exposure and reducing resistance to disease. During the last year of the war the blockade and the Union's scorched earth policy toward the land and civilians of the South significantly increased the chance of death to Southerners by sharply reducing the availability of medicines, leading to malnutrition and avitaminosis.

Therefore, it seems reasonable to assign 70% of the increased soldier deaths to the South, and this may be a conservative estimate. This brings the death toll among Confederate soldiers to approximately 350,000 men instead of the former 260,000. The Union death toll would be increased to 400,000. These figures include soldier deaths during the early years of Political Reconstruction caused by the War and the disruptions of those years incident upon the War. To begin to comprehend how this number of soldier deaths impacted the people who lived during the war, one must compare these totals to the men of military age and to the total populations.

It has long been said that the 260,000 Confederate soldier deaths represented approximately 25 percent of her white men of military age, dead, either killed in battle or died of disease, and to a much lesser extent, as in all wars, from accidents and other minor causes. This is a toll which the modern American mind cannot truly comprehend. Its impact on our society would be far beyond anything we can with any degree of real life experience imagine. If this proportion of men aged 18 - 48 died as a result of a war today, 17 million Americans would be dead. In Vietnam, America's losses were a mere 58,000, and the trauma wrought to the U. S. was great. Even in World War II, the loss of life was but 405,000. The figure of 17 million dead is approximately 300 times the number of men who died in the Vietnam War. But, if 350,000 Confederate soldiers died, the proportion of the white men of the majority Confederate areas of the South who died defending Dixie is close to 30 percent. Applying this ratio across today's American population, 21 million deaths would result from a war so deadly fought today.

The Southern proportion of dead was about three times the Union rate, the Union losing around 8 percent of its population of military age to the War by the 360,000 estimate, and about 9 percent by the 400,000 estimate. This rate of loss would result in 5,500,000 and 6,000,000 military deaths from a war fought today.

The Southern loss of life was so great that a prominent historian of the war, James McPherson, has estimated that the total mortality rate of the South from this war was greater than that of any country during World War I, which itself was so deadly that it set Britain, previously the world's great power, into a permanent decline and caused such severe disillusionment in the

Western World that confidence in Western Civilization has been in serious decline ever since. Only the region between the Rhine and the Volga in World War II suffered greater total mortality than did the South in America's epic war, according to calculations by McPherson.

A "harvest of death," a common term in the war, swept both North and South. Americans had never seen anything like it before, and have never seen anything like it since. But it was in the South that "the harvest of death" reached truly epic proportions. Two Southerners, one in a journal, one in a letter, expressed the ubiquity of the heart-wrenching commonality of death that Southerners came to know first-hand. Kate Stone in her journal recorded: "nearly every household mourns some loved one lost." A Confederate soldier, C. W. Greene, in an August 1862 letter, early in the war, before the bloodiest of the battles, wrote that death "reigned with universal sway." Some families lost many members; some, almost all. The Christian family of Christiansburg, Virginia lost 18 members in the War.

New studies have shown as never before the death and destruction to the civilian population of the South, to both blacks and whites. This is a topic scarcely touched upon in most histories of the War, concentrating as they do on the generals, the major battles, or political, cultural, and social issues, but not on the phenomenal death and destruction.

Civilians were caught up in the war in countless ways. "The war killed civilians as well, as battles raged across farm and field, as encampments of troops spread epidemic disease, as guerrillas ensnared women and even children in violence and reprisals, as draft riots targeted innocent citizens [the most famous one in New York City, involving Irishmen who lynched and killed a hundred or more blacks in expressing their opposition to the Union's draft law], as shortages of food in parts of the South brought starvation." (Faust, *This Republic Of Suffering*). Civilians were killed as the Union forces bombarded Southern cities. Some of these sieges lasted for very long periods. No one had been killed at the bombardment of Fort Sumter, Lincoln's excuse for beginning the invasion. But, later, the City of Charleston underwent the longest siege of any city in U. S. history. In these prolonged sieges not only were many buildings and much personal property destroyed, people were injured, maimed, and killed. Disease spread due to the confined conditions and serious catastrophic lack of food, medicines, and supplies of all kinds. The citizens of Vicksburg, Mississippi were so reduced that they ate rats. In these horrendous conditions disease and malnutrition spread, and people died. It was extreme malnutrition and accompanying disease which forced the well-publicized desertions from the Confederate ranks late in the war, when the Confederate Cause, to many, had come to seem hopeless. McPherson points out that until the last hard winter of the war, the desertion rate in the South and North was about the same, even though the Northern economy and war effort was flush with food, medicine, and the other necessities of life, as opposed to the meagre circumstances of Southerners under the blockade.

We will never know how many civilians died as a result of this bloodiest of America's wars, fought almost entirely on Southern soil. But if we count those who died during the early years of Reconstruction from the effects of the War, from wounds received, from diseases incurred during the War which brought death later, and especially death from starvation in the extremely harsh and disordered conditions of the post War South, as well as those who died of all causes during the War itself, we can see why civilian casualties were so large. The Northern armies had ravaged many of the richest and most productive areas of the Southern countryside, and much of the remainder of the South besides, leaving a destitute people barely able to find enough to eat, stripped of their control over their future, seemingly helpless against the victorious foe. There are even cases of the deliberate killing of Southern civilians by invading Yankee soldiers.

James McPherson, the leading historian of the War today, who is very partisan for the Northern side, though a very good historian, gives in his latest book (2015) a highly abbreviated look at the devastation to the South: ". . . . the victorious power . . . did all it could to devastate the enemy's economy as well as the morale of its home-front population. The Civil War wiped out two-thirds of the assessed value of wealth in Confederate states, two-fifths of the South's livestock, and more than half of its farm machinery – not to mention at least one-quarter of the Confederacy's white men of military age. While Northern wealth increased by 50 percent from 1860 to 1870, Southern wealth decreased by 60 percent." The average free Southerner, blacks included, was twice as wealthy per capita before the War than the average Northerner; ten years later the average Northerner was twice as wealthy as the average Southerner.

Perhaps the most prominent death from starvation was the loss of the Confederacy's Poet Laureate, the young and gifted Henry Timrod, during the early years of Reconstruction. If a person of Timrod's important connections could die of starvation, think of the thousands who must have died of insufficient proper food and nourishment throughout the Southern land both during the War and Reconstruction. It is estimated that 35,000 white civilians died of all causes during the War and the early years of Political Reconstruction up to 1870.

Even more arresting is the death of so many black people. Until recent years, the black experience in the War has been told principally as one of a triumph, of emancipation and freedom over slavery, almost as if everything turned up rosy for the black population. Jim Downs' relatively new book, *Sick from Freedom* (2012) proves with abundant contemporary sources the truly heart wrenching experiences of the freedpeople (the former slaves). Black people found an unknown and in many situations a hostile world with their emancipation. Many, believing that a great boon of freedom awaited them, rushed to the Northern armies as the invading forces made their way deeper into Southern territory, to find much anti-black feeling, almost universal discrimination, and exceedingly inadequate food, clothing, shelter, and medical care. One of the many distressing stories is that of a freedwoman who walked for 25 miles seeking medicine for her sick child, only to be told by the Freedmen's Bureau Office of the Federal Government that no medicine was to be had. So reduced were blacks in material circumstances that many of them earned a little money by scavenging for bones and selling them. Other black people begged for food, reduced to existing off of berries along the roadside and in the forest in the weeks after they "were freed."

The Northern Army, and, during the early years of Political Reconstruction, the Freedman's Bureau, saw the freedpeople more than anything else as potential laborers (the very underlining, basic reason for slavery, in all cultures, world-wide, from ancient to modern times). Both the Army and the Bureau put many black men to work, during the War on fortifications and the like, during Reconstruction also on public works projects, but, most of all, as common laborers on plantations, the work so many had done as slaves. In sending the men off to work projects, the women and children were usually left behind, leaving them even more destitute and with greater susceptibility to disease and death. Concentrating blacks together at "contraband camps" increased the chance of disease, sickness, and mortality.

The single most horrific disease that freed blacks faced was smallpox. Due to the overcrowded conditions of the black people who congregated in Washington, D. C. early in the War, amidst the general disorder, smallpox made an appearance first there in 1862. In 1864 it crossed into Virginia, and thence spread during the next several years over the South, reaching Texas in 1868. Though a few whites contracted the dread disease, the cases of smallpox were overwhelmingly among the freed blacks. One reason for the great prevalence among blacks was discrimination by the Northern Army and the Freedmen's Bureau, which favored whites over blacks in treating the disease. Medicines were slower to reach the blacks, and those that did reach them were often inferior. This was true for sickness in general. So great was death from smallpox that 800 blacks a week died on the Sea Islands in November and December 1865. Caskets of the black dead were lined up on the streets of Macon, Georgia during Political Reconstruction.

The Lincoln Administration had no plan for emancipation. Lincoln actually preferred that as many blacks as possible be deported from the United States to one or more foreign countries. But with the emancipation agenda that developed in the U. S. in 1863, no administrative structure was created to provide for the black people who had suddenly left their former homes and plantations within conquered regions.

In truth, the sudden emancipation of millions of former slaves, with no experience of freedom or independent living led to widespread dislocation, abject poverty, and widespread sickness and death. Families were split asunder by the Federal policies favoring the placement of the men in productive work to benefit the Northern war machine and by other Federal policies during both war and Political Reconstruction.

Furthermore, a widespread belief at the time among both Northerners and Southerners was that the blacks would slowly become extinct following emancipation. The Indians, it was believed by many, were going extinct. The Indian populations had by this time become greatly reduced in size, and most Indians on the reservations assigned to them lived in abject poverty. It was believed blacks would follow the fate of the Indians. Even the published U. S. Census of Population of 1860, written and published by the Northern Union, expected blacks after emancipation to increase less than they had under slavery. Observing that, in each of the three decades prior to 1860, the free black population of the U. S. had increased less than had the slave population, Census authors concluded that the black population of America "is doomed to comparatively rapid absorption or extinction."

Because a system of public records of deaths of people, black and white, in this period was almost non-existent, we will never know the actual extent of civilian deaths. However, the new evidence suggests that the rate of death among the freed blacks was exceptionally high, this ultra-high rate caused by the sudden emancipation imposed by the U. S. government without planning and the major disruptions and diseases and starvation caused by the War and its consequences, both during the War itself and during the early Political Reconstruction years. It would not be unreasonable to assume that it reached five or six percent of the Confederate black population, which would place deaths of blacks in the Confederate States caused by the War around the remarkable number of 200,000 people. The mortality rate of contraband camps may have reached 25%.

When we add the total deaths for Confederate soldiers and white civilians and black Southerners in the Confederacy (350,000 + 35,000 + 200,000) we get 585,000 deaths suffered by the Southern side. When we add to that 400,000 Union soldier deaths we arrive at the figure of 985,000 deaths.

White and black civilians also died in the Union dominated States as a result of the War. Fierce guerrilla warfare occurred in both Missouri and in the area of Virginia that became West Virginia. Civilian deaths in these Union dominated areas would almost certainly push the total number of deaths caused by America's epic war beyond one million.

Summation

If a war today should take as many lives in proportion to population as the South sacrificed for its independence in America's epic War Between the States, 21 million Americans would die.

The old Southern civilization which produced George Washington, Thomas Jefferson, John C. Calhoun, and a host of other eminent Americans and a rich, vibrant intellectual culture amidst an organic society rooted in family, the land, religion, tradition, honest agrarian self-sufficiency and a fierce legacy of self-government was swept away.

The South sacrificed far, far more than any other Americans ever have in any war or for any cause whatsoever in its heroic, epic struggle for the sacred virtues of Hearth and Home, Liberty and Independence. One Confederate lady wrote that everyone knew a friend who had died. The black population suffered terribly, with a proportionate loss of their population to death that may have been as high as that among Southern whites.

Suggestions for Class Discussion

Why are the horrors of the War Between the States largely hidden from students today? Chapter 36 will present "What If Bonded African Americans (Slaves) had Benefitted from Gradual Emancipation with Training and Freedom from Political Agendas? There was an alternative to horrific war. Talk about that, too.

Recommended Reading

- *This Republic of Suffering: Death and the American Civil War*, by Drew Gilpin Faust, pub. 2008.
- *Sick from Freedom: African-American Illness and Suffering during the Civil War and Reconstruction*, by Jim Downs, pub. 2012.
- *When the World Ended,* by Emma Leconte (ed. by Earl Schenck Miers), pub. 1957.
- "A Census-Based Count of the Civil War Dead," *Civil War History*, Vol. 57, No. 4 (December 2011), by J. David Hacker.

Chapter 30* – The Cost of the War in Financial Terms

By Joseph Stromberg of Georgia, S.I.S.H.

Introduction

You have just completed the chapter where the cost of the war is presented in terms of deaths and suffering by Federal and Confederate troops and sailors. Estimates of deaths and suffering by Confederate civilians were also presented. Now let us look at the cost of the war in financial terms. Here, you will learn that many men in the Northern states gained great wealth from the conflict, creating a class some called the "Robber Barons," and you learned that war-time financial loss in the land of the Republicans was rapidly recovered. But the South was devastated! Of course, on the financial books of people who owned slaves, the uncompensated and immediate loss of control over those persons looked like a huge financial loss – but not really. The Southern culture was beginning to arrive at the situation where maintenance of a slave family from birth to death was costing more than the alternative of hiring laborers by the day or by the season. So, let us just mention the book value of slaves prior to the WBTS, and move on to other areas of financial loss. The war against Confederate civilians in the last two years of the war produced huge financial loss. The loss to the economy from Confederate dead and wounded was great. The Republican's Political Reconstruction would intentionally produce further financial loss. You are fortunate to be reading this chapter at the hand of the learned Joe Stromberg. Be attentive as he tells this story.

History Relevant To Understanding the WBTS

Economies

In economic terms, the war of 1861-1861 pitted rising Northern industrial capitalism against an agrarian Southern economy resting on ownership of human labor (as of 1860, such property was the largest single capital investment in the United States). Those powerful Northern interests that political scientist Richard F. Bensel calls the Republican "developmental coalition" wanted to remove the South as an obstacle to their goals. Secession removed Southerners from (the U.S.) Congress, but separation was unacceptable to key Northern interests since it also removed Southern resources (land and labor) from potential Northern control. War was acceptable to key Northern leaders, especially if ordinary Northerners shouldered the costs, while they (leaders and entrepreneurs) escaped the hardships of battle.

Total War

Lincoln's theory of the Union (and of the war) implied total war. Treating secession as "rebellion," the Northern government felt entitled to wage war on the Southern people (John C. Calhoun predicted this in 1833). Rather than simply engaging Confederate armies, Northern forces directly assaulted the entire Southern social structure, to render support for Confederate armies impossible. (Northern practicality included preventing medical supplies from entering the South.)

Historian Edward Hagerman notes that "Sherman and Grant … knowingly accepted indirect civilian deaths from the intensified total war strategy as inevitable and just." These methods had the added advantage of inspiring terror. Southern morale was a target: hence the reckless bombardments at Charleston (shelled for 645 days) and Atlanta (with residential neighborhoods deliberately shelled). Criticized for his tactics in later Indian wars, Sheridan wrote defensively to Sherman in 1873: "Did we cease to throw shells into Vicksburg or Atlanta because women and children were there?"

Reckless Destruction

The move toward Total War began in mid-1862 with General Pope's campaign in Virginia. His army was to live off the country, "foraging" or stealing. He deported "disloyal" persons and burnt their houses. Lincoln took an active role in devising rules for this and later campaigns. In Virginia, Union operations made life between Blue Ridge and North Mountain "utterly untenable" (as historian James L. Sellers writes), burning barns and mills (and their contents), destroying or carrying off cattle and sheep, and clearing out a 92-mile corridor from Winchester to Staunton.

In Mississippi, Sherman looted and torched Jackson and Meridian. Farther west, A.J. Smith's bummers, on loan from General Sherman for the Red River campaign, marked their retreat by burning everything along their path. Wilson's "Raid" burned Tuscaloosa, Ala. (including university buildings) and much of Columbus, Ga. In Georgia and South Carolina, Sherman's forces used the same methods on a grander scale. Sherman estimated that his forces destroyed a hundred million dollars worth of property in Georgia, 80% of which was "simple waste and destruction." Shortly thereafter, Columbia, SC, was gutted.

Everywhere one sees the same pattern, which included massive deliberate destruction of livestock owned by Southern plain folk. Such was the Northern way of war, across this small time and space. According to Historian Alan Nevins (writing in 1962) it amounted to "general depredation" in 1862, "wanton destruction" in 1863, and "organized devastation" in 1864.

Plunder and Profit

For depriving the enemy of resources, confiscation worked as well as destruction and was very popular with its beneficiaries. Historian Ludwell Johnson describes the Northern government as conducting "a war of economic and political aggrandizement" – with profiteering and fraud "so pervasive that they seemed to be of the very essence" of the war. This "redeeming the South by stealing it" went forward under various legal doctrines. U.S. functionaries levied special taxes in captured territory and sold "abandoned" property to inside bidders. Hoping to grow cotton in conquered sections of Florida, using free (and cheap) labor, Boston textile manufacturer Edward Atkinson wrote in 1862 that if any former slave "refused to work, let him starve… still we must grow cotton."

Cotton was the item most demanded, whether confiscated, stolen, or obtained by trading with the enemy. (Lincoln personally issued special licenses for such trade.) Historian Clyde Wilson concludes that no more than ten percent of thirty million dollars worth of "legally" confiscated property ever reached the U.S. Treasury: "The rest was stolen by Republican appointees." Yet, Wilson adds, historians fully aware of such facts, still suggest that wartime and postwar corruption "mysteriously appeared after Lincoln's death, and somehow miss the obvious conclusion that it was implicit in the goals of the Lincoln war party."

Some Statistics

For the South as a whole, estimated wealth fell between 1861 and 1865 by about 40%, even without counting the value of slave property. Real estate values were down, as was livestock, 32 to 42%. As of 1870, farm tools were worth 55% of their 1860 values. Bank capital fell from sixty-one million dollars in 1860 to seventeen million in 1870. (See below.) More recently (1975), economic historians Claudia D. Goldin and Frank D. Lewis have estimated direct war costs in terms of expenditures, lost wages, etc., as $3,365,846 for the North and $3,285,900 for the South.

As reported in the previous chapter, the loss of lives in the Southern states was horrific. For many years the biggest item in the state budget of Mississippi was artificial limbs.

The New Economy

As historian Richard F. Kaufman puts it, the war brought about a "new industrial order ... composed largely of war profiteers and others who grew rich on government contracts ... and ... were able to influence the economic reconstruction." Many lasting capitalist fortunes arose from wartime contracts, e.g. those of J. P. Morgan, Philip Armour, Clement Studebaker, John Wanamaker, Cornelius Vanderbilt, the du Pont family, and Andrew Carnegie, to name some famous Robber Barons. The Republican Party's alliance of capitalists and farmers held together for a few decades, if only because ever-bigger pensions for Union veterans (America's first major welfare program) offset the costs of high tariffs and deflation to mid-western and western farmers. (A pension could come to four months' wages.)

War and Impoverishment

In 1937, Texas historian Walter Prescott Webb complained that railroads, which were built only in the North between 1860 and 1875, killed off Southern river traffic. Down toward the present, the North enjoyed major bounties: high tariffs, Union Army pensions (seven eights of which went to the North), Northern ownership of most industrial patents, and finally, the modern corporation as such, whose financial-capitalist "feudalism" was sustained by the U.S. Supreme Court's invention of corporate personhood in the 1880s (which in turn rested on the Fourteenth Amendment, a product of Political Reconstruction). Historian C. Vann Woodward added in 1951 that - ground down by tariffs and patents - the South had been reduced to a mere exporter of raw materials. Along with the famous freight-rate differential (lasting into the 1940s), these levers worked effectively to maintain the South as an economic colony of the North.

Another crucial piece of leverage involved banking and credit. Economic historian Gerald D. Jaynes notes that the capitalized value of human property had been central to the pre-war Southern credit. With emancipation, that credit system collapsed. Before Southerners could develop a substitute, U.S. national banking rules favorable to Northern interests "stifled recovery of the South's credit markets," as historian Jeffrey Hummel writes. Southerners' taxes helped to pay interest on the U.S. national debt (most of which went to Northerners) and to fund Union army pensions (29% of the Federal budget by

1875). On top of this northward net outflow, Southerners paid for state-level Confederate pensions and (for a while) interest on the debts accumulated by former Reconstruction state governments.

Historian Eugene D. Genovese commented in 1965: "Since abolition occurred under Northern guns... instead of under internal bourgeois auspices, the colonial bondage of the economy was preserved, but the South's political independence was lost." And Bensel has added: "The [American] developmental engine left the southern periphery to shoulder almost the entire cost of industrialization. ... The periphery was drained while the core prospered."

Summation

The War of 1861-1865 impoverished the South for long decades to come. Much of this damage resulted from plunder and reckless destruction which was not militarily necessary, even from the other side's point of view.

Suggestions for Class Discussion

Pursue the comparison between damage to the South in the 1860s and damage to various countries in World War One. Discuss what proportionate damages to the South would be like in terms of current population and other figures.

Recommended Reading

- **"Economic Incidence of the Civil War in the South,"** by James L. Sellers, *Mississippi Valley Historical Review*, 14 (September 1927), 179-191.
- **"Economic Cost of the American Civil War,"** by Claudia D. Golden and Frank D. Lewis, *Journal of Economic History*, 35 (June 1975), 299-326.
- **"The Plundering Generation: Uneasy Reflections on the Civil War,"** by Ludwell Johnson, *Continuity*, 9 (Fall 1984), 109-119.

Chapter 31 – The Cost of the War to the Northern States – They Also Lost Their State Rights

By Steve Litteral of Illinois, S.I.S.H.

Introduction

For those of you who already know a bit about "State Rights" and what is called the "Lost Cause," you might find it strange that we are presenting the "Loss of State Rights" as a loss suffered by the North. Why would the victorious Northern States damage themselves by loss of the State Rights that they had always enjoyed? Very good question. Keep that in mind as you read this chapter. In the long run, the loss of State Rights was equally destructive to the North as to the South. After the war and 10 years of Republican Political Reconstruction in the conquered states, and although the Democratic Party had once again become active, the people in every state found that they had lost the self-government that State Rights had afforded their grandfathers. It's as if the people in the North killed the big bad bear and then shot themselves in the foot. Here is the relevant history in the words of Steve Litteral.

Loss of Citizens' Rights on the Home Front

Before 1861, the Northern States had a long history of demonstrating to the Federal Government that they had the power to govern their own people. For example, the Hartford Convention was held in 1814 over concerns about the War of 1812 and encroachment of Federal power into the states. Delegates from five New England states attended the convention and discussed everything from secession from the Union to negotiating a separate peace with Britain. Only Andrew Jackson's victory at the Battle of New Orleans and the end of the war let the steam out of the New England secession movement.

During the prewar period, many, perhaps most, of the citizens of the Northern states accepted the right of a state to withdraw from the Union. This was not controversial before the war. (Illinois's state motto was "State Rights and Union.") At the start of the war, Republican editor Horace Greeley said that if Southern states wanted to leave the Union they should be allowed to go in peace. But when Lincoln claimed that secession was "rebellion," he assumed the right to imprison anyone who criticized his actions as guilty of being "disloyal" and treasonable. Eventually, thousands of people across the Northern states were imprisoned and hundreds of newspapers were forced out of business. Many newspapers were shut down, sometimes violently, by Union soldiers and Republican mobs across the Union for criticizing the Lincoln administration. Anti-Lincoln publications were also denied the use of the mails and telegraph.

In March 1863, Congress passed the Habeas Corpus Suspension Act which allowed the Federal government to arrest any U.S. citizen at the discretion of any army officer. Often arrests were for minor infractions: like criticizing Lincoln or the Republicans, whistling "Dixie," questioning the legality of the draft, or even, if you were a clergyman, refusing to pray for Lincoln. Often people were seized on the basis of anonymous accusations. Threats were made to arrest Chief Justice Taney of the Supreme Court and ex-President Pierce, though these were not carried out. In reality, Lincoln had been

doing this since 1861, but the Republicans passed the 1863 law to make it seem as if it was legal, because the Supreme Court and many State courts had ruled Lincoln's earlier action illegal. (Habeas corpus could constitutionally be suspended by Congress, not by the President.) For the first time the U.S. government was creating "political prisoners." Consider the experience of these victims. Soldiers knock down your door in the middle of the night and carry you away to a place in another State of which your family is not informed. You have no right to counsel, to confront accusers, or even to know what specific law you have violated. You will remain in a military prison until you take a forced "loyalty oath." Or you might be tried and punished by a court of army officers. This in the Northern States where the regular courts were open and no war was going on. Many thoughtful people realized that Northerners were being made victims of the government as well as the "rebels." These measures against civilians were even more harshly and comprehensively carried out in the Border States and occupied areas of the Confederacy than in the North.

Two Democratic governors replaced the Republican governors of 1861: Horatio Seymour in New York and Joel Parker in New Jersey. They attempted to challenge the legality of the Federal conscription laws and practices in the courts but were ignored. American citizens have ever since had no constitutional protection from military conscription at the order of the Federal Government.

Lincoln's harsh tactics did not sit well in his home state of Illinois. The unrest resulted in political victories by Democrats over the Republican Party. Democrats controlled the 1863 legislature in Illinois (13 to 12 in the Senate and 54 to 32 in the House of Representatives). There were many reasons why the Democrats were elected in Illinois – war weariness, army persecution of civilians, feeling that the Emancipation Proclamation had changed the purpose of the war from restoring the Union to overturning Southern society. Richard Yates, Governor of Illinois, was a staunch Republican. He was not interested in sharing power with the newly-elected Democrats. In an unprecedented act, Yates dissolved the two houses of the legislature on a technicality, disregarding the vote of the people and becoming a virtual dictator. The Republican governor of next-door Indiana acted even more arbitrarily and more brutally to critics. Lincoln had already set a dangerous precedent at the national level, and he became an example for governors to emulate at the state level. Citizens of the North were learning that their war on the Southern states had led to disregarding of the Constitution and robbing them of their basic freedoms on the home front.

Suppression of Labor

While Union soldiers were still conducting military occupation of the South after the war, many of the soldiers who returned home found out that labor conditions and public ethics had changed dramatically. Corruption stretched from the workplace to the White House (particularly during the Grant presidency, the most corrupt in U.S. history). There was a period of good wages during the war, but after the war and disbanding of the huge Union army, workers found themselves at a great disadvantage. Factory workers often endured horrible and dangerous conditions with long hours and low wages. Family living conditions in the vastly expanded cities were atrocious. By 1870, overcrowding and unsanitary living conditions for factory workers in New York caused the infant mortality rate to be 65% higher than it had been in 1810. Northern miners and steel workers were working in very dangerous conditions as well. Hundreds were killed in work place accidents every year. The men who had returned from the war found that a restored Union meant the rule of ruthless Republican industrialists, bankers, and crooked stock speculators.

A National Labor Union was formed in 1866 to fight for goals such as an eight-hour work day. In 1867 there was a general strike in Chicago to help enforce the new eight-hour workday law in Illinois. This strike ended peacefully, but many others ended in violence. In July 1877, Chicago workers supported a national railroad strike. At one point over 10,000 men, women, and children filled the streets in support of the strike. Soldiers and police were called out to disperse the workers. By the end of the day, 30 workers were killed and over 200 were wounded. The same government that forced people back into the Union at bayonet point was now suppressing labour organisations with bloody violence. Republican money men had fought the war against the South to guarantee their control and profits. They were not about to give up their advantages.

Immigration was used by the Federal Government to keep enlistment numbers high during the war. This same strategy was used by Northern industrialists to keep wages low after the war. Waves of European immigrants came to the United States during the 19th Century, and many of them ended up in the urban areas of the North as cheap factory labor. A Contract Labor Law passed during Lincoln's presidency meant that companies could bring gangs of European immigrants to the U.S., paying their way in exchange for a contract to work for so many years. Often this practice was abused by the companies by withholding wages from the immigrants, who were also used as strike breakers and to create division within working class communities. A good example: in Lowell, Massachusetts, the mill owners would bring in a new wave of immigrant workers about every 10 years to keep the unions out of the factories and the wages low. This was all done with the blessing of the Federal Government. The same war profiteers who earned a lot of money off of the war were now turning their backs on the returning veterans. The Union veterans had returned home to a country they did not recognize. Political Reconstruction was not only happening in the Southern states, but the federal and state governments were being run for the benefit of Republican corporations. Legislators were bought and paid for by corporations on a large scale. The North as well as the South was irrevocably changed by "saving the Union."

Other Changes

The same U.S. army officers who had burned Southern cities to the ground and were breaking strikes now unleashed their tactics against the Indians of the Great Plains and Rocky Mountains like the Apache and Sioux. For the first time in the long history of pioneer/Indian wars, the Federal Government pursued a policy of deliberate genocidal ruthlessness. And much of the Indian resistance was caused by the corruption of Republican Indian agents and contractors who cheated the Native Americans of what they had been promised. Native Americans who did not comply with Federal orders were labeled as 'rebellious,' just like Confederates. This gave the military free range to kill anyone who was not submissive to Federal power. If we want to find out why the military was so ruthless at this time, all we need to do is look at the leadership. William T. Sherman was Commanding General of the Army from 1869 to 1883. During that time he was in charge of the Indian Wars that were fought in the west. All of his generals were Union war veterans. Sherman was a ruthless commander who had no problem destroying American cities in the South, and his methods found their way to conflicts against Native Americans. It was Sherman who made the famous remark that the only good Indian was a dead one. And when Republicans would take over the Philippines after the Spanish-American War, they would compare the natives to rebellious Southerners and institute the same ruthless tactics against them.

The Republicans kept the Northern public in line in several ways. Their election campaigns "waved the bloody shirt," reminding people that they had saved the country from Southern evils, real and imagined. Pensions for Union soldiers and their dependents were a large item in the Federal budget for years. A Homestead Law allowed families to acquire western land on fairly easy terms. Much more and more valuable land was given away to railroad and mining corporations and none was available to African Americans, whose assigned role was to stay in the South and vote Republican. Among the consequences of the Homestead Act were over-production and falling prices, and over-cultivation of areas of insufficient rainfall that led to the terrible "Dust Bowl" of the 20th century. High tariffs were said to protect the jobs and wages of American workers, although this was questionable.

Summation

Although the war was mainly fought on Southern soil, the conflict forced radical changes on those living in the Northern states as well. Northern victory was a defeat for individual and State Rights throughout the country. It is a harsh reality, but America's founding documents have been dead letters since 1861.

Suggestions for Class Discussion

Imagine the kind of individual freedoms that people had in the United States before 1861. Do you think citizens were more or less free at that time in history? What would you think of the current American President if he halted the presses of your local newspaper because he disagreed with what they were writing?

Recommended Reading

- *North Against South: The American Iliad, 1848—1877*, by Ludwell H. Johnson, pub. 1993.

Chapter 32 – Political Reconstruction in Delaware, Maryland, West Virginia, Kentucky and Missouri.

By Joyce Bennett of Maryland, S. I. S. H.

Introduction

In the previous chapter you learned about the loss of State Rights during War and the Republican's Political Reconstruction of the conquered Confederate states. Also experiencing these events, but sooner and to a lesser degree, were the states that had not been allowed to secede and join the Confederacy: the subjugated Democrat-controlled states – the so-called "Border States" of West Virginia, Kentucky, Missouri, Delaware, and Maryland. This chapter presents the history of these states during the years of their Political Reconstruction. Joyce Bennett tells that story below.

History Relevant To Understanding the WBTS

During the secession crisis, people in the Upper South, while loving the old Union of the sovereign countries we call States, still reserved the right to board the "dissolution wagon." Just as meaningless reconstruction-era Republican victories at the polls in the Border Southern States do not constitute evidence of a prevailing love for Unconditional Unionism, neither do the alleged high numbers of men from these States who wore blue. Many were Northerners brought down to fill draft quotas and Irish and Germans imported to kill "the Dixies," the foreigners making up about 25 percent of Union forces. Still others were readily available bonded or free African conscripts or enlistees, a manpower pool denied the Federals in States yet unconquered.

The Republicans had to keep the Upper Borderland from seceding at all costs because of the region's natural resources, harbors, navigable waterways and industrial potential. And the Upper South was seen as a strategic buffer zone between the armies of the Confederacy and the North. Soon disabused of the notion that the Radical Republicans would behave Constitutionally – or allow them neutrality – the citizens of the Border Southern States were to grow increasingly rebellious under an unlawful Federal occupation. And the complete abandonment of the terms of the U.S. Constitution by the Republicans and President Abraham Lincoln was to foster widespread chaos and political complications in the region. The key to understanding the internecine contest of the 1860s and its consequences is knowing the truth about the Federal's Political Reconstruction of the Upper South. That story is faithfully told here.

West Virginia

For many of the tough, egalitarian frontiersmen west of Virginia's Blue Ridge Mountains, the War Between the States offered a long-awaited chance to separate from the "effete" eastern planters. But in spite of West Virginia's "loyalty," it was not to be spared military occupation. And it was not until 1872 that the State's onerous Reconstruction would end.

After Virginia seceded from the Union, an action that did not violate the U.S. Constitution, some of the citizens in the western counties, refusing to recognize the government in Richmond, helped to form an unlawful "Restored" Government in Wheeling. It was this illegal "Virginia" that allowed the separation of those western counties from the Old Dominion. But under the U.S. Constitution, only the parent State, in this case "legal" Virginia, whose capital was Richmond, had the power to approve the creation of a new State within its borders. While admitting the extra-legality of West Virginia's admission to the Union, President Lincoln called it a necessary measure to advance the "restoration of the National authority" over the States, an authority not found in the Constitution.

Significantly, it was under Northern occupation that West Virginia had been created and had been admitted to the Union, many West Virginians coping with Federal subjugation by embracing "neutrality," others just staying home on election day. The absurdly lopsided vote in favor of the secession of the western counties from Virginia (18,408 to 781) is suspect because of Federal disfranchisement of anti-secession voters. When they were finally out from under Republican rule, West Virginians immediately repealed and replaced a Radical reconstruction-era state constitution. They hoped to be a sovereign people again.

Missouri

Mainly Constitutional Unionists or outright secessionists, the people of Missouri early on professed a desire to "remain neutral" during the War Between the States. Removed by the illegitimate Republican-friendly State Provisional Government, Missouri Governor Claiborne Jackson promptly convened the legal Legislature which passed an ordinance of secession severing ties with the Union. This Missouri government-in-exile joined the Confederacy. Towards the end of the WBTS, iron-willed Missouri Radicals aided by "outsiders" were to rise to power through voter intimidation and other malfeasance and were to impose an even harsher form of Political Reconstruction.

Continuing to deny that Missouri was conquered territory, the Provisional Government, allegedly a stalwart of State Rights, frequently found itself at odds with Republican military commanders. And Provisional Governor Gamble walked a fine line between serving the Lincoln administration and his own people. Not finding military abuses entirely objectionable, Gamble even asked the Federals to "suppress" a newspaper critical of him.

Biding his time, President Lincoln hoped that Radical Republicanism would eventually tip the balance of power against the more conservative Unionism of the Provisional Government. He was not to be disappointed. The 1865 election of Radicals and their subsequent reign were to leave Missouri prostrate, bankrupt and broken But in the early 1870s, Southern Democrats regained power and home rule. The Radical state constitution was repealed and order was restored at last to Missouri.

Kentucky

Even the infamous William Tecumseh Sherman protested the abuses suffered by Kentuckians during Political Reconstruction. Given Kentucky's intricate politics at the time, it is only safe to say that her people desired a Constitutional Federal Government and opposed a forced Union. A sovereign convention, favored by Governor Beriah Magoffin and Southern Democrats, was feared by Northern-style Democrats and Constitutional Unionists because it might have led to separation from the Union and invasion from the nearby North. Many Kentuckians thought the Union could be saved by their example of neutrality, but neutrality was not an option for Kentucky.

The Kentucky Legislature accommodated itself somewhat to the Republican occupation army. But, revolting against military tyranny and the Federals' so-called public safety measures, sixty-five counties seceded from the State and joined the Confederacy. Their Provisional Government – the legality of which is debatable – declared that because a "majority of the Legislature of Kentucky" had cooperated with the Lincoln Administration's armies and abandoned neutrality, no allegiance was due this government. The Kentucky Ordinance of Secession further declared that the Federal Government had trampled on the "reserved powers" of the States.

But by 1867 deliverance was at hand. With the return of Democrats to power, Kentucky was liberated from the reign of the Republicans and their German and carpetbagger allies in Louisville. A once-more "reliable, rebel old Kentucky" was now to begin righting the wrongs committed by her Northern occupiers, a Republican not being elected governor until 1895. In 1917 Confederate supporters built at Jefferson Davis' birthplace at Fairview, Kentucky a 351-foot-high Davis Monument that resembles the 555-foot Washington Monument.

Delaware

In spite of an avowed loyalty, Delaware was eyed with suspicion by the Republicans who thought she had rebellion in her heart. Declaring martial law in this tiny Border Southern State, military commander General Schenck banned "seditious" language and harassed "evil-disposed persons." And 3,000 occupation Union troops engaged in voter intimidation and sundry misdeeds.

The Delaware Legislature protested the unjust arrests of citizens, but Republican Governor Cannon, elected by a slim majority in 1862, insisted that the Federal Government was omnipotent. Suspending the writ of habeas corpus, Cannon so enraged the Legislature they tried to impeach him. At the beginning of the WBTS, Delaware had held Union rallies and had dutifully supplied men to the Federal war effort, but by 1863 she was growing ever more hostile to her occupiers, even circumventing her Federal draft quota by appropriating to draftees money to pay for substitutes.

As a result of the usual Republican electoral intrigue, Lincoln in 1864 enjoyed a victory in Delaware, a State which had been won by the Southern secessionist John Breckinridge just four years earlier. Nevertheless, the Democrats managed to hold on to the Legislature and in 1870 elected a State Rights governor. Although in 1872 the much-reviled U.S. Grant won Delaware (along with other Southern States still under Political Reconstruction), by 1876 she was fully unreconstructed and solidly Southern Democrat again.

Maryland

Maryland's people were repulsed by what they considered Republican aggression. The first Southern blood was shed by Marylanders who were killed at the hands of Northern troops passing through Baltimore on 19 April 1861. In an attempt, in the words of U.S. Senator Henry Wilson, to "crush out her boundary lines," the North conquered Maryland in a matter of weeks. As Confederate President Jefferson Davis wrote in his memoirs, she was the first Southern State to fall to Federal forces.

Maryland Governor Thomas Hicks was the only Southern governor not elected as a Democrat – he was a Know Nothing. Quisling over his predicament, Hicks, realizing the advantage of siding with the Republicans, stopped protesting all together the occupation army's depredations against his increasingly restive and secession-minded constituents. Even in supposedly more Unionist Western Maryland, the Radicals found it necessary to control the ballot box. On 8 November 1861, Col. J. W. Geary, of the Twenty-eighth Pennsylvania Regiment, informed his superiors that, "owing to the presence of ... troops, everything progressed quietly," and he was "happy to report a Union victory in every place within [his] jurisdiction." Col. Geary also arrested "disloyal" political candidates.

In 1867 not only was the vote restored to pro-secessionists and returning Confederates, the illegal Reconstruction-era State constitution was replaced. Beginning with the 1868 election, the first free Presidential election since 1860 when she overwhelmingly rejected Lincoln and the Republicans, Maryland was at liberty once more to express her Southern Democrat sentiments.

Summary

Although the bloody sectional strife of the 1860s was rooted in the irreconcilable cultural differences between Northerners and Southerners as much as in old political quarrels, this chapter has examined only the latter. It was in the States located immediately below the Mason-Dixon Line that the Radical Republican-controlled Federal Government, declaring an extra-constitutional supremacy, began the Political Reconstruction of the South. Thus in the Upper Borderland, consolidation first triumphed over subsidiarity. The original Union of free and independent States was supplanted by a Union of States who would become over the next century and a half increasingly obedient to an ever more powerful central government.

Class Discussion

To what extent has the "Unionism" of the Border States been overestimated or overemphasized?

Recommended Reading

- *The Civil War and Readjustment in Kentucky*, by E. Merton Coulter, pub. 1966.
- *Turbulent Partnership Missouri and the Union 1861-1865*, William E. Parrish, pub. 1963.
- *History of Maryland from the Earliest Period to the Present Day: 1819-1880*, vol. 3, by J. Thomas Scharf, pub. 1879.

Chapter 33* – Political Reconstruction in the Defeated Southern States

By Egon Richard Tausch of Texas, S.I.S.H.

Introduction

It takes little imagination to recognize that the people of the conquered Confederate States would never vote for a Republican in their life time, nor would their children, not likely even their grandchildren. So how was the Republican Party to win elections in the conquered states? By Political Reconstruction! The idea was to deny the vote of people who had supported the Confederacy, which were the vast majority of the whites, and enable and organize the vote of people who had been slaves, which were the vast majority of the blacks. Then, to make the process run smoothly, send in Republican adventurers, called "Carpetbaggers," from the North to organize the blacks into a regimented political bloc and, at the same time, gather to themselves as much wealth as possible. Republican military governors and Federal troops would ensure Republicans remained in control. We should make clear that "Reconstruction" was a strictly political term. It had nothing to do with *rebuilding* the devastated South. Not at all.

The Radicals Take Over

Within two years after the war, the U.S. Congress curtailed a relatively peaceful period of Presidential Reconstruction and established military government over the defeated South. This was accomplished by marginalizing the new President, Andrew Johnson, whose powers were unconstitutionally assumed by the Radical Republicans in Congress. Unionist governors who were appointed by President Johnson for each of the ex-Confederate States right after the war were removed and the South was divided into military districts under martial law. The great Commonwealth of Virginia was now Military District No. 1, and the families of its great patriots deprived of American citizenship. The war had been fought by Lincoln on the theory that it was impossible for a State to secede, but now, the victory won, the rules were changed. The seceded States were not States but "conquered provinces," as Thaddeus Stevens, the leader of the Radical Congress, expressed it.

Although the welfare of African Americans was unimportant in Republican motives for waging war, the freedmen were easily made into a major weapon by the Radicals against the South during Political Reconstruction. Exclusionists, former Abolitionists, and Northern money men were united in this – though many Northern States still had laws against blacks voting or having any civil rights. The newly freed African-Americans were not only enfranchised but were manipulated by Federal military and civilian agents into voting as a bloc for Republicans. Voting was not by secret ballot, so it could be supervised. African-Americans were bribed with false promises of benefits and threatened if they failed to vote as told.

Thaddeus Stevens called for the confiscation of every Southern estate worth $10,000 or of a size of 200 acres, though this was not implemented except by confiscatory taxation. The South was desolate. Cities like Columbia, Charleston, and Atlanta, and countless small towns had been shelled or burned into rubble, with their schools, businesses, and churches. Farms had been devastated and lacked the means to start again.

"Carpetbaggers," Northern scavengers who were of low repute in their home communities, swarmed over the country to pick the bones of the impoverished South. They had all their worldly possessions in one carpetbag, a cheap form of luggage. In the early days of freedom, the loyalty which Southern African-Americans felt toward their white families and neighbors, which allowed the latter to leave their homes to fight, remained. White and black could have worked together as in other countries in the Western Hemisphere which had had slavery. But this was not the game intended by Washington. Soon anarchy reigned, except around Union Army camps. "Young colored women, gaily making their way to Northern Army camps for freedom were used for immoral purposes by the soldiers." There were violent conflicts here and there. The Radicals circulated tales of outrages by Southern vigilantes against blacks and carpetbaggers which were routinely exaggerated or deceptively misrepresented by Republican newspapers. Even some Union generals were furious over false reports.

Looting was widespread by the new Southern State officials, recently arrived from the North. Federal agents combed the South confiscating all cotton and whatever else they could find. One in Alabama stole $80,000 worth (almost a million in today's money) within a month. In Texas, thieves caught red-handed were freed from jail by Federal soldiers. A Secretary of the Treasury remarked that a few of the agents he sent south may have been honest, but none remained that way very long. Most of the proceeds went into carpetbagger pockets rather than to the Treasury. Even Indian Territory (now Oklahoma), home to the Confederate, Southern-assimilated "Five Civilized Tribes," was not spared the ravages of Political Reconstruction.

The Radicals Ride High

"The laws of War, not the Constitution," Stevens shouted in Congress. "Who pleads the Constitution? It is the advocates of the rebels." Stevens had no "higher law" to restrict him; he followed no creed and, according to those who knew him personally, "had been all his life a scoffer of sacred things." He declared himself an enemy of the Constitution until it was amended "to secure perpetual ascendency of the Party of the Union" – Republicans. The 13th Amendment, which freed the slaves, had been readily ratified by the Southern States, and most Southerners expressed satisfaction at the end of slavery. The 14th Amendment was a different matter. It was deliberately so written that it has been used ever since to nullify parts of the Constitution itself and State constitutions and laws. This has brought vast judicially ordered changes to American society that have not been voted by the people. The Republicans engaged in illegal procedures to get the 14th amendment through Congress. When presented to the States for ratification, Southern States and a number of Northern States rejected it. The problem became: how to count the Southern States for the purpose of ratifying the 13th Amendment, but not let them vote on ratification of the 14th? Simple: count them as States for the former, declare them back out of the Union ("conquered provinces" again) for the latter, then readmit them into the Union on the condition that they *first* ratified the 14th Amendment. Congress decreed it so, and the courts have not dared reopen the matter.

Congressional Republicans usurped the President's power as commander of the Army. The "Freedmen's Bureau" was given absolute judicial powers to be exercised at will, backed by an army of petty officials to scour the country. Radical Republicans purged Congress of non-Radicals on various invented charges so that all of President Johnson's vetoes of their measures could be easily overridden. "Every government is a despotism," said Stevens: "Better ours." Congress passed the *Tenure of Office Act*, which made it a crime for the President to fire any of his appointed officials. Secretary of War Stanton and his ally, General Grant, had been sabotaging Johnson in favor of the Radicals, so Johnson fired Stanton. The House impeached him for this "crime" and Republicans carried on a major press hate campaign against him. In the Senate trial, Johnson escaped being removed from office by one vote, but he would no longer bring restraint to Political Reconstruction.

The presidential race of 1868 was between Gen. Grant, Republican, and New York Governor Horatio Seymour, for the Democrats. After the most corrupt campaign in American history, Grant won, though losing four Northern States, because corrupt Republican regimes delivered him all but one Southern State. The Radicals now had their President, but were losing hearts and minds. Under Grant, the country's economy was run on governmental monopolies, embezzlement, and bribes. Members of Grant's family and Cabinet and his close friends were exposed for major corruption. Wall Street was considering moving to Washington, where the power and money was.

The defeated States have a Political Reconstruction histories that differ in details. The process and the timing of redeeming each from corrupt governments and military occupation varied. A combination of popular resistance and growing Northern disgust with blatant stealing and with State governments that had to be upheld by the army brought an end to Political Reconstruction everywhere after ten years. Unable to tell the whole complicated story, we will now consider how three States were "Redeemed" from Political Reconstruction.

In **Georgia**, the Radical Republican governor knew that his party would not win the election of 1870, so he demanded that Washington delay the election for two years. Senator Charles Sumner of Massachusetts, the Radical leader of the Senate, fought for this unconstitutional request, but lost by a few votes. Georgian Benjamin H. Hill addressed the Reconstruction Legislature, attended by Union officers, the Freedmen's Bureau, and Radical politicians. Hill had readily taken the Oath of Loyalty to the Union after the War, and the Republicans thought he was one of them. Until his speech. He lashed out at the "unholy work" of Reconstruction:

Go on confiscating; arrest without warrant or probable cause; destroy habeas corpus; deny trial by jury; abrogate State Governments. . . On, on with your work of ruin, ye hell-born rioters in sacred things. . . You are but cowards and knaves." To the freedmen he said, "They tell you they are your friends – it is false. They tell you they set you free – it is false. . . They came down here to seek to use you to further their own base purposes. . . Improve yourselves; learn to read and write; be industrious; lay up your means; acquire homes, live in peace with your neighbors.

Hill's denunciation of Political Reconstruction was published throughout the civilized world: "[T]he Military Bill leads to the ultimate but complete change of all American government from the principle of consent to the rule of force and to a war of races. . . All the guarantees of liberty wrung through the centuries from the hands of despotism are abrogated and withdrawn from ten million people of all colors, sexes, and classes. . . A conquered people are [rightfully] subject to the terms of the conquest, made known and demanded before, or at the time of the conquest. . . [But] every demand in the Military Bill originated after the war; not one of them was demanded during the war or made a condition of surrender. . . They are rushing all sections and all races into wild chaotic anarchy." Hill's protest was "discussed in the streets of London and the boulevards of Paris." The London *Telegraph* described Reconstruction thus: the United States "may remain a republic in name, but [half] of the people are subjects, not citizens." Georgia was lost to Political Reconstruction.

In **Louisiana**, stealing from the people by State officials reached massive proportions. In response conservatives elected a governor and a legislative majority. The defeated Radical Republican, William Kellog, wired President Grant that their Party was in danger. Grant sent troops to overrule the election. The legitimately elected government and the Republican forces confronted each other in the streets of New Orleans. The Republican police, backed by artillery, broke within ten minutes. Grant sent more troops. Then General Sheridan arrived. He demanded that Grant declare all Louisianans "banditti" – outlaws – so he could wage total war against them. Even the Northern Radical *Nation* magazine called Sheridan's demand "The most outrageous subversion of parliamentary government by military force ever attempted in this country." The troops did not leave until 1877.

In **South Carolina**, the Radical Governor complained to Congress that Political Reconstruction could not be eased. "[T]here are five years more of good stealing in South Carolina," he said. The Republican Legislature tended to stay in session, partying until 4:00 A.M. daily and ordering in cases of whiskey, barrels of wine, and "Westphalia hams, bacon, cheese, smoked beef, buffalo tongue, nuts, lemons, oranges, cherries, peaches," and the same for the houses of their mistresses. As State Senator C. P. Leslie said, "The State has no right to be a State unless she can afford to take care of her statesmen." The drafted "Negro Militia" were often drilling, with fixed bayonets, intimidating citizens of both races and forcing them off the streets. This militia had 7,000 new Winchester repeating rifles. The Governor imported a gang of gunmen from New York whose orders were "to defend the Governor and kill his enemies." When all this did not satisfy him, the Governor called on President Grant for troops, which Grant supplied.

The redemption of South Carolina was led by planter and former Confederate Gen. Wade Hampton. As described by the historian Claude G. Bowers, Hampton "was symbolical of the finest flowering of pre-War Southern chivalry and aristocracy. Patrician by birth, instinct, training, his manner was democratic." His prewar speech in the SC Senate against reopening slave importations had been described by the Abolitionist Horace Greeley as "a masterpiece of logic, directed by the noblest of sentiments of the Christian and Patriot." During the war, Hampton's genius for command, his quiet poise and daring, had endeared him to Lee, to his men, and to his people. "In one engagement he had seen one son fall; and, sending another son to his aid, had seen him fall, too, and had ridden back to kiss the dying youth and whisper in his ear – then back to the fight and to sleep on the ground that night in the rain." The close of war found his fortune and home gone, but no word of bitterness escaped him. Urging conciliation and peace, abstaining from politics, he faced hard times with courage, and with his former slaves, who clung to him, turned again to farming.

In 1876 Hampton was nominated for Governor of South Carolina by the Democrats. The Republican candidate was assured that "President Grant will bring the strong arm of the United States Government to support and keep the Republican Party in power." Black voters were in the majority, but many of them were tiring of the game, and many admired Hampton. "Negro Democratic Clubs" were quickly formed all over the State. Groups of Hampton's Red Shirts formed human shields to protect conservative blacks. (Forbidden to have a militia, South Carolinians formed clubs, wearing traditional red hunting shirts.) Hampton's Red Shirts faced down Radical gangs but did not open fire. They let it be known everywhere that they would harm no African-Americans, but if there were any bloodshed, they would "kill every white Radical in the country." The Radicals did not mind a slaughter of blacks which would cause Grant to send an army, but they were unwilling to risk their own lives.

Hampton addressed countless meetings. He insisted: "The only way to bring prosperity in this State is to bring the two races in friendly relations together." The Radicals declared Martial Law and called for Federal troops, but Hampton wired the Army to send troops to protect black Democrats. News of all this got into the Northern papers, hurting the Radicals. Hampton was elected despite massive Republican voter and vote-counting fraud. Even Union soldiers, disgusted with the officials they were upholding, voted for Hampton. Washington had no excuse to intervene, and a huge parade of both races marched and rode down the streets, through tumultuous throngs, flags, and bunting, led by former Generals Hampton and John B. Gordon of Georgia. Republicans began boarding northbound trains with the loot they could get away with.

The Election of 1876

In 1876 the presidential election was between Rutherford B. Hayes, Republican, of Ohio, and Samuel J. Tilden of New York, Democrat. Republicans knew they had to "wave the Bloody Shirt" – trumpet Northern casualties during the War – to keep the Northern vote, so they went all-out in their speeches, hoping voters would forget their corruption. But they also needed the electoral votes of the three Southern States that still had carpetbagger governments upheld by the army – South Carolina, Louisiana, and Florida. In the presidential election, Tilden, the Democrat, received a majority of the popular vote nationally but was one short of a majority in the Electoral College. South Carolina, Florida, and Louisiana sent in two conflicting sets of election returns, one from the governments still run by Radicals and one from the legitimately elected redeemer governments. After a great deal of wheeling and dealing, Democrats allowed the Republicans to put the cheating votes through Congress and Hayes was elected, on the promise that he would remove the last Federal

troops. Anyway, by now the South was too poor to loot much more.

Washington was still run by competing gangs of rent-seeking businessmen and greedy politicians enjoying centralized power – the true legacy of Political Reconstruction. The Republicans were assured repeated victories at the polls until they ran out of Northern war-heroes (Grant, Hayes, Garfield, McKinley) to run. With one exception: President Grover Cleveland, Democrat, who served from 1885-89 and 1893-97, and was an honest man. Although he could not *reverse* the centralization of American government, he could refuse to increase it. It has been said that if the Constitution had been a huge mediaeval castle destroyed to ground level, Cleveland rebuilt it to a five-foot retainer wall, on the original plans.

After Cleveland, the Republicans returned to power. But the new Progressive Party which also had no interest in Constitutional rule, began taking votes from both major parties. Naturally, both parties decided to co-opt it and adopt its platforms. Although originally from the Midwest, the Progressives did institute segregation in the South attempting to enlist poor whites there, and urged contraception and abortion on African-Americans to "improve the National race."

But the Republican Party regained domination of the North, and the Democrats the South. It would be about a hundred years after Reconstruction before the former Confederate States voted Republican in a presidential election, and then only after the Democratic Party had turned even more Radical than the Republicans had been. We show the long-lasting effects, State by State: Virginia did not vote Republican for 100 years after 1870; Tennessee for 90 of 100 years after 1871; Georgia for 131 years after 1872; Arkansas for 93 years after 1874; Alabama for 113 years after 1874; Texas for 105 years after 1874; Mississippi for 116 years after 1876; North Carolina for 92 of 96 years after 1877; Florida for 102 of 110 years after 1877; Louisiana for 103 years after 1877; and South Carolina for 99 years after 1877. The longest-lasting effect of Political Reconstruction was the damage to race relations, which are still strained because of the animosities and mistrust raised by it. Other countries which had more extensive African-American slavery than America do not have these tensions. And, of course, Political Reconstruction did permanent damage to the U.S. Constitution.

Suggestions for Class Discussion

Lincoln had tentatively outlined a less destructive and vindictive Reconstruction policy than was adopted, and Andrew Johnson tried to carry out Lincoln's policies, although he lacked Lincoln's political standing and will. How might American history have been different if Johnson had not been overruled?

Recommended Reading

- *The Story of Reconstruction* by Robert Selph Henry, pub. 1938.
- *The South During Reconstruction*, by E. Merton Coulter, pub. 1947.
- *North Against South: The American Iliad, 1848—1877* by Ludwell H. Johnson, pub. 1963.

Chapter 34 – How Political Reconstruction Affected the Lives of African American People and Native American People.

By Gail Jarvis of Georgia, S. I. S. H.

Introduction

For many of you, this will be the most important chapter in this booklet, for here we again present the story of bonded African Americans – the story of their being emancipated, made immediately independent, and directed to make a living for themselves and their families. A very important event in American history, this story needs to be truthfully presented and we accept that mission. The lives of the African American people were difficult in that era. They were forced to immediately make their own way in what was often a devastated and bankrupt land and to be simply used for political purposes by not-so-caring Carpetbaggers. Also, in what is now Oklahoma, Native Americans would suffer the loss of their land. We hope we have truthfully given balance to this delicate subject. The heroes are the African Americans and Native Americans who endured and raised families in spite of imposed hardships. We now proceed with the story in the words of Society author Gail Jarvis.

Relevant History

When the War Between the States ended, Northerners generally felt that the Federal Government should concentrate its efforts on stabilizing economic conditions rather than attempting a realignment of the South's social structure. Although the North supported the 13th Amendment that outlawed slavery, there were fears that there would be a massive inflow of freed slaves into the region, upsetting the social structure as well as the economy. Many states in the North had vagrancy laws to restrict the movement of blacks, as well as exclusion laws, which forbade blacks from migrating there. Ohio enacted laws to "regulate blacks and mulatto persons." Similar laws were passed in Illinois, Indiana, and other states in the region. Essentially, these laws created separate facilities for blacks – blacks were prevented from voting, serving on juries, holding public office, or owning property.

Unfortunately, neither fixing the economy nor ending slavery was uppermost in the minds of congressional Republicans. Their essential interest, which could not be publicly stated, was the exploitation of the chaotic conditions created by the war in order to establish a power base for themselves. In the defeated Confederate states, they saw an opportunity to create the apparatus necessary to accomplish their goal. This involved assembling a tremendous voting bloc that would cast ballots in accordance with Republican wishes. By disallowing the vote to white Southerners, and registering vast numbers of freed slaves, they felt that an accommodating voting bloc could be created. The numbers looked convincing. For example, South Carolina alone had roughly 415,000 Negroes to only 290,000 whites.

The Freedmen's Bureau, created to assist freed slaves in the South, never lived up to its expectations. Also, no one could predict how much it would cost the government, or how long its services would be needed, as its responsibilities were not clearly defined. The Freedmen's Bureau did produce some benefits for the slaves; primarily assisting with food, housing, and medical needs, but its purpose was gradually altered. Republicans converted it to a device to promote Republican causes. So, when its one year authorization ended, the Republicans, over President Johnson's veto, extended the Bureau's life.

Although public schools, for both whites and blacks, rarely existed in the antebellum South, some slaves had been educated in various degrees by ministers and family members of plantation owners. Some slave children were taught to read by their white childhood companions – and even during the war years, members of Northern benevolent societies established schools for blacks in the South – the most famous being the Penn Center on South Carolina's St. Helena Island. The Freedmen's Bureau did help build schools and furnish textbooks, but it did not provide teachers. Students were instructed by local white and black volunteers.

The Freedmen's Bureau gradually became more of a political machine than a charitable agency. Staff members recruited freed slaves into the Loyal League, originally created for persons loyal to and supportive of the Union, which now meant supporting the Republican Party. Freed slaves were told that by registering and voting the Republican ticket, they could prevent their former Democratic masters from re-enslaving them. They were also led to believe that land would be taken from their former owners and redistributed to them. Its Propagandizing of slaves became more vicious – vilifying their former owners, the South, and the Democratic Party.

Many freed slaves did not understand what registering to vote meant. Staff told them that "registration" would be very "beneficial," so many believed it involved the distribution of food, clothing or other items; that it would lead to grants of land forcibly taken from Southern planters. Most had heard the story that each slave would receive "forty acres and a mule." Many slaves were awarded so-called "abandoned" land, and an immense area along the Southern coast was confiscated and set aside for homesteading by slaves. But outright confiscation without compensation is prohibited by the Constitution and President Johnson's Attorney-General formally prohibited outright confiscation.

Northerners who began migrating to the South were called "Carpetbaggers," implying that all they owned could be carried in a carpetbag. They were soon taking advantage of the unstable conditions, not only by exploiting white citizens, but also freed slaves. One swindle involved a variation of the "forty acres and a mule" story. Portraying themselves as government representatives, swindlers sold red and blue pegs to slaves, claiming that they were official government pegs, and could be used to legally mark off the land grant each wanted to get upon distribution. Each slave had to purchase numerous pegs to demarcate the land he wanted.

The South Carolina Freedmen's Bureau decreed that marriages conducted while persons were held as slaves were not legally binding. So, these couples had to pay substantial fees in order to remarry. One unscrupulous minister, a former pastor of a Massachusetts Methodist church who had relocated to the South during Reconstruction, amassed quite a sum of money by performing re-marriage ceremonies for previously wedded slave couples.

In South Carolina, a state militia was created, comprised primarily of black Loyal League members. This state militia was allegedly needed to protect blacks from intimidation by whites, but antagonistic acts against blacks were only sporadic until after the militia began menacing white communities. In one legislative session, roughly $375,000 was spent to staff and provide rifles to the state militia ($7,500,000 in today's money). This organization gradually became more aggressive, holding secret meetings at night, parading through unprotected neighborhoods, firing weapons, chanting antagonistic slogans, and otherwise harassing already frightened households. There were reports of arson and even murder.

In response, former South Carolina Confederates established their own clandestine organizations patterned on other secret societies throughout the South. The most notorious of these secret societies was the Ku Klux Klan. The South Carolina Klan lasted only three years, until the election of Democrat Wade Hampton to the office of Governor. In those years it sought to balance the impact of the Loyal League and the state militia. At times the Klan became overly aggressive, engaging in unacceptable behaviors as vicious as those perpetrated by the state militia. When no longer needed the Klan disbanded.

The Indian tribes that fought on the side of the Confederacy also felt the ill effects of Political Reconstruction. Those five Indian nations: Cherokee, Choctaw, Creek, Chickasaw, and Seminole, were never given full citizenship rights, but they lost even the marginal rights that former treaties conferred on them when the Federal Government resettled them in what became known as "Indian Territory." For aiding the Confederate war effort, these tribes had to agree to a treaty of peace with the Union, and give up land as war reparations (The government actually wanted to relocate all unwanted indigenous people in the Indian Territory). The tribes were also required to agree to a future forfeiture of land that would become "rights-of-way" for railroads. They had to emancipate any slaves they owned, and incorporate them into their tribes or otherwise make provisions for them.

The Federal Government felt it could consolidate all the tribes into just one, but that was just another of the unrealistic Political Reconstruction ploys. Each of the Indian nations negotiated separately with the government's representatives, but a Choctaw phrase was suggested for the Reconstructed territory: *Okla Humma*, translated as *Red People*.

We also wonder why, during and immediately after Political Reconstruction, the Northeast and Midwest gave jobs primarily to European immigrants from economically depressed countries, while ignoring the desperate employment needs of recently freed slaves in Southern states. Former slaves should have been as able as European immigrants to fill the kinds of jobs available at mills, factories, railroads, and coal mines. While promising them free land in the South, no Republican considered allowing them to settle the free land in the West that was being massively given away to immigrants and corporations.

Even while Political Reconstruction was occurring in the Southern states, the Statue of Liberty was being built to stand in New York harbor to welcome struggling European immigrants. At its unveiling, a few years after Reconstruction ended, a poem, which would later adorn its base, was read. It contained these words: "Give me your tired, your poor, your huddled masses yearning to be free. . . Send these, the homeless, the tempest-tost to me." These descriptive words could easily have depicted freed slaves. But no such enthusiastic invitation was extended to former Southern slaves, who were closer at hand, and certainly as destitute and "tempest-tossed" as indigent Europeans. Many of the freed slaves emigrating to the North, hoping to find work, were soon disillusioned.

The Freedmen's Bureau led slaves to believe that simply being independent would bring about their economic salvation. If the transformation from slavery to independence had been accomplished gradually, giving time for survival skills to be acquired, it might have brought economic redemption. Indeed, in the years before Reconstruction, over 250,000 Southern slaves had earned their freedom, and become independent in this manner; now supporting themselves in such occupations as carpenters, tailors, seamstresses, shoemakers, butchers, and barbers. But immediate freedom without any means of livelihood was disastrous. Ironically, the only economic ventures that had long-lasting benefits for the slaves were renewed working relationships with former owners.

Slaves and former owners made use of the ancient farming relationship of working the land on shares – mentioned in both the Talmud and the Bible. This latest version of "sharecropping" allowed freed slaves to work without overseers or drivers. Tillable land, farm implements, seeds, housing, food, and other basic necessities were provided to erstwhile slaves in return for their labor. After crop expenses and family maintenance were satisfied, the income remaining was allocated between farm owners and laborers according to contractual provisions.

"Tenant farming" was also a viable alternative for many black and white farmers. Unfortunately, the War and Political Reconstruction had decimated the finances of both groups, so they had to contract costly crop-liens with local merchants, who, in turn were financed by Northern creditors. Although paying off crop-liens seriously reduced the profitability of this venture, it sustained struggling farmers for many years.

Summary

Looking back on the Political Reconstruction debacle, we wonder why slavery in the South wasn't eliminated in stages similar to its gradual phasing-out in the North. Although the immediate removal of slave labor certainly punished prominent Southerners for their war efforts, it left the slaves without any means of supporting themselves. Removal of whites from government positions and replacing them with carpetbaggers, scalawags and blacks was also based on vindictiveness, and it severely strained the relationship between the races. This was certainly a contributing factor for the enactment of Southern "black codes," which were patterned on black codes in Northern states.

Suggestions for Class Discussion

In what ways did Republican Reconstruction policies fail to benefit African Americans in the South?

Recommended Readings

- ***Reconstruction in South Carolina, 1863-1877***, by John S. Reynolds, pub. 1905.

Chapter 35 – How Political Reconstruction Affected the Lives of the White Southern People.

By Gail Jarvis of Georgia, S. I. S. H.

Introduction

Here we present another follow-up to Chapter 33, "Political Reconstruction in the Defeated Southern States." Because Republican Political Reconstruction was a complex process and because the history differed in each of the 11 conquered Confederate States, we authors of *Understanding the War Between the States* – in presenting the impact on the personal lives of the white people – have chosen to do so primarily in one state, South Carolina – the first to secede and the last to regain home rule. Also glimpses of the overall picture are provided. Gail Jarvis presents the history.

Relevant History

War obviously engenders hostile feelings, and the winning side often feels that there should be some kind of retribution against the losing side. But warring factions are restrained by international protocols that prescribe the rights and treatment of both combatants and non-combatants. Although such protocols, as well as unwritten humanitarian principles, were in existence when the War Between the States ended, they were not observed.

"Unconditional surrender" was the demand Union forces made of the defeated Confederacy, and almost a century later, as World War II ended, Allied powers would make the same demand of Japan. Note the contrast between the two eras. The Supreme Commander for the Allied Powers, General MacArthur, realized that the traditional Japanese culture should not be radically altered, nor should Emperor Hirohito be deposed, even though he had sanctioned Japan's war effort and the surprise attack on Pearl Harbor. Japanese military leaders suspected of serious war crimes were independently tried by an international military tribunal, presided over by judges from various nations. But those not accused of serious war crimes were allowed to resume their civilian roles. The occupying Allied forces left most of Japan's social structure intact, and worked in conjunction with the Emperor, albeit restricting his authority. The Allies assisted the Japanese in recovery from wartime desolation, and provided supplies and materials for the rebuilding of their infrastructure, as well as providing food for the starving citizens. Because they approached their reconstruction efforts without ulterior motives or vindictiveness, the Allied powers were able to withdraw in a few years, leaving behind an island nation well on its way to normalcy.

A radically different occupation and reconstruction occurred in the defeated Southern states. The Confederacy never officially surrendered; instead, individual Confederate armies surrendered in stages, with some simply disbanding. These piecemeal surrenders began in early 1865 and continued throughout the year. Finally, in August 1866, President Johnson issued a formal declaration that the war was over (Proclamation 157). Following the reunification plan proposed by President Lincoln, Johnson sought an expeditious reunification of North and South, basically requiring that Southern states repeal secession ordinances, abolish slavery, and take an oath to support the U.S. Constitution.

President Johnson dispatched Union General Ulysses Grant to the conquered states in order to assess the prevailing mood of Southerners. Although Grant's report to the president stressed the demoralization of their white citizens, it said: "I am satisfied that the mass of the thinking men of the South accept the present situation of affairs in good faith." In conclusion, the report said: "My observation leads me to the conclusion that the citizens of the Southern states are anxious to return to self-government within the Union as soon as possible."

In March 1865, Federals established a Freedmen's Bureau, supposedly to help former slaves. Although created with good intentions, the Freedmen's Bureau soon became corrupted. The Bureau was authorized for one year, but, over President Johnson's veto, Republicans extended its existence because it served their political purposes.

In December of 1865, Congress passed the 13th Amendment to the U.S. Constitution to outlaw slavery. This amendment, coupled with the fact that both Northerners and Southerners eagerly sought reunification, should have signaled the softening of sectional enmity, and the return to peacetime relations. But Republicans gained a lopsided advantage over Democrats in the congressional elections of 1866, a newly-acquired dominance that emboldened them to seek a permanent power base. Denying that the war was fought to preserve the Union, congressional Republicans decreed that Southern states were *not* states, but "conquered provinces." Consequently, they replaced the lenient readmission policies of Lincoln and Johnson with draconian Political Reconstruction measures, including the imposition of military rule.

Congressional Republicans were able to inveigle another constitutional amendment codifying the slavery issue. This amendment, the 14th, is often considered our most controversial constitutional amendment. It granted basic civil rights and protections to all citizens, excluding Indians. But while the amendment granted freed slaves the right to vote and hold office, it took those rights away from former white Confederates. Also, the amendment validated the North's war debt, while the South's war debt was repudiated. As former white Confederates were a substantial segment of the South's population, they were reluctant to endorse an amendment that essentially denied them any voice in their government. In a typical maneuver, Congressional Republicans made the endorsement of the 14th Amendment a *requirement* for readmission to the Union.

Many legal scholars maintain that the 14th Amendment was not legally ratified, but adopted in a way that violated the Constitution, and that several other aspects of Political Reconstruction were likewise unconstitutional. At the 1868 Democratic convention in New York, the platform declared that the Reconstruction Acts authorizing military control of the South were unconstitutional. The Republican platform stated the opposite opinion and argued that Congress should decide who had voting rights in conquered states, whereas Northern states should decide for themselves.

In its 1866 *ex parte* Milligan decision, the Supreme Court held that suspending *habeus corpus* rights and placing civilians under military control was unconstitutional, as long as civilian governments and courts existed. With that precedent, William McCardle, a Mississippi newspaper editor, appealed his arrest by occupying military forces (McCardle's offense was publishing articles critical of Political Reconstruction). Although the infrastructure and other parts of Southern states had suffered extensive war damage, the states still had functioning civilian governments and courts. Nonetheless, the Republican-controlled Congress used oblique and questionable legal justifications to prevent the Supreme Court from ruling on this case, so McCardle remained under military arrest.

Many Republicans personally profited from the scandals that plagued the Grant administration, and, with the ratification of the 14th Amendment, many felt all hindrances to their power grab were removed. But in the 1874 congressional elections many were voted out of office, somewhat restoring balance and much needed integrity. Although the reign of these dissembling Republicans lasted only eight years, the damage they inflicted on Southern states took almost seven decades to repair.

Many former members of the Union army remained in the South after the war, and became part of the Republican leadership during Political Reconstruction. But Republicans with good intentions, to the extent they existed, were eventually subverted by the more corrupt officials. Other Northerners began relocating to the South, and were referred to as "Carpetbaggers." Many of these perhaps arrived with good intentions, but soon succumbed to the temptations of personal enrichment so easily obtainable in the loosely structured region. Unfortunately, many locals, called "Scalawags", were eventually drawn into the relatively effortless plundering.

As Southern states qualified for readmission to the Union, military rule was withdrawn. But the Radical Republicans who controlled the governments were determined to maintain their control. They left nothing to chance, especially elections. The ballots of Southern whites that did manage to vote were screened by the "Returning Board," made up of a few highly placed Republican officials who reviewed ballots to determine if they had been "properly" cast, and therefore allowable. Of course, when the Returning Board completed its review, the election results nearly always favored the Republicans.

The Freedmen's Bureau in South Carolina, recruited massive numbers of freed slaves to join the Loyal League, and become loyal supporters of the Union, i.e. the Republican Party. After joining the Loyal League, blacks were immediately registered to vote, and the Bureau used fear tactics to secure their votes for Republicans. Loyal League members were also an essential part of the statewide militia. The justification for the militia was the claim that black voters needed to be protected from "intimidation" from whites during elections. Actually, the militia was heavily involved in disrupting Democratic Party meetings, and intimidating Democratic voters, prompting one historian to claim ". . . election outcomes depended as much upon the balance of armed force as upon the distribution of political popularity."

Toward the end of 1872, South Carolina was visited by the Abolitionist/Republican James S. Pike; a distinguished writer and statesman from Maine. In his book *The Prostrate State*, Pike addresses the previous seven years of Reconstruction in South Carolina. The following comments from his book will help put the degeneracy of the Reconstruction Era in perspective. "The experience of South Carolina during and since the war is one of the most tragic episodes in history. . . The rule in South Carolina should not be dignified with the

name of government. . . They rob the poor and the rich alike, by law. They confiscate your estate by law."

Members of South Carolina's legislature were bribed into authorizing the issuance of questionable bonds to finance railroad lines in the state. Dishonest officials enriched themselves by deviously obtaining immense stock holdings in the railroad company. An investigating committee uncovered one case of fraudulently issued bonds exceeding six million dollars. ($100 at that time would equal roughly $2,000 today.)

A land commission that claimed to be purchasing homes for indigent African Americans, illegally inflated prices of land and structures, with the excess payments going to the commissioners themselves. Much of the land was unsuitable for either home-building or agriculture, and few if any homes were provided to indigent African Americans. The state lost roughly $600,000 on this swindle. In the 1871-72 legislative session, $300,000 was appropriated for free schools primarily for African Americans. Sadly, these state funds were largely squandered or pilfered by dissolute officials, with little or no benefit for school children.

The personal bills of members of the legislature were falsely classified as "state supplies," and paid for by the state – luxury items such as clothing, gold watches, fine horses, diamond pins, imported wines, liquor, and cigars. In one legislative session alone, the bill for these "supplies" was $350,000. Crafty officials also created a sham printing company, and obtained the contract for the state's printing requirements. Most printing was done by other organizations with the dummy company simply issuing grossly-inflated billings to the state. The phony company also submitted billings for printing never done – investigators found a single printing invoice for $98,000.

The magnitude of the corruption in South Carolina during Political Reconstruction can never be determined with any degree of accuracy, but what is known indicates an enormity of theft and plundering almost beyond belief. The cost of projects to repair the infrastructure was inflated to include bribes and kickbacks and, often, any repairs that were done were substandard. Property taxes continued to rise until many landowners, unable to pay, suffered seizure of their property. The Political Reconstruction years brought South Carolina's government and its citizens close to bankruptcy.

Conclusion

Not only did Political Reconstruction fail to physically "reconstruct" the devastated Southern states, it also put white families in dire financial straits, blacks, too. The War, Political Reconstruction, and government policies in the following decades essentially reduced the Southern states to colonial bondage; a condition that lasted well into the 1940s.

Suggestions for Class Discussion

Compare the Political and Economic Reconstruction of Germany, Italy and Japan following WW II to the mere Political Reconstruction of the conquered Confederate States.

Recommended Readings

- *The Story of Reconstruction*, by Robert S. Henry, pub. 1938.
- *The South During Reconstruction, 1865-1877*, by E. Merton Coulter, pub. 1947.

Chapter 36* – "Recapping the Big Puzzle:" Simply Understanding Why the War Between the States was Not "About" Slavery.

By Paul C. Graham of S. C., S. I. S. H.

Introduction

By now, we, the sixteen authors of *Understanding the War Between the States*, have surely presented sufficient history to justify the conclusion in your mind that the WBTS was not "about" slavery. But let us look at this again as a special study. In considering the posed statement, a focus on the operative word "about" is merited. In the English language, when a man declares that "so-and-so" was "about" "such and such" he is saying that his "such and such" was the cause of the "so and so," not just some related event we might call a side-line issue. If Joe stabs John with a butcher knife and kills him, are we talking about murder or improper use of the kitchen butcher knife? Properly framing a question is so essential to the understanding of the issue that the question presumes to concern. So, the question concerning the role slavery played in the WBTS must be asked this way: "Did the North invade the South to emancipate its slaves?" With that introduction and lesson, and the importance on properly framing one's question, author Paul C. Graham proceeds to address the subject of this chapter. As you read his words be sure to distinguish between the passions for Exclusionism, versus Abolitionism, versus Deportationism.

Relevant History

In today's accepted historical narrative, there is only one acceptable answer to the questions concerning the cause and/or meaning of the WBTS, namely, that it was "about slavery." This position, more than any other, makes the task of articulating the Southern position difficult, if not impossible, for those who have not carefully studied the historical record. Most often the claim that the war was "about slavery" is tied to the question of why the South seceded. Even if, however, it could be shown that the South seceded over the issue of slavery, it does not follow that this caused the *war* or that this was the reason the two sides engaged in mortal combat. There is a fundamental difference between why one political body may separate from another and why an armed conflict would ensue. Both must be considered if the claim that the war was "about" slavery is construed to be even a theory worth consideration.

Secession and Slavery – Let us begin by looking at Southern secession, especially as it relates to slavery. Before commencing, however, it is important to understand that "The South" did not secede from the Union, but rather, *individual* Southern states did. The causes for the secession of these individual Southern states did not occur simultaneously or for the exact same reasons. During the first wave of secession, beginning with South Carolina on December 20, 1860, many of the Deep South states were forthright in stating that their actions were, at least in part, motivated by the perceived threat to the institution of slavery. Other "slave states," particularly those of the upper regions of the South, remained in the union until Abraham Lincoln called for 75,000 state militia to reinforce the suppression of the "rebellion" following the incident he contrived at Fort Sumter. Still other Southern states did not secede at all, but stayed in the Union – coerced except for Delaware.

Insofar as slavery was linked to any motive for secession, it was specific to one or more of the following related issues:

1. The *preservation* of slavery (where it existed)
2. The *extension* of slavery (into the territories)
3. The fugitive slave laws (when/where unenforced)

Of these three, only number 1 can be a legitimate candidate when considering whether or not the war was "about" slavery.

2. Out of the Union, the Southern states had no influence about how and by whom the territories would be settled.
3. The U.S. fugitive slave laws became irrelevant for the Southern states.

The Corwin Amendment – Between December 1860 and April 1861, seven states had declared their independence from the United States *without a single shot being fired*. During this interim, the 36th U.S. Congress set to work to find a compromise to bring the seceded states back into the Union, or at least to avert the exodus of the eight other Southern states that where considering secession at that time (NC, TN, AR, VA, DE, MD, KY, MO)

Among the many proposals put forth, one gained significant bi-partisan support in both houses of Congress. It was to be an amendment to the Constitution, what would have ironically become the 13th amendment. Named after Representative Thomas Corwin of Ohio, The Corwin Amendment would have *unambiguously* and *permanently* protected the institution of slavery from any action taken by the U.S. government:

> Art. 13. No amendment shall be made to the Constitution which will authorize or give Congress the power to abolish or interfere, within any State, with the domestic institutions thereof, including that of persons held to labor or service by the laws of the said State.

Although largely symbolic, this resolution was put forth to *assure the South there would be no effort made by the U.S. government to interfere with slavery in the Southern States*; that they were willing to put it in writing and *guarantee* that the issue would never again be a cause of concern to them, *if* they would return to the union and/or remain therein.

Senator Stephen Douglas, one of the Senate's most enthusiastic supporters of the resolution, characterized the Corwin Amendment as evidence that the North was *neither* hostile to the South *nor* to its domestic institution of slavery:

> [I]f the northern states will by three forth majority come forward and insert this clause in the Constitution, it proves conclusively that there is no such sentiment [in] the North.

The resolution passed the House on February 28, 1861 and the Senate on March 3, 1861. President James Buchanan signed the amendment that same day, his last day in office (but could not be law until ratified by the States).

The very next day, in his inaugural address, Abraham Lincoln said:

> I understand a proposed amendment to the Constitution...

has passed Congress, to the effect that the Federal Government shall never interfere with the domestic institutions of the States, including that of persons held to service.... [H]olding such a provision to now be implied constitutional law, I have no objection to its being made express and irrevocable.

Thirteen days later Lincoln sent a copy of the amendment to the governors of *all* the States, including those states that were out of the Union, an action that can only be interpreted as a lobbying effort to affect the passage of the amendment.

His efforts failed. Not one of the states that had left the Union returned. In fact, four of the eight Southern states contemplating secession during the attempted compromise would eventually leave the Union, bringing the total number of independent Southern states to eleven.

The Emancipation Proclamation – Much has been made of what Lincoln's *Emancipation Proclamation* actually did or did not do, but little has been said of what it *intended* to do. As a "fit and necessary war measure" to suppress the "rebellion," its purpose was *not* to end slavery, but to end the war.

When the preliminary proclamation was issued on September 22, 1862, it provided a 100 day window in which those states or parts of states which were designated as being "in rebellion against the United States" could, through their own actions, *preserve slavery* in their own territory *by returning to the Union*. If any or all of the states in the Southern Confederacy would have complied with the conditions enumerated in the proclamation, they would have extricated themselves completely from the threat of abolition, yet no state did.

Although the Emancipation Proclamation has been hailed as a great moral achievement, one wonders how this interpretation came about. It did not immediately free one single slave where it was intended to have an effect, namely the Confederate States that *were not* under Union control, and it held in bondage all those slaves residing in MD, KY, MO and those states or parts of states, and Confederate areas under occupation, that *were* under Union control. In fact, an honest reading of the actual document reveals that it was nothing more than an offer to *perpetuate* slavery. The *moral* content attributed to the Emancipation Proclamation results from the Confederacy's failure to comply with Lincoln's demands, thus triggering an emancipation that, according to American mythology, freed the slaves, but according to the plain facts of history, did no such thing.

Ask yourself this: How would the Emancipation Proclamation be viewed *today* if the Southern states had chosen to return to the union?

Slavery in the Territories – Because we have been conditioned to view the extension of slavery into the territories as a great moral crisis, it is appropriate to briefly consider the issue of slavery in the territories in order to better understand the nature of this crisis.

It is an undisputed fact that Lincoln was inflexible and unwavering in his opposition to the expansion of slavery into the territories. His opposition to slavery in the territories, however, had *nothing* to do with the actual institution of slavery. Insofar as Lincoln was in favour of keeping the territories free, it was to keep them free *for* white immigration

and free *from* black immigration. According to Lincoln,

"The whole nation is interested that the best use shall be made of these territories. We want them for the homes of *free white people*. This they cannot be, to any considerable extent, *if slavery shall be planted within them*."

This was not merely a position of political expediency. For Lincoln it was a *moral imperative*. "Is it not rather our *duty*," he rhetorically asked, "to make labor more respectable by preventing *all black competition*, especially in the territories?"

Lincoln's position on slavery in the territories had nothing to do with whether slavery was right or wrong, but only his desire to keep the territories "Negro-free" zones.

Conclusion

If we are to intelligently address the question of whether or not the war was about slavery, we need to address the question of how it was about slavery.

1. Was the war "about" slavery because some of the Southern States seceded because they perceived the election and ascendancy of Republican Governors and President Lincoln as a threat to the institution itself?

2. Was the war "about" slavery because the South wanted to preserve the institution for themselves, to protect it from the machinations of the Federal Government?

3. Was the war "about" slavery because of the threat of having slavery excluded from the territories?

If these issues (and many others could be included) are not even considered when appraising the actions and motives of the Southern states, then the characterization that the war was "about" slavery is not only questionable, it is slanderous and morally reprehensible allegation.

Suggestions for Class Discussion

If "about" slavery, how do we deal with the fact that Congress passed a resolution that would have expressly and permanently removed the perceived threat to slavery by amending the Constitution itself and that Lincoln was in favour of its passage during his first days in office?

If "about" slavery, given the Corwin Amendment that *preceded the war* and the Emancipation Proclamation that occurred *during the war*, both of which offered the *preservation of slavery in exchange for re-entering the Union*, why was there a fight to begin with? Why did the fight continue as long as it did?

If "about" slavery, how do we deal with the fact that the Southern States voluntarily relinquished any claim to the territories they might have accessed if not seceded?

Recommended Reading

• ***Bloodstains, An Epic History of the Politics that Produced the American Civil War and the Political Reconstruction that Followed***, vol. 2, ***The Demagogues***, by Howard Ray White, pub. 2003.
• ***When in the Course of Human Events: Arguing the Case for Southern Secession***, by Charles Adams, pub. 2000.

Chapter 37: What If Bonded African Americans (Slaves) Had Benefitted from Gradual Emancipation with Training and Freedom from Political Agendas?

By Barbara G. Marthal of Tennessee, M. Ed., S. I. S. H,

Overview

The subject of this chapter is too vast to permit a comprehensive treatment of the question posited in the title. But our author knows that great success would have followed a sincere program of gradual emancipation with training and freedom from political agendas. People of full and partial African descent arrived on our shores numbering only 600,000 (equal to the population of Baltimore, MD today). In spite of that small number they raised families and played a major role in building America – yes, in building America. Of that accomplishment all of their descendants, living today, should take great pride. If you are still in school, listen up while our storyteller, Barbara Marthal, speaks to your heart and mind.

A History Seldom Taught

Hello students. I am Barbara Marthal. Much of my ancestry is derived from Africa. I have a great passion for teaching history but my major was not History; it was Sociology with a minor in Anthropology. I have a Master of Education with a concentration in Reading and Story Arts. My knowledge of African American History is driven and informed by my research as a storyteller. That research has provided me with a history of African Americans that I have seldom seen published in school history texts.

I have strong opinions on what is needed in telling the History of people of African descent in colonial America and the 1800's. We should require textbooks that reveal the lives of slaves and free people of color – capable, intelligent, talented, living and breathing people – books that connect the contribution of their labors, skills, talents, and ethnic cultures to the making of this nation and to the building of our country.

In general, most texts about African Americans are rather informative, but do not sufficiently illuminate their achievements – just a continuation of the same old story – about how our African ancestors were victimized and how the great political, social, and economic structure of America dehumanized and degraded them until the crusade of President Lincoln and his Federal army.

Some recent texts include the North in this process of victimization, but, as a teenager, you need to understand that slavery was an accepted worldwide legal institution and that in spite of that institution, slaves of African, European, and New World descent, through the use of their labors and skills, helped to build a country that was committed to a concept of freedom that up until the end of the 1700's had not existed anywhere in the world.

I will tell a few stories that are generally omitted from the standard school textbooks. We start with **William Ellison** who was born a slave and apprenticed to a carpenter and cotton gin maker. After purchasing his freedom in 1816, Ellison set the course of his life, becoming known as a master cotton gin builder and planter and one of the richest men in South Carolina. There was **William Tiler Johnson** born a slave; yet, when apprenticed and given his freedom in 1820, he became a successful Natchez, MS barber and planter. In 1801 there is the documentable history of "**Black Bob**," a slave who owned a tavern and inn in Nashville, TN, which was so successful he solicited his most influential white clients to petition the state legislature for his freedom and changed his name to Robert Renfro. Where in today's texts do we hear of the slave, **Dr. Jack**, who in 1830, doctored on members of his community that were free, slave, male, female, black and white, in Maury County, TN? There are surprises in state archives such as the account of a Tennessee free black man, who, in 1832, petitioned for the right to marry a white woman with the signatures of his white male neighbors affixed.

What about the history of **Elizabeth Keckley**, who authored her 1868 biography, *Behind the Scenes or Thirty Years a Slave, and Four Years in the White House*? Keckley was the highly skilled seamstress whose clients included Mary Todd Lincoln, Varina Davis (wife of Jefferson Davis), and other elite women of the Washington D.C. governing class. And let us not forget the story of the African American slave woman, **Marie Thereze Coincoin** of Natchitoches, LA, who, when freed at some point in the late 1700's, established the Yucca Plantation (today known as Melrose Plantation) which eventually encompassed 18,000 acres of fertile land, which was tilled by hundreds of slaves owned by Marie and her descendants. You can visit the Coincoin plantation as well as the home of William T. Johnson.

No story is more inspiring than that of Booker T. Washington, the African American educator who founded the Tuskegee Institute in 1881. He and his faculty believed in a skill and trade based program that would make people self-sufficient. They believed in the philosophy of cooperation and cultural solidarity. They built their community with the aide and respect of their white neighbors. If this mutual respect had been nurtured in the absence of a war torn society and absent of divisive political agendas, more institutions such as Fisk University and Howard University could have prospered.

The history shared above and many others are too numerous and important to be excluded from our school history texts. Historians: we need inspired students with a thirst for scholarship that propels them into the process of research and deliberation, if we are to conscientiously tell the history of this nation and the opportunities that it held out to all people in spite of having to come to grips with the institution of slavery. By producing textbooks that include stories such as those mentioned above, students will begin to understand that if you are thorough with your historical research, you will discover that all people are descended from serfs, slaves and free people, all of whom they can be proud.

Now to address the subject in the title of this chapter, gradual emancipation and training, free from political agendas. When reading the title, many historians will immediately dismiss it as speculation and chide the author with "There is no place in the science of History for speculation!" The author's response: if you can find evidence that supports a point of view, that evidence should be researched and tested, thus transitioning it from the shadow of speculation into building a reasonable hypothesis worthy of exploration. Let us proceed.

The *Anti-Slavery Examiner*, of New York, published in 1839 an article titled "On the Conditions of the Free People of Color in the United States." In it we read that in 1840, African

Americans made up approximately 5% of New York City's population. Racial discrimination barred them from most crafts or professions and forced blacks to work as servants, waiters, seamen, dock workers, or at menial jobs that rarely paid enough to support a family. "... There is a conspiracy, embracing all the departments of society, to keep the black man ignorant and poor. As a general rule, admitting few if any exceptions, the schools of literature and of science reject him – the counting house refuses to receive him as a bookkeeper, much more as a partner ...."

It is not an overstatement to say most white Northerners and a substantial number of white Southerners supported such restrictions on African Americans and certainly Abraham Lincoln did. That is why during all of his political career, he supported the American Colonization Society which was committed to freeing slaves and shipping them all out of the country. In Lincoln's ideal America, there was no place for African Americans to live in our country as free people because they took jobs away from white men.

Now, let us examine conditions of African American slaves and free people of color in the South. Although their story is far from ideal, you see a significant difference when looking at the typical Southern attitude. A story about John Berry Meachum, a free black man in Missouri, is helpful. "... [B]orn a slave, in Goochland county, Virginia, May 3d, 1789. I belonged to a man by the name of Paul Meachum who moved to North Carolina ... He was a good man and I loved him, but could not feel myself satisfied... So I proposed to him to hire my time... By working in a saltpeter cave I earned enough to purchase my freedom." John went on to purchase and free his father, his wife, his children, and men not related to him. He inspired those men to purchase land and to establish businesses. In 1821 he was ordained and became pastor of the African Baptist Church in St. Louis.

John Berry Meachum's story is not unique. Throughout the south, during the era of our study, stories similar to his can be documented. The point is, the South had a running successful track record of freeing slaves and integrating them into society. Albeit the timing was far, far too slow, and many times limiting, but it was a proven record. More free successful black people lived in the south during antebellum times than anywhere else in the United States. Many of them owned land which was illegal in most Northern states. A few owned large plantations with slaves, others owned small farms that made them self-sufficient.

Self-sufficient, that is the key word. In the South, an owner had to appear before a panel of his peers to assure his fellow white neighbors that the person being freed was of good character and could provide for himself/herself and any future family members. The slave usually had a skill that would secure his/her future and many times that was a skill almost monopolized by free people of color. It was a system that had worked for generations in the South and there is no reason to believe that Southerners would have abandoned that system if a devastating army had not invaded, thus disallowing the option of gradual emancipation and training of slaves.

One last word on training: the myth that the majority of slaves were without skills is just that, a myth. Many slaves were skilled craftsmen and mechanics. Others were the best skilled

and qualified people, both physically and mentally, in the industry of farming anywhere in this country, skilled and productive at agriculture (plant and animal husbandry), the industry that was the foundation upon which America was built. And on successful farms and large plantations (contrary to what is usually taught: antagonistic whites as overseers and drivers), a significant number of those positions were filled by competent free people of African descent or by slaves.

Now, we have a very feasible working hypothesis. Slavery was a legal intuition throughout the countries of North and South America. And this is key – **Every single one of those countries with the exception of Haiti, ended slavery without a war**. Had the Republican North not invaded the Democrat South and had politicians not used slavery to promote the personal agendas of conflict and competition, the South could have produced more men and women such as those at the Tuskegee Institute, founded by Booker T. Washington. It is even feasible (some believe probable) that integration and racial tolerance, elements which were already present within the Southern Antebellum culture, would have progressed and flourished more rapidly had the South not suffered a catastrophic war and Political Reconstruction.

Our Close

We hope your heart and mind were stimulated by Barbara Marthal's stories and commentary. Now, a look at some numbers – of the 3,653,770 people of African descent living in the Confederate states, 3.6% were free, the remainder slaves (1860 census). Between 5% and 11% in three states were free; less than 1% in five states. Together, people of African descent (slave and free) were 33% of the total population of the south. In a famous 1858 debate with Senator Stephen Douglas, Illinois Republican Party leader Abraham Lincoln predicted more than 100 years would pass before all Southern slaves would be free. Of course, that was cut to "8 years" by his WBTS, a horror that took the lives of 1,000,000 people – sailors, troops and civilians of all races. We authors believe that, if the Confederacy had been allowed to go its own way, avoiding that horrific war, all Confederate slaves would have been free by 1890 (Brazil freed its last in 1888).

The student is encouraged to open his or her mind to the possibility of saving the 1,000,000 lives lost in the WBTS and exploring an alternate path to freedom for 3,521,010 Confederate African American slaves. Reflect on Ms. Marthal's stories and revelations during your discussions.

Suggestions for Class Discussion

Discuss how a program of gradual emancipation, with appropriate training, would have influenced the lives of Confederate African Americans and of subsequent generations, from 1861 up to today. Let Barbara Marthal's stories and revelations help you "think from the heart and from the mind."

Recommended Reading

- **Behind the Scenes or Thirty Years a Slave, and Four Years in the White House**, by Elizabeth Keckley, pub. 1868.
- **Up From Slavery**, by Booker T. Washington, pub. 1901.
- **The Chronological History of the Negro in America**, by Peter M. Bergmam, pub. 1969.

Chapter 38 – What Was the War of 1861-1865 All About?

By H. V. Traywick, Jr. of Virginia, S.I.S.H.

Names tell a lot, and that conflict had many names. The one that seems to have stuck is "The Civil War." But is this an accurate description? Civil wars by definition are wars waged between two or more factions within a country struggling for control of the government. But Robert E. Lee was not fighting to take over the government of Abraham Lincoln any more than George Washington was fighting to take over the government of George III. Quite to the contrary, both were fighting to get out from under those governments, and Lincoln and George III were fighting to prevent them from doing so. Why?

Did the North wage war against the South because the South fired the first shot? South Carolina – with far more provocation - did no more than Massachusetts did when she seceded from the British Empire and fired on the British troops at Lexington and Concord.

Did the North wage war against the South to preserve democracy? Notwithstanding Lincoln's stirring rhetoric in his Gettysburg Address, government "of the people, by the people, and for the people" did not "perish from the earth" when the Southern States withdrew from the Union. It perished when they were driven back into it at the point of the bayonet. Furthermore, while Lincoln was issuing this stirring address, his suspension of the writ of *habeas corpus* had been in effect for ten months and up to *38,000* of his critics and political enemies had been languishing in his dungeons without trial from one end of his domain to the other. At home, opposition printing presses had been destroyed by Mr. Lincoln's Army and editors threatened with death, while Lincoln was conducting total war against a Southern people who only wished to be let alone, and whose attempt to peacefully withdraw from a voluntary Union would not have in any way prevented the North from having all the democracy it desired.

We are very often told the War was fought over slavery. "Just look at the Ordinances of Secession," we are told. "They had slavery written all over them." A little research will show that this generality did not apply to all of them – such as Virginia's. But even if it did, so what? The Ordinances of Secession were not Declarations of War. Where slavery was mentioned it was in the context of legal briefs giving examples of Northern state's violations of the Federal Constitution. They were Declarations of Independence. However, one will notice that this is never mentioned in the National narratives, because it would directly repudiate the National legacy of the Declaration of Independence that the thirteen *slaveholding* colonies signed in 1776. So to cloud the issue, the contention that slavery caused the war is emphatically and always implied – but never explained! Lincoln himself could not even explain it. In his Second Inaugural Address, Lincoln said of slavery:

> All knew that this interest was, somehow, the cause of the war. To strengthen, perpetuate, and extend this interest was the object for which the insurgents would rend the Union, even by war; while the Government claimed no right to do more than to restrict the territorial enlargement of it.

Let us take another look at this. "All knew," Lincoln claims, that "somehow" slavery was the cause of the war. We see here in Lincoln not some infallible Oracle of Truth, but merely an obfuscating lawyer arguing his case by ignoring the question of "*How?*" – the very question fundamental to his accusation.

The fallacies of Lincoln's accusations are readily apparent. The Southern States – far from withdrawing from the Union in order to expand the territorial limits of slavery – essentially *gave up* their claims to the territories rather than live under a Northern despotism, and thereby *restricted* their avenues for the expansion slavery! This not only brought about what Lincoln said was the Federal Government's sole object – to restrict slavery's expansion – it went most of the way towards peacefully removing slavery from the United States altogether! As for rending the Union, "even by war," I would ask: Who rebuffed Southern diplomatic overtures of peace from December 1860 to April 1861? Whose garrison committed the first act of war by spiking the guns at Ft. Moultrie and slipping into Ft. Sumter in the dark of night in direct violation of the truce then in effect? And who deceived the South diplomatically until he could send a powerfully armed armada to Charleston to provoke the South into firing the first shot?

If the North was fighting a Crusade of Liberation, why didn't she wage war on New York City and Boston, the largest home ports for slave-trading ships in the world in 1861? Or on Africa herself and her slave-raiders – such as the Kingdom of Dahomey – the largest exporters of African slaves in the world? Or on New England and her manufacturing profits gleaned from slave-picked cotton? Why? Because slavery was not the issue of the "Irrepressible Conflict," as William Seward contended. The "Irrepressible Conflict" was between the "opposing and enduring forces" of an agrarian economy and an industrial economy. The respective labor systems of the antagonists were just as irrelevant in this conflict as in any other war of conquest.

Why did Northerners abolish slavery in the first place? Was it because of their superior morality? Or was it because in an industrialized economy a free-labor system is more profitable to an employer than a slave-labor system? Adam Smith – in his classic treatise on economics entitled *The Wealth of Nations* – explained it all in 1776 and set the Abolition ball rolling. And if abolishing slavery in their States was because of the Northerners' superior morality, why did they first sell their slaves "down the river" before the abolition laws went into effect? Did they wish merely to rid themselves of a troublesome and unprofitable labor system, or to rid themselves of their African population as well? Alexis de Tocqueville makes some interesting observations on this in his classic work, *Democracy in America*.

But did the North in fact abolish slavery? Or did she merely transform it into something a little more discreet and a lot more profitable? Slavery is as old as Egypt, and the Preacher tells us there is no new thing under the sun (Ecclesiastes 1:9). If the borrower is the servant to the lender (Proverbs 22:7), then some of us have voluntarily sold ourselves into indentured servitude to our mortgage bankers, but our children have been sold into involuntary servitude with a seventeen trillion dollar national debt. And when did this happen? It was all inaugurated during Political Reconstruction of the conquered former Confederate States. Lt. Gen. Richard Taylor, CSA, son of President Zachary Taylor, described the carpetbagger as being worse than Attila the Hun, for Attila could only steal existing wealth, while the carpetbaggers stole the labor of unborn children with their invention of public credit. And they are still waxing fat on the backs of our enslaved children.

No, the North was not fighting to free the slaves. Lincoln said so himself. He specifically stated that he was fighting to save the Union. What he neglected to add, however, was that he was fighting to save the Union *for Northern financial and industrial interests!* And what were some of these interests? The industrializing North, with her sectional majority, was rapidly gaining control of the Federal Government and wielding it to accomplish her political ambitions to centralize its power, and use her control of that power to accomplish her industrial ambitions for high protective tariffs, bounties for transcontinental railroads, and the creation of national banks to manage it all, all at the South's expense, turning the Southern States into her agricultural colonies – of the sort that England had earlier created with her thirteen Colonies. With the election of Lincoln and the triumph of his strictly Northern sectional party, the Cotton States saw it all coming and got out from under the North's control once and for all through State Secession.

So what was the War all about? Quite simply, it was the North's war against the South's secession. Secession is an Imperialist's worst nightmare. When the thirteen Colonies rebelled against England's economic exploitation by seceding from the Empire, England sent in the Redcoats. When the Southern States rebelled against Yankee economic exploitation by seceding from the Union, the Yankees sent in the Bluecoats.

With the secession of the Southern States, the North lost her largest source of tariff revenues, her source of cotton for her mills, a large portion of her markets for her manufactured goods, and control of the mouth of the Mississippi. (So the North propagandized, but Confederates were pledging to keep that key river open to steamboats engaged in international trade.) If the South were to be allowed to leave the Union and get out from under the control of the North and her sectional majorities, the North feared its economy might wither on the vine.

So the North provoked the South into firing the first shot, blockaded the Confederate coasts, and marched her armies across the South to the tune of the Puritanical and militantly intolerant "Battle Hymn of the Republic" – burning and pillaging and raping and killing – until she drove the Southern States back into the Union. Then – by the Reconstruction Acts that dis-franchised Southern intelligence and enfranchised Southern ignorance under the control of unscrupulous and predatory Northern carpetbaggers and demagogues propped up by Federal bayonets – the North passed Amendments that effectively gutted the Constitution of its federative nature, and put the Federal Government under her unlimited control. With the stumbling blocks of the South and the Constitution finally out of the way of her ambitions, the North then sent Sherman, Sheridan and Custer out to the Great Plains to tend to the Indians, who were in the way of her transcontinental railroads. But this doesn't look very good on the pages of a school history book or in a National Park Service film presentation, so the North's war of conquest must be cloaked in robes of morality and turned into a war of liberation. To the victor belong the spoils, and the "Official History Book" – written by "Court Historians" – is one of the spoils of war.

It should come as no surprise, then, that the South has been made the nation's foil, the scapegoat, the traitor, the guilty one, fighting not to defend herself from invasion, conquest, and coerced political allegiance, but fighting to defend slavery. And it should come as no surprise that the North has been made the righteous one, the "good guys," fighting not a war of imperialism and conquest, but fighting a noble war of liberation under the tragic benevolence of "Father Abraham." But the truth is that when Abraham Lincoln got the war he wanted, he suspended the writ of *habeas corpus*, secured for himself dictatorial powers, and – with the collaboration of newly elected Republicans – implemented the very usurpation that the Founders had struggled to prevent.

With the possibility of secession and nullification destroyed by force of arms in 1865, the States – who created the Federal Government in the first place – are no longer the final arbiters of the limits of Federal power granted by the Constitution. The Supreme Court is. But the Supreme Court is part of the Federal Government. Therefore the Federal Government is the final arbiter of the limits of its own power – and that is the very definition of despotism. This, then – the exact opposite of Emancipation – is the true legacy of Abraham Lincoln and his War to Prevent Southern Independence. The Confederacy – the last remnant of the Republic of sovereign States bequeathed us by the Revolutionary Founders – was the American Empire's first conquest.

A Co-Editor's Closing Comments

By Howard Ray White, S.I.S.H.

The writing and publication of this booklet would not have been possible without the guidance, reputation and writings of Clyde N. Wilson. All who wish to express their appreciation for this, the work of the Society of Independent Southern Historians, should always remember the essential nature of Dr. Wilson's role in making possible this contribution to the education of America's future leaders with regard to a truthful understanding of America's greatest tragedy – The War Between the States.

Appreciation is also due to the writers whose breath of backgrounds made this booklet one of broad experience.

But the most important way to express your appreciation for this work is to make financial contributions to the Society. If a student, I suggest you turn to parents, relatives, and older friends and encourage them to contribute money toward printing and distribution. And don't forget the grandparents. You will be surprised how much many of them know about the WBTS. Engage in conversation, share what you all know and encourage their help in furthering this, the first project of the Society of Independent Southern Historians. Go to www.southernhistorians.org .

Dr. Wilson's final chapter is next. Give it special attention as you consider further study.

Chapter 39 – How and Why to Study History

By Clyde N. Wilson of S. C., Ph.D., S. I. S. H.

Introduction

How to study history has been a passion of co-editor Howard Ray White, a retired chemical engineer who became interested in history at midlife. He emphasizes biography, judging the character of important leaders, looking at what they did instead of what they said, keeping history in strict chronological order to see action, reaction, action, etc. (cause and effect), sorting propaganda from fact. He purposefully transports himself back in time to the era being studied, choosing to know what people of that era knew, forgetting subsequent history for the moment. Dr. Wilson has taught truthful history all his life. This editor considers him an expert of the highest order. So pay close attention as he gives worthy instruction concerning "How and Why to Study History." And keep in mind that, if a student, you will soon be in charge of leading America, sifting through propaganda in search of truth. You must know the past to wisely steer forward. Dr. Wilson explains "How and Why to Study History," using as the basis of his instruction the hugely confusing story of the War Between the States.

How and Why to Study History

How should 21st Century Americans T\think about the War Between the States? We human beings are peculiar creatures, half angel and half animal, as someone has said. Alone among creatures, we have a consciousness of ourselves, of our situation, and of our movement through time. We have language, and by symbols can communicate knowledge to one another and across generations. We can learn something about humans from the Divine Revelation in the Bible. We can also learn something by scientific examination of our physical selves. But most of what we know about human beings is in our knowledge of the past. But what kind of human "knowledge"? – truthful knowledge or accepted propaganda? You see, what makes us human is our ability to distinguish truth from falsehood, and that is the theme of this chapter. As a philosopher puts it: we must live forward but we can only think backward. I am, of course, making a plea for the importance of history, or to be more exact, historical memory, something that is undergoing catastrophic destruction today in the United States.

People without truthful knowledge of their past would be scarcely human. What makes us human is the culture we inherit. It has been truly said that we are what we remember. Let me emphasize: What we remember determines what we are. What we take from the past is crucial to our identity. And it follows, as Dr. Samuel Johnson said, that there is hardly any worse crime against humanity than to falsify its records.

Every society of any worth has revered those who came before. Romans, in their period of greatest freedom and achievement, kept images of their ancestors by the fireside as minor gods. The Greeks at their highest point thrived in a belief in a Golden Age of Heroes that preceded their own lesser times. Perhaps you know of personal ancestors who fought for the Confederacy. Then be proud that those ancestors not only won a place in the hearts of us, their descendants, they also won the lasting admiration of everyone in the civilized world who values courage, skill, sacrifice, and an indomitable spirit in defense of freedom. They are admired by the world to a degree seldom granted to lost causes. I find that thoughtful Europeans speak respectfully of the Confederacy, as did Winston Churchill. Foreigners have a great advantage in judging the right and wrong of the War Between the States. They do not start out with the automatic assumption that all the good is on one side and all the bad on the other.

Lord Acton, an English historian who published many deeply-researched volumes on the history of liberty, wrote to General Lee in 1866. The defeat at Appomattox, Acton said, was a blow to the entire civilized world because it had reversed the progress of humanity toward constitutional liberty. And Lee replied: "All the South has ever desired was that the Union, as established by our forefathers, should be preserved and that the government, as originally organized, should be administered in purity and truth." But there has long been a campaign within our society aimed at wiping out our historical memory and replacing it with a made-up history that serves the political and social needs of a multicultural empire.

And what do we mean when we say a war is "about" something? Was the American Revolution "about" the price of tea? Was the War Between the States not also "about" economic interests, as was believed by a former generation of historians, or cultural conflict, or constitutional questions, or issues of invasion and defense?

Most current historians seem to be invoking a doctrine of "the Lost Cause Myth," which claims to explain that everything favourable that anyone believes about the Confederacy is false, manufactured propaganda. According to this rendering, Confederates were evil people who tried to destroy the best country on earth to preserve slavery. Not only were they evil, but they were weak and stupid. They made a pathetic effort that was inevitably defeated. Then after the war, those evil Confederates, it is claimed, made up a mythology about a supposedly honourable and heroic "Lost Cause" which never really existed. In other words they covered up their bad deeds and failure with a pack of lies packaged as "The Lost Cause." In order to understand truthful history, which is keenly important, the student must be discerning and sort truth from falsehood. Often all that is needed is good common sense. The records are there to be examined.

The biggest American myth is that of Lincoln, which is untrue and pernicious. But Americans have experienced another myth, now mostly forgotten. For a long time, from the late 1800s through the first half of the 1900s, Americans enjoyed a comforting myth about the war. North and South agreed that it was a great tragedy, with good and bad on both sides, which had fortunately resulted in a stronger, united country. This was a good myth – a myth of reconciliation and harmony that allowed the national memory to cope with an immense and ugly event. Those days are gone forever. The Lincoln myth and the myth that the War was "about" slavery, end of story, dominates the teaching of history.

Victors write the history and the first prevailing interpretation of any great event is that the winners were the good guys and the losers the bad guys. With the passage of time and research by trained and supposedly dispassionate historians a more complex and balanced picture emerges. It is seen that the winners were not always angels and that the losers actually had something to be said for their side. This kind of revisionism governed the understanding of the war for much of the 20th century. But now there is a concerted effort underway by so-called professional historians to deny and denigrate the extraordinary heroism and sacrifice of the South in that war.

The Southern understanding of the Constitution was never refuted, and it can't be. It was simply crushed. Preserving the Union? You cannot preserve the Union, or government of, by, and for the people, by a massive military invasion that destroys the constitutional, democratically elected governments of nearly half the states and converts them into conquered provinces with puppet governments and their citizens deprived of rights. The most basic simple fact about the war is that it was a war of invasion and conquest. Once you get clear on this basic fact, all other truths tend to fall into place. This is no secret. It is plain in the record. The Northern war party openly declared that it was a war of conquest, to crush resistance to government, to promote a powerful state, and to keep the South as a captive source of profits. People love Lincoln's pretty words because they put a happy face on a great crime.

Furthermore, historians' assumption about the Northern public's support of the war is wrong. We are led to believe that the opposition consisted of a few Copperhead conspirators and the New York City draft riots. Not true. Northern opposition to the war was much more widespread, more respectable, and more articulate than that. This is the biggest untold story in American history. It was a Republican Party war. Lincoln and his supporters knew that their support was shaky and they saw conspirators under their beds every night. We know about the suppression of newspapers and arrest of dissidents by the government without any legal due process. What does it tell us that detention of the Chief Justice and of a former President were seriously considered? Dissent was suppressed not only by the military but by violent mobs of Lincoln supporters. Lincoln bought support with patronage on a scale previously unimaginable in the United States. The supposed "loyalty" of the Border States has been greatly exaggerated. Why did all the Border States including West Virginia start electing ex-Confederates and Democrats to public office as soon as the Federal army left?

Here is something else to keep clearly in mind as a vital part of the history of the South. It took 22 million Northerners four years of the bloodiest warfare in American history to conquer 5 million white Southerners. Confederates mobilized 90 per cent of their men and lost nearly 30 percent. Not only Confederate self-government but more than half of the property of its citizens was lost. The war impoverished the South and enriched the politically connected in the North. Foreign visitors to the North in 1861-1865 said that they could see little sign that there was even a war going on.

Confederates were true heroes. Man for man they marched harder, risked their lives more often, fought better, endured impossible hardships, and won many battles against superior forces. Let me give you a comparative statistic. About 12,000 North Carolinians lost their lives in World War II. If we project the loss of men in the Confederate War against the larger population of World War II, as a percentage, it would require 300,000 North Carolina deaths to equal the State's loss of men in the 1860s. No other group of Americans has EVER made a sacrifice that remotely approaches that of the South in

its war for independence. Losses of the North in that war, a huge 400,000 deaths, larger than the United States in any other war, are negligible when compared to the South as a percentage of population. Very late in the war, when defeat seemed inevitable, Northern generals were complaining that the Confederate soldier refused to give in and admit defeat, that Southern women remained indomitable in spirit, and that Southerners from the richest to the poorest were determined to keep on.

Southerners are too quick to be generous in their accounts of the war, and thus detract from the honour due their forefathers. One example is the so-called great Union victory at Gettysburg. Some victory! Lee's army maneuvered freely on enemy territory for several weeks, even though the nearest Union army outnumbered him greatly and there were several other sizable Union armies within a few days' march. The Confederate army spent three days attacking a much larger force on its home territory and barely failed of victory. Then stopped attacking and went home. Lee's army trekked back to the Potomac with vast herds of cattle and hogs, a 50-mile long wagon train, prisoners, and wounded, in knee deep mud without any serious harm from the larger, supposedly victorious, army, and remained an undefeatable fighting force for more than a year longer. Furthermore, something like 5,000 black men, bond and free, accompanied the Confederate army to Pennsylvania – and back. The British observer Col. Fremantle observed one of these men marching a Yankee prisoner to the rear. He wondered what the abolitionists in London would think if they saw that.

Finally, we come to slavery and the noble crusade to free the suffering black people. How can the war be "about" slavery when the government formally declares that it is not fighting to free the slaves but to preserve the power of the politicians in Washington? And it would seem that the vast majority of Northern soldiers doing the fighting agreed. Certainly no Confederate thought he was fighting just to preserve slavery. In fact, by the third year of the war many Southerners would have willingly given up slavery to secure independence.

Confederates were truly admirable, and decent people all over the world know it. Historians need to tell that story. And, if an inquisitive student, you need to find it, dig it out. Use this booklet as a jumping off place. Then march forward.

Summation

Regarding "How" to study history the inquisitive student must be discerning and investigate diligently. Regarding "Why" to study history, be assured that productive citizenship and personal liberty requires truthful knowledge of it.

Suggestions for Class Discussion

How does a student of history sort truth from falsehood, the right story from the propaganda? Why must the student transport himself or herself back into the times of the history being studied to truly understand the events of that era?

Recommended Reading

When seeking to understand the War Between the States, look for histories and biographies written before 1940. The era of 1900 to 1940 will provide the most truthful histories and biographies.

Chapter 40 – Thanks to Our Authors and Our Encouragement to Student Readers.

By Howard Ray White of N. C., co-editor, S.I.S.H.

As co-founders of The Society of Independent Southern Historians and co-editors of *Understanding the War Between the States*, Dr. Clyde N. Wilson and I have volunteered our time in support of the Society and in creating this booklet to deliver truthful knowledge to inquisitive Americans, especially students, who thirst for real understanding of our country's history and what it means to people living in today's world. We are both retired grandfathers, eager to share our life's experiences with the youth of today. Please use our Society's offering to your advantage, for knowledge is power.

I first must express my appreciation to Dr. Wilson for his vast knowledge of our subject and his expert guidance. Without that guidance – often gentle, sometimes firm – not even one page would have been produced. When he offered stern advice, normally beginning with "My friend," I bent, but did not break; I became stronger through the experience. I know no one who is more respected, more informed and more dedicated to unraveling with truth our often-distorted history.

Yet, the help of others was essential to the success of this project. And it is toward them that most of the words on this page are dedicated. To Karen Stokes of South Carolina much is owed. She quickly wrote for us two moving chapters that tell so much: one on the War Against Civilians, the other on Prisoners of War. Drawing on decades of research and historical knowledge, Joseph Stromberg and William Cawthon wrote two important and revealing chapters. I speak of Stromberg's presentation of the Cost of the War in Financial Terms and Cawthon's diligent research and presentation of the Cost of the War in Lives Lost and Families Shattered.

Egon Richard Tausch, writing from his home in Texas and drawing from a life-time of study and publication experience, has contributed two fine chapters. I speak of his chapter starting with the Mexican War and ending with the Compromise of 1850, plus his very important chapter on Political Reconstruction.

We are blessed to have African American writers telling important history. Heart-felt is the chapter by Earl L. Ijames of North Carolina concerning those African American men who supported the Confederates and those who supported the Federals. Also heart-felt is the "What If" chapter by Barbara Marthal of Tennessee, which ponders the consequence of possible gradual emancipation, had that been history's path.

The Society is fortunate to have additional writers who hail from diverse backgrounds and experiences. Two chapters by Steve Litteral of Illinois provide examples. Note his chapter on analysis of the "Two Armies" and the "Cost of the War in the Northern States." Another example is the writing of Paul C. Graham of South Carolina, who addresses "Recapping the Big Puzzle." Gail Jarvis of Georgia takes on "Political Reconstruction." Also valuable to the project were the contributions of writers Joyce Bennett of Maryland, Patrick Kealey of California and Leslie R. Tucker of Oklahoma.

We concluded our booklet with a wrap-up chapter by H. V. Traywick of Virginia. Mr. Traywick demonstrates that a fine student of history and writer on the subject need not always be a career university professor of history to understand his subject and tell about it in a clear and truthful manner.

Others contributed to our thinking on this project and offered appreciated support. Among these is Dr. Bob Butterworth of TN, Rebecca Calcutt of SC, Roger Busbice of LA, Gene Kizer of SC, Loy Mauch of AR and Dr. W. Kirk Wood of SC.

You are at the age where teenagers face peer pressure to conform, to be liked, to fit in. Will you become "other-directed" and bend to those pressures or will you be "self-directed" and grow into the person you wish to become. There is no human, anywhere on earth who it exactly like you: you are unique. So thirst for understanding, question what you hear and see, and choose wisely. Do not be a slave, a captive bound by perceived obligations to fit in. Choose freedom. Adopt the following philosophy going forward:

> In all of your studies
> On your journey through life
> Always Seek the Truth –
> For the "Truth Shall Set You Free."

In closing our booklet, *Understanding the War Between the States*, Society historians and authors assure you that we are:

1. Dedicated to delivering truthful history of the American people via **all available communication technology** – Low cost printed booklets and free digitized text for viewing on computers, tablets and e-book readers, and to print as .pdf. Go to www.southernhistorians.org for details and free downloads.

2. Delivering this to **all available learning environments** – Self-guided Instruction, Libraries, College, Home School, Private School, Charter School and Public School.

And **Public School** remains the mainstay of American education. The late John Andrew White – Tennessean, grandson of a Confederate soldier, educator, poet, pubic school superintendent, and my grandfather – encouraged Public Schools in the 1920's with this poetry, viewing the institution as our "Pillar of Progress;" the "Light of our People;" our "Mother of Justice," and the "Mainstay of our Nation." These are worthy goals every public school should strive to meet. With this tribute to America's public schools we bid you farewell, adiós and adieu.

> Oh **Pillar of Progress** be strong!
> Yes, teach us to use all our strength;
> Then point out all weakness and wrong,
> That we may outstrip them at length.
>
> Oh **Light of our People**, shine on!
> Dispel superstition and fear;
> The bondage of serfdom is gone,
> The day of true freedom is near.
>
> Oh, **Mother of Justice**, be firm!
> Give mercy and vision to youth;
> Though haughty tradition may squirm,
> Broadcast each decision of truth.
>
> **Mainstay of our Nation**, hold fast!
> Though ignorant surges embrace.
> Oh bind us together at last,
> United through wisdom and grace.

Appendix 1: Our List of Society Members Who Wrote this Work and a Bit about Each.

Clyde N. Wilson, Ph. D., co-editor and Society Founder, of South Carolina.

Emeritus Distinguished Professor of History at the University of South Carolina; author or editor of more than 30 books and hundreds of articles, essays, and reviews in a wide variety of books and journals, both popular and scholarly; editor of the multi-volume *The Papers of John C. Calhoun;* founder of the Stephen D. Lee Institute; M.E. Bradford Distinguished Professor of the Abbeville Institute; winner of the Bostick Medal for South Carolina Letters. Among major works: *Carolina Cavalier: The Life and Mind of James Johnston Pettigrew; From Union to Empire; Defending Dixie.*

Howard Ray White, co-editor and Society Founder, of North Carolina.

Retired chemical engineer, historian and writer. Major publications include *Bloodstains, An Epic History of the Politics that Produced and Sustained the American Civil War . . .* (4 volumes); *Understanding Abe Lincoln's First Shot Strategy; Understanding Uncle Tom's Cabin and The Battle Hymn of the Republic,* and *Understanding Creation and Evolution: a Biblical and Scientific Comparative Study.*

Joyce Bennett of Maryland

Author of many articles on Maryland life and history and of the recent *Letters from the Outpost: The Cultural Cleansing of a Small Southern State.*

Vance Caswell of North Carolina

Free-lance writer and tobacco farmer.

William Cawthon of Alabama.

Among the most informed of the authors who contributed to this project; the author of numerous essays on Southern history and a diligent and energetic researcher.

Paul C. Graham of South Carolina.

Professor of Philosophy at Midlands Technical College, popular public lecturer on the WBTS and other subjects, and editor of the, *Palmetto Partisan.*

Earl L. Ijames of North Carolina

Curator of African American History at the N.C. Museum of History and co-producer of the documentary video, "Colored Confederates."

Gail Jarvis of Georgia.

A retired CPA and historian, Mr. Jarvis has published articles at LewRockwell.com, AbbevilleInstitute.org, and many journals.

Patrick J. Kealey of California.

A commercial real estate agent, Patrick is passionate about telling the truthful history of the WBTS.

Steve Litteral of Illinois.

Museum director and editor whose writings we appreciate.

Barbara G. Marthal of Tennessee

A popular African American story-teller and the author of the children's book, *Fighting for Freedom: A Documented Study.*

Karen Stokes of South Carolina.

Archivist for the South Carolina Historical Society, historian and writer. Major publications include the historical works *Faith Valor and Devotion; South Carolina Civilians in Sherman's Path,* and *The Immortal 600,* as well as a series of novels about South Carolina during the WBTS.

Joseph Stromberg of Georgia

A widely learned and published independent historian, former college instructor and internet columnist.

Egon Richard Tausch of Texas.

A wide-ranging career as an army officer, history professor, attorney, and writer. Author of over 50 articles for many publications. Notable books include *The Secret Ledger of an Early Texas Doctor.*

Leslie R. Tucker of Oklahoma.

Historian and writer. Major publications include *Maj-Gen Isaac Trimble, Baltimore Confederate*; *Magnolias and Corn Bread,* and *Brig. Gen. John Adams.*

H. V. "Bo" Traywick, Jr. of Virginia.

A veteran of diverse careers, including tugboat captain, now retired, and also a well-researched Historian. His recent book, *Empire of the Owls, Reflections on the North's War Against Southern Secession,* is noteworthy.

Want to Help Promote This Project? Here is How!

Join the Society of Independent Southern Historians – See our website at www.southernhistorians.org – Seek application at southernhistorians@gmail.com. Mail check for $25 or more to S.I.S.H, 6012 Lancelot Drive, Charlotte, NC 28270.

Purchase a bundle of 25 printed booklets and distribute them. A great project for any group. Call 704-846-4411 for details.

This booklet is **free to download** as a pdf and print on your printer at home or at the office. It is formatted for 8-1/2 by 11 paper. Download at www.southernhistorians.org/freebooklet, read and promote.

Today most people communicate via the **worldwide web** using computers, tablets, smart cell phones, etc. Ask those you know to link to www.southernhistorians.org/freebooklet.

Contribute money to subsidize producing and delivering a printed booklet to students who prefer paper booklets over reading on a computer, tablet or e-book reader.

Distribute booklets to libraries, schools, colleges, home school groups, newspaper editors, historical groups, students, descendants of Confederates, etc. We suggest a contribution of $5.00 each for printed booklets plus shipping (for 10 shipping is $8.00; for 25 it is $14.00; for 50 it is $20). For smaller quantities, go to Amazon.com.

Appendix 2 – Resources for Further Study.

By Dr. Clyde N. Wilson and Howard Ray White, co-editors.

The Society of Independent Southern Historians maintains an expanding website which presents a large bibliography of Southern literature, history, biography, etc. for your viewing. Every item in this bibliography has been endorsed and recommended by the Society. Members continually add to the bibliography with recommendations and book reviews. See us at www.southernhistorians.org . There, you can also download this booklet for free and learn how to join and help the Society.

Overview

Albion's Seed: Four British Folkways in America, by David Hackett Fischer (1989).

Bloodstains, An Epic History of the Politics that Produced and Sustained the American Civil War and the Political Reconstruction that Followed, 4 vols., by Howard Ray White (2002-2012).

Democracy in America, by Alexis de Tocqueville, (English translation, 1848).

Redcoats and Rebels, The American Revolution through British Eyes, by Christopher Hibbert (1990).

Westward Expansion: A History of the American Frontier, by Ray A. Billington (1949).

From Union to Empire (2003) and *Defending Dixie* (2006), Clyde N. Wilson.

Historical Consciousness, or the Remembered Past, by John Lukacs (1985).

North Against South: The American Iliad, 1848-1877, by Ludwell H. Johnson (1963).

Understanding the Constitution

A Constitution for the United States of America. (Note Amendment dates. Note Federal power before the War and its growth afterward.)

A Better Guide Than Reason (1977); *Original Intentions* (1993); *Founding Fathers* (1994), by M.E. Bradford.

The Founding Fathers Guide to the Constitution, by Brion McClanahan (2005).

Is Jefferson Davis a Traitor?, by Albert T. Bledsoe (1866).

Nullification, A Constitutional History, 1766-1833, 4 volumes, by Walter Kirk Wood (2008-14).

The South was Right, by James R. and Walter D. Kennedy, (1991).

This Constitution. . . Shall be the Supreme Law of the Land, . . ., by David Loy Mauch (2014).

The Webster-Hayne Debates on the Nature of the Union, Herman E. Belz, editor (2000).

Conflict of the Northern and Southern Cultures

The Missouri Controversy, 1819-1821, by Glover Moore (1953).

Bleeding Kansas, by Alice Nichols (1954).

Nativism and Slavery, The Northern Know Nothings, and the Politics of the 1850s, by Tyler Anbinder (1994).

The Story of the Democratic Party, by Henry Minor (1928).

The Origins of the Republican Party, **1852-1856**, by William E. Gienapp (1987).

The Secret Six, John Brown and the Abolitionist Movement, by Otto Scott (1979).

The American Conscience, The Drama of the Lincoln-Douglas Debates, Saul Sigelschiffer, editor (1973).

Lone Star, A History of Texas and the Texans, by T. R. Fehrenbach (1968).

The Essential Calhoun, Clyde N. Wilson, editor (1992).

The Coming of the Civil War, by Avery O. Craven (1942).

Clash of Extremes: The Economic Origins of the Civil War, by Marc Egnal (2009).

North Over South: Northern Nationalism and American Identity in the Antebellum Era, by Susan-Mary Grant (2000).

The Politics of Dissolution, The Quest for a National Identity and the American Civil War, Marshall L. DeRosa, editor (1997).

When in the Course of Human Events: Arguing the Case for Southern Secession, by Charles Adams (2000).

Yankee Leviathan: The Origins of Central State Authority in America, by Richard F. Bensel (1990).

The War Between the States

Understanding Abe Lincoln's First Shot Strategy (Inciting Confederates to Fire First at Fort Sumter), by Howard Ray White (2011).

Maryland, The South's First Casualty, by Bart R. Talbert (1995).

The Civil War and Readjustment in Kentucky, by E. Merton Coulter (1926).

Turbulent Partnership, Missouri and the Union, 1861-1865, by William E. Parrish (1963).

The Civil War: A Narrative, 3 volumes, by Shelby Foote (1956-74).

The Civil War, Day by Day, by E. B. and Barbara Long (1971).

The Story of the Confederacy, by Robert Selph Henry (1936).

A History of the Confederate Navy, by Raimondo Luraghi (1996).

Memoirs of Service Afloat, During the War Between the States, by Raphael Semmes (1868).

The Siege of Charleston, 1861-1865, by E. Milby Burton (1976).

Northern Opposition to Lincoln's War, D. Jonathan White, editor (2014).

Lincoln Unmasked, by Thomas DiLorenzo (2006).

The Confederate War, by Gary W. Gallagher (1997).

Mr. Lincoln Goes to War, 4 volumes, by William Marvel (2006-2011).

Destruction and Reconstruction: Personal Experiences of the Late War, by Richard Taylor (1879).

Merchant of Terror: General Sherman and Total War, by John B. Walters (1973).

War Crimes Against Southern Civilians, by Walter Brian Cisco (2007).

South Carolina Civilians in Sherman's Path, by Karen Stokes (2012).

A City Laid Waste: The Capture, Sack, and Destruction of the City of Columbia, by William Gilmore Simms (1865; new edition 2005).

Civil War Prisons: A Study in War Psychology, by William B. Hesseltine (1964).

Elmira, Death Camp of the North, by Michael Horigan (2002).

To Die in Chicago, Confederate Prisoners at Camp Douglas, 1862-1865, by George Levy (1999).

Portals of Hell: Military Prisons of the Civil War, by Lonnie R. Speer (1997).

The Immortal 600: Surviving Civil War Charleston and Savannah, by Karen Stokes (2013).

Let Us Die Like Brave Men, by Daniel W. Barefoot (2005).

The Fremantle Diary, by Col. Arthur J. L. Fremantle (1865).

Recollections Grave and Gay, by Mrs. Burton Harrison (1912).

Blood and War at My Doorstep: North Carolina Civilians in the War between the States, 2 volumes, by Brenda Chambers McKean (2011).

Empire of the Owls, Reflections on the North's War against Southern Secession, by H. V. Traywick, Jr. (2013).

Partisan Warfare in the American Civil War, by Bertil Haggman, upcoming e-book (title tentative).

Slavery was Not the Cause of the Civil War: The Irrefutable Argument, by Gene Kizer Jr. (2014).

About African Americans of the Southern Culture

The Making of New World Slavery: From the Baroque to the Modern, 1492-1888, by Robin Blackburn (1997).

The Chronological History of the Negro in America, by Peter M. Bergmann (1969).

Roll Jordan Roll: The World the Slaves Made, by Eugene Genovese (1976).

The Nat Turner Slave Insurrection, by F. Roy Johnson (1966).

Time on the Cross: The Economics of American Negro Slavery, by Robert W. Fogel and Stanley L Engerman (1974).

Legend of the Underground Railroad, by Larry Gara (1961).

North of Slavery, by Leon R. Litwack (1965).

"What Shall We Do with the Negro?": Lincoln, White Racism and the American Civil War, by Paul D. Escott (2009).

Sick From Freedom: African-American Illness and Suffering During the Civil War and Reconstruction, by Jim Down (2015).

Behind the Scenes, or Thirty Years a Slave, and Four Years in the White House, by Elizabeth Keckley (1868).

Fighting for Freedom: A Documented Story, by Barbara G. Marthal (2015).

Up From Slavery, by Booker T. Washington (1901).

Slavery Remembered: A Record of Twentieth-Century Slave Narratives, by Paul D. Escott (1979).

Political Reconstruction

Reconstruction, Political and Economic, 1865-1877, by William A. Dunning (1907).

The South During Reconstruction, 1865-1877, by E. Merton Couther (1947).

The Story of Reconstruction, by Robert Selph Henry (1938).

Wade Hampton: Confederate, Warrior, Conservative Statesman, by Walter Brion Cisco (2004).

The Prostrate State: South Carolina Under Negro Government, by James S. Pike (1874).

Reconstruction in South Carolina, 1865-77, by John Reynolds (1905).

Reconstruction in Mississippi, by James Wilford Garner (1902).

Dixie after the War, by Myrta Lockett Avary (1906).

Biographies of Major Leaders

George Washington, 7 volumes, by Douglas S. Freeman (1948-1957).

The Life of Francis Marion, by William Gilmore Simms (1844).

Jefferson and His Time, 6 volumes, by Dumas Malone (1948-1981).

James Madison and the Making of America, by Kevin R. C. Gutzman (2012).

James Monroe and the Quest for American Identity, by Harry Ammon (1946).

The Life of John Randolph of Roanoke, 2 volumes, by Hugh A. Garland (1850).

The Life of Andrew Jackson, by Marquis James (2 volumes, 1933, 1937).

James K. Polk, Jacksonian, by Charles Sellars (1957).

John Tyler, Champion of the Old South, by Oliver P. Chitwood (1964).

The Raven, A Biography of Sam Houston, by Marquis James (1929).

John C. Calhoun: American Portrait, by Margaret Coit (1950)

Franklin Pierce: The Young Hickory of the Granite Hills, by Roy F. Nichols (1969).

John Brown: The Making of a Martyr, by Robert Penn Warren (1929).

Jefferson Davis, volume 1*: American Patriot (1808-1861);* Volume 2*: Confederate President;* Volume 3*: Tragic Hero,* by Hudson Strode (1954-1964).

Jefferson Davis, Unconquerable Heart, by Felicity Allen (1999).

First Lady of the South, The Life of Mrs. Jefferson Davis, by Ishbel Ross (1958).

Stephen A. Douglas, by Robert W. Johannsen, (1973).

Charles Sumner, 2 volumes, by David Donald (1960, 1970).

Old Thad Stevens: A Story of Ambition, by Richard N. Current (1942).

Lincoln, a biography by David Herbert Donald (1995).

Lincoln, the Man, by Edgar Lee Masters (1991).

The Real Lincoln, A New Look at Abraham Lincoln, His Agenda, and an Unnecessary War, by Thomas J. DiLorenzo (2002).

The President's Wife: Mary Todd Lincoln, by Ishbel Ross (1973).

R. E. Lee, 4 volumes, by Douglas Southall Freeman (1961).

Life and Campaigns of Lieut.-Gen. Thomas J. Jackson, by Robert L. Dabney (1865).

That Devil Forrest: The Life of General Nathan Bedford Forrest, by John A. Wyeth (1899).

Breckinridge: Statesman, Soldier, Symbol, by William C. Davis (1974).

Major-General Isaac Trimble: Baltimore Confederate, by Leslie Tucker (2005).

Grover Cleveland, a Study in Courage, by Allan Nevins (1932).

Literature and Culture

Eight Revolutionary "Romances" by William G. Simms (1806-70).

New Orleans: The Place and the People, by Grace King (1895).

The Unvanquished, by William Faulkner (1938).

The South in American Literature, 1607-1900, by Jay B. Hubbell (1954.)

Understanding "Uncle Tom's Cabin" and "The Battle Hymn of the Republic" -- How Novelist Harriet Beecher Stowe and Poet Julia Ward Howe Influenced the Northern Mind, by Howard Ray White (2003).

The Rise and Fall of the Plantation South, by Raimondo Luraghi (1978).

The Southern Essays of Richard Weaver, edited by George M. Curtis (1987).

Patriotic Gore: The Literature of the American Civil War, by Edmund Wilson (1969).

The Long Roll (1911) and *Cease Firing* (1912), by Mary Johnston.

Our Fathers' Fields: A Southern Story, by James E. Kibler (1998).

Letters from the Outpost: Essays on the Cultural Cleansing of a Small Southern State, by Joyce Bennett (2014).

Magnolias and Cornbread: An Outline of Southern History for Unreconstructed Southerners, by Leslie R. Tucker (2010).

Shadows of Blue & Gray: The Civil War Writings of Ambrose Bierce, Brion M. Thomsen, editor (2002).

Traveller, by Richard Adams (1988).

I'll Take My Stand: The South and the Agrarian Tradition, by twelve "Fugitive Agrarians," (1930).

Made in the USA
Columbia, SC
29 June 2019